# Print Reviews

"Awe-inspiring accounts pack enough adventure, suspense, turmoil and intrigue for a Hollywood film...Although Alexy's aim in writing this book was the redemption of her "disowned Jewish self", her accomplishment is higher: a meaningful contribution to the literature of the Holocaust."—*San Francisco Chronicle*

"Best reading of 1993...the kind of book you'd have no idea you'd want to read until you opened it to Page One and found you couldn't put it down."—*The Progressive*

"A woman discovering her Jewish roots...and the Jewish past of Spain viscerally brings home the complex layers of history. Alexy cracks open the historical events to reveal Spanish efforts on behalf of Jewish refugees...while at the same time discovering the fearful heart of the Marranos, remnants of another persecution."—**Lilly Rivlin**, director of *Conversos, The Secret Jews*

"A compelling, multi-dimensional look at Judaism and Spain—a land infamous for its medieval anti-Semitism, but as yet unheralded as a haven from Hitler....Alexy guides us through the perilous tension between faith and identity, helping us to understand the complex psycho-spiritual reverberations of the Spanish Expulsion and Inquisition...still quivering from the aftershocks of 500 years. ."—*Kirkus Reviews*

"The first-person narratives make fascinating reading, as do Alexy's own musings about her life and history...A story of hope rather than despair."—*Booklist*

"*The Mezuzah in the Madonna's Foot* tells of a rare journey: Jews again becoming Conversos to escape Hitler by fleeing to Spain. Trudi Alexy recaptures that period of flight—an odyssey uniquely told in this riveting book."—**E. M. Broner**, author of *The Telling* and *A Weave of Women*

"Contributes to our common history with a very important and not very well-known chapter."—**King Juan Carlos I of Spain**

Trudi Alexy with King Juan Carlos I and Queen Sophia of Spain

# The
# Mezuzah
## in the
# Madonna's
# Foot

# Marranos And Other Secret Jews: A Woman Discovers Her Hidden Identity

# The Mezuzah in the Madonna's Foot

## in the

## Madonna's Foot

**TRUDI ALEXY**

AN AUTHORS GUILD BACKINPRINT.COM EDITION

*The Mezuzah in the Madonna's Foot*
*Marranos And Other Secret Jews: A Woman Discovers Her Hidden Identity*

All Rights Reserved © 1993, 2006 by Trudi Alexy

AN AUTHORS GUILD BACKINPRINT.COM EDITION

Published by iUniverse, Inc.

For information address:
iUniverse, Inc.
2021 Pine Lake Road, Suite 100
Lincoln, NE 68512
www.iuniverse.com

Originally published by Simon & Schuster

**Designed by Levavi & Levavi**

ISBN-13: 978-0-595-41159-7
ISBN-10: 0-595-41159-2

Printed in the United States of America

For my son, Peter, and my daughter, Debra, with love

# Contents

# *Preface*

"Marrano" is a pejorative name meaning "swine," given to secret Jews by suspicious Christians during the Spanish Inquisition. I have used it in the book reluctantly—only because it is a historical term with which most people are familiar and because it illustrates the demeaned status and fear suffered by Jews who were forced to convert during that terrible time.

Why does this ugly term have so much resonance for so many people? Why does a book such as mine, which deals primarily with the experiences of Jews in Spain during the past fifty years, keep inspiring conversation and debate about the mysterious Marranos? What is it about the Marrano experience that provokes such intense fascination?

The drama of the Marranos' dogged determination to cling to their way of life, holding fast to their beliefs and practicing their

9

laws and traditions when being found out meant torture and death, symbolizes for many the importance of connection to one's ancestral roots and the miraculous survival of the spirit, even in the most hostile climate..

One of the many stories recounted in the book compares Judaism to the straggly cactus, which, unlike other beautifully flowering but more fragile plants, not only survives in an arid climate under a burning sun, but thrives. Marranos are the human counterparts to that cactus.

Speaking with people throughout the U.S. and Canada about Spain, the Jews and the Holocaust, it is the history of the Marranos that seems to have the most powerful impact—stirring the imagination, rousing the curiosity, and touching the hearts of nearly all who learn about them. I should not be surprised. After all, the Marranos' influence on my own life was profound: finding out about them inspired me to search for my lost Jewish heritage.

Seldom before has the pull towards one's own people, the need to belong, the stubborn resistance to assimilation, and the challenge to prevent the blurring of identity, emerged with more urgency than now. Today, when frustration over centuries-old suppressed ethnic and religious differences are erupting all around us with atrocities such as the world has not witnessed since the Holocaust, the Marranos' stubborn but contained commitment to their spiritual heritage stands as a shining example of courage under fire. But the burden of secrecy inherited from their martyred ancestors by present-day crypto-Jews living in Majorca, Portugal, South and Central America, as well as throughout our own American Southwest, passed from generation to generation through five fear-ridden centuries, is graphic evidence of the enormous price they are still paying. May their tragic legacy help us create a world in which all peoples can safely and openly affirm their true identities.

—**Trudi Alexy**, March 1994

# Foreword

This is the story of a personal quest, set in motion by an event that happened fifty years ago.

I was eleven years old when World War II broke out in 1939. My parents, nine-year-old brother, and I were living in a small village in Normandy, France, when Father suddenly announced that we were going to Spain. He added that we would also be baptized as Catholics, because it was not safe for us to remain Jews.

Until that moment I never knew we were Jews. Only later did I discover how dangerous it was in those times to be Jewish.

Years after we settled in America I heard rumors that thousands of other Jewish refugees had fled to Spain during the Holocaust, but that, unlike my family, most of them had done so without converting or hiding the fact that they were Jews.

The paradox of Jews seeking and finding refuge in Spain at that time, *as Jews*, hounded me. Why would Fascist Spain ignore its own people's reputation for anti-Semitism by openly defying the anti-Jewish racial laws of Hitler and Mussolini, who had helped Generalissimo Francisco Franco win the recent Civil War, while other, more likely, democratic governments ignored the plight of the Jews and kept them out?

Even without taking into account Spain's long history of persecuting Jews, which culminated in the infamous Spanish Inquisition and the 1492 Expulsion of all Jews who refused to convert, Franco's Axis connection made all these "facts" too incongruous to accept without considerable skepticism. Spain was clearly not safe for Jews at that particular time, because of the oppressive presence of Franco's victorious Fascist Falange troops as well as of German soldiers who were still actively involved in mop-up operations long after the Spanish Civil War had ended. So why would Jews, by the thousands, dare seek refuge there? Was there any truth to the story that nearly all who did not only survived but found the Spanish people to be remarkably hospitable, generous, and willing to risk arrest (or worse) to help them? This was a mystery I felt compelled to unravel.

To sort out the many intertwined facts and fictions I encountered, my quest took me back to my childhood and to several countries, where I discovered my own connection to a past that seemed lost in a jumble of denials and contradictions, and to roots from which my family was cut off long before I was born. It also revealed a heretofore hidden yet meaningful kinship link with the Marranos, a people who, for centuries, suffered the same sense of dislocation as did I, never feeling safe, forever strangers in a hostile environment where their survival depended on disguising or hiding their Jewish identities.

My family originally came from Romania, but we moved to Prague, Czechoslovakia, when I was a baby. When Hitler tested his expansionist ambitions in 1938 by annexing Austria (the Anschluss) without encountering either local resistance or foreign protest, we abruptly left Prague and fled to Paris.

I did not know what to make of the cataclysmic events suddenly creating chaos in our lives. But, even though this was by far the most dramatic event of my ten years, I had always been keenly aware of things I could not explain, events that seemed mysterious and frightening: people and pets became ill and died, anger erupted without apparent reason, friends disappeared without saying good-bye, adults acted in secretive ways, pretending nothing was wrong, vague threats lurked in unlikely places. Since no one ever offered anything comforting or reassuring to counteract my confusion, I was forced, from very early on, to find my own way to cope with the turmoil around me. My way was to lose myself in books and to create a fantasy world around the characters in them whose realities became my own.

These books revealed a world where the gods of ancient mythology wielded unlimited power and meted out justice, where witches and wizards wrought magic, sainted martyrs performed miracles, and heroes risked their lives for noble causes. Although that world seemed no less tumultuous for the inhabitants of those pages than the one from which I was trying to escape, *their* reality relieved my anxiety by providing answers to questions I did not even know how to articulate. What mattered was that in *that* reality nothing happened by accident; everything had logical explanations and predictable consequences. Mysterious signs and random intuitions proved meaningful, even if only in retrospect. Those who were good were rewarded and those who were bad got punished—here on earth, or after death. Life felt more stable: I was convinced that whatever happened, no matter how unexpected or irrational, *someone, somewhere, was in control.* "Magical thinking" (ascribing symbolic meanings to ordinary events, investing them with mythical relevance and power) became my religion, my spiritual security blanket.

Until that fateful day in 1939, when Father announced we would become Catholic because "it was not safe to be Jews," religion had been a non-issue in our thoroughly assimilated family. I did not know what being Jewish was all about, any more than what it meant to be Catholic. But I was sure what we were doing was wrong: to say we were Catholic was a lie. Would any of the heroes I had read about ever have lied in order to be safe? Of course not. *They* were brave and good. Father was telling us to be cowardly and bad. My protests went unheeded. We were baptized. I felt sure we would never be forgiven.

In spite of this, a strange sense of wonder and peace enveloped me as we crossed the border into Spain. I did not question why I felt that way. I simply welcomed it as a good omen: Spain was sure to be a magical place where we would all be safe and where I would feel good again.

I had no clue, back then, how important Spain would become in my life. Not until decades later did I uncover personal details of the stirring history of the Marranos, Spain's Secret Jews (Catholics in name only, baptized under duress), and feel a rush of recognition: just as my family sought to escape Nazi persecution by pretending to be Catholic, so centuries before, the Marranos had hoped to escape the Inquisition's savagery by submitting to baptism. For them, being found out meant torture on the rack and death by fire. For us and others like us, getting caught meant the horrors of concentration camps and death in gas chambers.

However, unlike the Marranos, who had powerful traditions and spiritual laws to sustain them, and unlike the rest of my family, for whom baptism had been a mere technicality that created no moral conflict, I had nothing to help me reason away my certainty that what we had done was terribly wrong. Thus, I salved my guilty conscience by losing myself in the pomp, pageantry, and seductive security of Catholicism. Later, when reality set in and the magic wore off, my guilt over surviving by fraud while so many others perished as Jews pursued me into my adult life.

• • •

As I began to explore the history of the Jews in Spain, I found it full of controversy and contradictions yet strangely familiar. Although Jews lived in Spain before either the Christians or the Moors (Islamic followers of the prophet Muhammad), it was not surprising that Jews were easy scapegoats and always vulnerable to the political and economic whims of the ruling majority, because they never governed any of the land and never commanded armies of their own. The Moorish conquest of Spain, launched from North Africa during the early seventh century, ushered in a seven-hundred-year-long tug-of-war between the separate Christian and Moorish kingdoms. Despite this on-again, off-again struggle, interspersed by years of peaceful and productive coexistence, Jews not only managed to maintain a working relationship with both warring factions but prospered in professions and in businesses, owned land, and often attained positions of great power and influence in the courts of their Christian and Moorish rulers.

During the two years I lived and attended school in Barcelona, I heard only vague allusions to the "Golden Age," none of which mentioned that, for nearly seven hundred years, Jews and their contributions were, to a great degree, responsible for placing Spain at the cultural, economic, and political center of the world. History classes failed to reveal that Córdoba, Granada, and Seville in the south, and Toledo, Barcelona, and Gerona* in the central and northern regions had been renowned centers of learning maintained by flourishing Jewish communities. Names like Yehuda Halevi, Moses Maimonides, Abraham Zacuto, Moses Nahmanides, Abraham ibn Ezra, and Shlomo ibn Gabirol were unknown to me while I lived in Spain and for years after I left. They are, however, in the words of Spain's present king, Juan Carlos I, "inscribed with golden let-

---

*Gerona is the Castilian Spanish spelling of the town known today in Catalan Spanish as Girona. Until the death of Franco in 1975, Castilian spellings were mandated for Catalan place names. In this book, the Catalan forms are used only when appropriate for the period being covered.

ters in the books of literature, philosophy, and science" (see his address, in the Epilogue).

Later, while attending Catholic schools in the United States, I was given a rather slanted and sanitized version of the Spanish Inquisition. No mention was made of the fact that brutal persecution of Jews and mass baptism forced on them under threat of death became routine, and increased in frequency and severity as Christian armies slowly reconquered the land from the Moors. Or that mobs, whipped into murderous frenzy by fanatical preachers, slaughtered, plundered, and destroyed entire Jewish communities long before 1478, when Queen Isabella and King Ferdinand finally persuaded Pope Innocent VIII to send in the Church's watchdog tribunal, the Inquisition, to protect Spain's Catholic integrity.

It was easy to see why newly baptized Jews never felt safe, despite their attempts to escape persecution by blending into Spanish society. Suspicious Catholics never trusted or accepted the new Conversos. They also never tired of spying on them and needed little cause to accuse them of Judaizing. Great heresy trials became commonplace. But the Jews' worst fears came true in 1492, when Queen Isabella and King Ferdinand's armies finally routed the Moors from their last stronghold in Granada, and all the warring kingdoms were at last united under the crest and crown of the Catholic Monarchs.

Tomás de Torquemada, a confidant of the queen, was named Grand Inquisitor. Believed to be descended from Jews, he had long been obsessed with weeding out all backsliding Jewish converts. Now, convinced that "Judaism was an incurable disease" and that practicing Jews were contaminating the new Christians, he committed himself to the ideal of "one people, one kingdom, one faith." To achieve this goal, he conspired with his queen to rid Spain of the remaining "infidels" threatening the security of her realm. The 1492 Expulsion Decree forced all unbaptized Jews either to convert or to leave Spain forever.

After being an integral part of Spanish life for so many centuries, one half of Spain's 200,000 to 300,000 Jews chose to flee rather than submit to religious blackmail, leaving behind vast estates, commercial holdings, and orchards and vineyards that were immediately appropriated and divided between the crown and the Church. I mentally followed them into exile, south to North Africa, east to Turkey, Greece, and the Balkans, and north to the Netherlands. I felt their rage over being allowed to take with them only what they could carry (with the exception of gold coins, precious jewelry, and other such portable treasures) and felt an incongruous mixture of pride and guilt that no one could seduce those steadfast Jews into abjuring their faith or deprive them of their culture, their professional and business know-how, or their language, Ladino, an ancient form of Spanish that survives among Sephardic Jews to this day.

Recalling the seductive appeal Catholicism had for me when I was first exposed to it in Spain as a young girl, it came as no surprise that, among the 100,000 to 150,000 Jews who chose baptism over exile, a fair number actually became true converts, going so far as to join the Catholic clergy as priests and nuns. Some of them even rose in the Catholic Church's hierarchy to bishops and cardinals, while others, like Teresa of Ávila and John of God, were canonized.

As I uncovered more and more details about the continuing torment suffered by the great majority of Jews who remained in Spain as Marranos, the irony of their fate did not escape me. Although they had hoped their Christian cover would protect them, the opposite happened. As Catholics, they now fell under the direct scrutiny and stringent control of the Inquisition's fanatical heretic hunters, who tortured and burned at the stake anyone even vaguely suspected of clandestinely practicing the "crime of Judaism." Thousands of Marranos, hoping to find a measure of freedom and safety, eventually followed Columbus to the New World. So did the Inquisition, which remained in operation until 1820, even across the ocean. Although Spain has since abolished the

Catholic Church's status of official state religion and now has a constitution that guarantees freedom of worship for all faiths, the five-hundred-year-old Expulsion Decree has (as of 1992) never been formally rescinded.

The more I learned about the Marranos and their stubborn efforts to maintain their essential connection to their spiritual wholeness, the more I identified with them, or, perhaps more precisely, the more I longed to be one of them. *They* had something deep inside that kept alive their link with one another and with their heritage, even under the most stressful circumstances. I, on the other hand, never saw myself as anything but a failed, flawed outsider during all the years I practiced Catholicism and long after I stopped doing so, cut off, forever banished from my own people because there had never been anything experiential in my own past to bind me to Jews. More than anything I longed to have what the Marranos had: a sense of *belonging*.

Little did I suspect, when I began my research, that it would lead me to meet some of the Marranos' direct descendants, who, to this day, maintain their traditions in secret and suffer the same fears, in the twentieth century, as did their medieval ancestors.

Long before I became aware of the Marranos or my mystical connection to them, something intangible yet increasingly persistent kept gnawing at me, urging me to search for my lost birthright. I did not know how to proceed or what to expect. One thing was certain: Spain held the key to my finding that lost Jewish part of me.

Thus I began my journey into my own past and into a deeper exploration of the history of the Jews in Spain, as a way of reconnecting to a spiritual core of which I was not even aware as a child, but whose lack had left a gaping void.

I was also curious to know more about those refugees who, unlike my family, chose to seek shelter in Spain during World War II *as Jews*, and what that experience meant to them and to those who helped them. My parents never wanted to talk about the past. In order to find out what happened, fifty years after the fact, I knew

I had to return to Spain and speak to others who had been there.

When I began, I had no idea my search would take four years to complete and lead me to speak with sixty people in four languages, in five countries on three continents! Aware they would be quite elderly and that their stories might be lost forever if I did not hurry, I immediately began contacting anyone who might lead me to survivors or those who had helped rescue them. I was amazed how quickly potential contributors materialized in Toronto, Jerusalem, Tel Aviv, Mexico City, Rio de Janeiro, and closer to home in New York City, Chicago, and southern California. Reluctant at first, most of these survivors let down their guard and agreed to cooperate once they found out I was one of them. Many had never spoken about their experiences to anyone before.

By the time I left on the first of my several trips to Spain, in December 1988, I had the names of eighteen persons in Madrid and Barcelona willing to meet with me: not only refugees and those who helped them, but leaders of Spain's Jewish and Catholic communities, historians, and diplomats, some of whom had been in Spain since before the war.

As more and more people agreed to tell their stories, I realized that my personal quest was turning into something far richer than I had expected, and far more complex.

The book that emerged out of this journey begins with my own story, covering my childhood in Prague and Paris, and, our two year stay in Barcelona until 1941, when my parents finally obtained our United States entry visas. It also describes my struggle to maintain some connection to my fragile Jewish identity once we settled in America, while surrendering to a conflicted fascination with Catholicism, which, for some years, had satisfied my religious hunger.

It includes harrowing personal stories of Jewish men, women, and children braving the dangerous climb over the Pyrenees Mountains into Spain during the worst period of Nazi persecution, and dramatic accounts of their rescues by those who risked their own lives to save and sustain them.

It focuses on the efforts and extraordinary devotion of ordinary Spaniards, both Jews and Gentiles, to the ideals of peaceful coexistence, mutual understanding, and respect for others' differences, which brought about and continues to deepen these changes in Spain since Franco's death in 1975.

It traces the suffering endured by the Marranos, as recorded in their diaries and in official Inquisition documents, and offers startling testimony by many of the hundreds of present-day descendants of those Secret Jews who followed Columbus to the New World. Nearly five hundred years later they still hold on to their Christian cover while hiding their Jewish identities, Jewish rituals, and Jewish laws, right here, in the American Southwest. It is through their eyes that we see the tragic but proud legacy they have inherited.

It ends with a stirring statement by King Juan Carlos of Spain, expressing his personal feelings about the deep connection still linking Jews and the Spanish people today, five hundred years after their expulsion.

When I set out, there was no way of knowing whether I would find what I so deeply longed for: the redemption of my disowned Jewish self. What I *did* know early on was that, whatever the outcome, I would never regret the effort, for the quest itself promised to be the adventure of a lifetime.

# PART ONE

# LOST AND FOUND:

## A Jewish Identity

# · 1 ·

# Girlhood in Prague

When my father was born in Czernovitz, the capital of the province of Bukovina, it was part of the Austro-Hungarian Empire, ruled by Kaiser Franz Joseph, and most of the people who lived there spoke German. After World War I, Czernovitz was assigned to the kingdom of Romania. By the time I was born there, in 1927, its name had been changed to Cernauti, and its official language became Romanian. After World War II, the Soviet Union incorporated it and, of course, changed its name again. It is now part of the Republic of Ukraine, called Černovci, and, with the rapid changes occurring as I write, I won't even try to guess what language is prevalent there today.

In the late 1920s Czernovitz was a charming university town, alive with a bustling cultural life. My father's family owned a combination pharmacy-barbershop. His father was the druggist, and his mother, the official cast hairdresser for several theater companies in town, worked in the store with him. My father, Georg, was the middle child between a younger brother, Milos, and an older sister, Frieda.

My mother, Norma, was born in Vienna and was an only child. In her family were well-to-do landowners with extensive farm, forest, and farm-machinery interests located close to the Russian border. Her father was killed during the first year of World War I, when she was only nine years old, and by war's end all of the family's holdings were lost to the Russians, never to be recovered. Her mother, my Oma Jenny, raised her alone.

My father, whose photos as a young man reveal a striking resemblance to the dashing King Carol of Romania, was introduced to my mother when she was visiting her Czernovitz relatives, and was immediately captivated by her blue-eyed blond beauty and patrician air.

After they were married, Father brought Mother to Czernovitz. Oma Jenny soon joined them, and my brother, Fredo, and I were born there, eighteen months apart. In 1929 all five of us moved to Prague and remained there for nine years.

Several childhood memories stand out, not only because of their content but because of the exaggerated symbolic meaning they came to hold for me. Only much later did I recognize this flight into "magical thinking" as a child's attempt to explain the inexplicable, to make order out of chaos and to create a spiritual world where none exists.

The first such event happened when I was two and a half years old. A minor throat infection turned into streptococcus sepsis, a type of blood poisoning for which there was no cure at that time. Fever kept me delirious for weeks. Huge boils, which appeared all over my body, had to be lanced without anesthetic due to a mild heart murmur. I have a clear picture of me sitting on a padded window seat in our flat, with my parents holding me still while the doctor cut open the abscesses on my legs, wrists, and back as blackish blood spilled into a basin on the floor.

Later, one end of a strange glass coil resting on our dining-room table was inserted into my father's wrist, with the other embedded in my own. I can still see the blood coursing from his body into mine through the transparent coil while my own poisoned blood poured out through a cut next to it.

This primitive blood transfusion saved my life. I have no memory of pain. I do, however, remember the color of the blood: my own was nearly black while my father's, bubbling through the glass coil, was bright red. That color contrast, and the fact that I soon felt better, made Father suddenly appear bigger than life, and the possessor of magical powers.

Father's personality actively perpetuated this superhuman projection. His booming voice and his domineering manner discouraged all challenges to his authority. His frequent loud outbursts frightened us all, and I knew early on that the only way to escape his wrath was to do as I was told and ask no questions.

Despite his stern manner, Father and I shared a frequent ritual. On many Saturday mornings, just he and I had lunch together at Lippert's. This was a most unusual automat-delicatessen, where each of the open-faced sandwiches, displayed in little cubbyholes along a wall, was a fanciful work of art. At the drop of a coin, a glass door would pop open on such edible masterpieces as the replica of an ocean liner, with asparagus smoke stacks and rolled-up anchovy portholes resting on layer upon layer of alternating ham and cheese decks, all floating on a sea of mayonnaise whitecaps; or an airplane with a lobster body, artichoke leaves for wings, and silvery sardine propellers stuck with toothpicks to red radish engines.

Eating at Lippert's was an exciting adventure, but there was an ordeal I had to wrestle with each time we went there. The restaurant was located on the third floor of a tall building at the foot of Wenceslas Square in the heart of Prague. In order to get upstairs we had to take a strange tandem elevator made up of several individual doorless cabins, spaced just a foot or two apart and attached to perpetually moving pulleys. One had to jump on and off the open elevator cabins as they slowly passed by the exit on each floor. Every time I faced this contraption (oddly named "Paternoster," "Our Father" in Latin), I stood before it frozen in terror till Father jumped on, pulling me with him. Getting off was even more frightening. In my fantasy (which was to recur as a nightmare well into my adult years) I was certain I alone would somehow miss the last moment to get off and be trapped inside. I had no doubt that the cabin would turn upside down as soon as it reached the top floor, spilling me out, to fall down, down, down . . . Each time I survived intact but dizzy, sweating, with my heart pounding, I marveled at my father's ability to know exactly when to make our move. This merely confirmed what I already knew: he had special powers, among them an uncanny instinct for timing that filled me with awe and turned terror to blind trust whenever danger threatened.

There was nothing about our life to indicate that our family was Jewish. If others knew we were Jews, I was not aware of it. Religion was not discussed. Neither was politics. There were no traditions or rituals, no reliable guidelines to tell me what to do, no rules that confirmed I was good or reassured me that I had not crossed some invisible line, committed some unknown crime for which some unspeakable punishment would be meted out by some all-knowing power.

Christmas and Easter were part of our life, as they were for everyone else around us, but devoid of meaning beyond the most obvious: they were fun-filled holiday festivities. Christmas meant Father's calling us into the parlor on Christmas Eve to see a pine tree ablaze with candles and sparklers, and with tangerines, apples, marzipan fruit, and nuts wrapped in colored papers hung on its branches amid gilded cardboard angels and birds. After opening our presents, we had midnight dinner: chunks of carp swimming in a tasty broth of onions and potato dumplings. For dessert we had traditional sweet breads filled with almonds and raisins. Easter meant new clothes, candy eggs, and chocolate bunnies in straw-lined baskets. No religious connotation was apparent.

Nothing could have adequately prepared any of us to deal with the dramatic changes that turned our lives upside down in 1938, when I was just ten years old. Most of the world had chosen to ig-nore the darkening clouds gathering over Europe, although Hitler had revealed his intentions for territorial expansion (Lebensraum) and the scapegoating of Jews in his prison manifesto, *Mein Kampf,* well before he became chancellor in 1933. Few believed they had reason to take him or his wild threats against Jews seriously until the night of November 9, 1938, when carefully orchestrated anti-Semitic riots erupted across Germany and Austria. As his hench-men smashed and plundered Jewish homes and businesses, burned hundreds of synagogues, and brutalized and carted off thousands of Jews to concentration camps, Hitler challenged the civilized world to intervene on their behalf. While those Jews who remained watched their civil rights and privileges as citizens disappear, the rest of the world looked away. Many Jews, elsewhere, also mini-mized the ominous warning of Kristallnacht and chose to see it as an isolated incident. Few recognized it as the beginning of the end for European Jewry.

Until then life seemed peaceful enough for my family. We lived in a large, sunny apartment facing a park. Father was an engineer and an inventor of mechanical gadgets and traveled often. Mother, a talented milliner, made elegant hats at home on wooden head forms and took care of Fredo and me. Oma Jenny, who became a corsetiere as a young widow, constructed fancy, lace-trimmed corsets on a wooden body form in the small flat where she lived alone. We were not rich, but we had everything we needed. The rest of our small family had remained either in Romania or in Austria. One exception was Father's younger brother, Uncle Milos, who left home as a teenager in the early twenties to make his fortune in the New World, and thus established our family's foothold in America. Twenty years later, it was Uncle Milos who secured our escape from war-torn Europe.

My parents made sure our family was as invisibly woven into Prague's life fabric as was possible for foreigners. We spoke German at home, but Fredo and I were encouraged to speak Czech everywhere else. Later we attended Czech state schools and joined Sokol, the national gymnastic society, which specialized in performing the tightly choreographed mass exercises so effective during spectacles like the Olympic games. Our nursemaid was Czech. I wore Czechoslovakia's embroidered costumes and flower wreaths when performing folk dances or marching in parades through Wenceslas Square on state holidays. I often went to the Prague National Theater to see *The Bartered Bride, Rusalka,* and other folk and classical operas, plays, and ballet. Puppet shows, popping up here and there in public parks on makeshift stages atop wooden wheelbarrows, were a particular favorite. I loved watching the Noble Prince triumph over the Wily Usurper and the Evil Witch get her violent comeuppance, collapsing under a hail of blows while we cheered on the Avenging Hero. Hot roasted chestnuts and *topinki* (toasted butter-soaked rye bread rubbed with raw garlic) sold from sidewalk brazier carts were a special treat.

I remember only two close friends. One was Yutzi, whom I watched waste away and die of leukemia when we were both eight years old. The other friend was Hans, who lived across the hall from our flat. His mother, Pauli, Viennese like my mother and her closest friend, often took me along when she and Hans went to the opera. We would take a rear seat in the tram and listen, entranced, to Pauli's scene-by-scene preview of the Sturm und Drang we were about to see, complete with renditions of the key arias! By the time we had arrived at the theater a half hour later and settled into our seats, Hans and I were experts on the opera of the day.

We skated together on the ice-covered tennis courts along the Vltava (Moldau) River and swam in it in summer. When Hans and I were six and seven years old, respectively, we each pricked a forefinger with his penknife, mingled our blood, and swore to be friends forever.

For several years Hans and Pauli joined my family during our summer vacations in Miechenice, a mountain resort near Prague. We rented two of the ten cottages that surrounded a country lodge, where we ate all our meals.

During our last summer in Miechenice, when I was about nine years old, something happened that concretely confirmed, beyond a shadow of doubt, what I had always known: that some being, somewhere, watched everything everyone did and meted out punishment when bad deeds were done.

One evening, while all the guests were at supper at the lodge, a torrential rain and violent thunderstorm flooded the path back to our cabin so badly it became impassable. The owner of the lodge offered to put Fredo and me to bed in one of the rooms upstairs while everyone else remained downstairs.

We were put into twin beds in a small room at the end of a long hall, and we quickly fell asleep. I awakened with a start when I felt someone in bed with me, pressing up against me and fussing with my clothes. At first, in the dark, I thought it might be Fredo, but no, this body was much bigger. Stark terror kept me pretending I was asleep as hands passed over my upper body and down between my legs, pulling at the elastic of my pants. Just then footsteps came down the hall, toward the room. I tried to pull away, only to be pinned down tight by one strong hand while the other clamped my mouth shut. "If you tell anyone about this I will kill you!" a voice hissed in my ear. With that he got up, listened by the door as the footsteps outside the room faded, and let himself out. In the light, as he opened the door, I recognized the teenage son of the lodge owner. I stayed awake the rest of the night, too frightened to move.

Early next morning Mother came to get us. I said nothing, and it was clear Fredo had slept through everything. The rain had abated during the night, but lightning and thunder were just starting up again. The dining room was full. Behind the bar, the owner's son was dispensing beer from a huge old-fashioned brass pump. I tried to avoid his eyes, but when I stole a peek, I saw him glare at me. Just then a lightning bolt struck the lodge and he began to scream. All the lights went out and I stared in shock as he stood there, shaking violently, unable to let go of the brass handle, then fell to the floor. A wild commotion ensued as people rushed up to help. I sat, frozen to my seat, pressing my eyes shut. Suddenly I felt scalding liquid pour down my back. A waitress, distracted by what was going on, had accidentally spilled hot coffee on me.

As my back blistered beneath my shirt, there was no doubt in my mind about what had just happened. The connection was instant and inescapable: the boy who had come into my bed and touched me and I, who had failed to stop him, had done something bad, and now we had both been punished. It was clear that someone, somewhere, had the power to see, judge, and condemn.

Both my parents worked, and my emotional connection with them during that time remains a blur. As Hans became more and more involved with boy activities like soccer and hockey, I felt increasingly isolated and alone. Books and those who inhabited their pages became my best friends. I found a mythical home in the world of Greek and Roman gods, for which I made rough genealogical charts to keep straight who was related to whom. The age of chivalry came alive in *The Song of Roland*, *The Ring of the Nibelungen*, and in stories of King Arthur and the Knights of the Round Table. To learn more about the past of my own immediate world, I also worked my way through *The History of the Bohemian Kings*.

Everything around me conspired to reenforce the magical world I was creating inside: Prague was an artistic and architectural fairyland where every cobblestoned street and square in the inner city reflected a rich historic past. The Baroque houses had exterior walls that were etched, painted, and encrusted with bas-relief figures. Opulent palaces, massive Gothic churches, and treasure-filled museums were everywhere. These sights served as a never-ending source of fantasy and wonder to someone as steeped in folktales, mythology, and chivalry as I was. Every house had a story, every statue its legend. I knew them all. I often forgot what century it was and imagined I was back in the time when all of that magic was happening.

On school excursions I wandered through the vast arched naves of Saint Vitus Cathedral and climbed up and down the narrow streets leading to Hradčany Castle, a labyrinth of mirrored halls and frescoed galleries high on a hill overlooking the city. I knew all about the generations of nobility who had lived behind its massive walls.

I remember returning again and again to the tiny, pastel-colored cottages where medieval alchemists had lived along the narrow, winding street just below the castle. I puzzled over the tools and vessels on display and wondered how I, too, could learn to magically transform base metals into gold or, if that failed, just find the Philosophers' Stone, which grants one access to all the wisdom of the world.

I could never guess how many times I walked across Old Charles Bridge. The oldest among many in this ancient city, it is lined on both sides with statues of historic and religious personages, interspersed by Gothic gas lanterns. Saint John of Nepomuc, the chaplain to one of Bohemia's long-ago kings, stood tall and erect near the center of the bridge, wearing a crown of stars. Because he refused to divulge the queen's sins to the king, he was shackled and thrown off the bridge to drown in the freezing Vltava River. The moment his soul left his body, they say, a circle of stars appeared just above the water, a sure sign of God's approval of him.

Another of my favorite places was the Gothic Quarter, with its Old Town Hall tower and its unique astronomic clock. This clock had a tragic story. A king commissioned a young clockmaker to create the most elaborate timepiece in the world for the tower. But when the clock was finished, the king ordered the artisan's eyes put out with burning pokers to keep him from duplicating his masterpiece for anyone else. When the clockmaker broke the complicated mechanism to punish the king, no one was found who could repair it. The king had no choice but to ask its creator to put it back into working order. Satisfied that he had made his point, the blind man agreed to rebuild it. I remember being deeply moved by his noble generosity.

Whenever I passed the statue of Jan Hus, which stood facing the church of Our Lady of Tyn, near the Old Town Hall with its famous clock, I shuddered at the horror of being burned at the stake. Here Hus, an accused heretic, chose to die rather than renounce what he believed to be the truth.

These, then, were some of the haunts and heroes of my early childhood. Their stories stirred my imagination and provided me with standards of nobility of spirit to which only a child would dare aspire. I admired these heroes' willingness to suffer, even to die for what they believed. I knew I was not one of them, but I wanted more than anything to be like them. How wonderful to be swept up in something grand and heroic! I wished I, too, had something important enough to die for.

One part of Prague was unknown to me. I did not learn about Prague's Jewish heritage and thriving religious community until long after we left, long after the community ceased to thrive.

I never saw the nearly five-hundred-year-old Altneuschul Synagogue, the one structure related to Jews that Hitler had wanted to preserve. I did not see even one of the hundreds of tombstones in its cemetery, with their Hebrew inscriptions memorializing Prague's Jewish dead back to the twelfth century. I did not see the ornate silver candelabra and embroidered Torah covers spirited out of Prague during the Nazi occupation until I recently visited a traveling exhibit of Czechoslovakian Jewish artifacts. I did not know about Prague's renowned rabbinical tradition or about the philosophers, scholars, and writers who long ago lived in its Jewish quarter. And I did not hear of Rabbi Judah Löw, the famous master of the Kabbala, to whom legend credits the creation of the Golem of

Prague, a giant robot-like servant made of clay whose task it was to protect the ghetto Jews against their enemies.

One day, shortly before my tenth birthday, gas masks were distributed to each student at school. Teachers showed us how to use them and told us what they were for, but nobody explained why we had to carry them with us everywhere we went. "If you hear a loud siren, put them on" was all we were told. There was no war, so why would anyone want to drop gas on us? It made no sense. Even if I had known that Hitler had just occupied Austria without firing a shot and had made Jew baiting into an accepted sport for his storm troopers, I would not have known that those were *my people*, or worried that some day *my family* might be personally affected.

One night Father awoke us shortly after midnight.

"We're going to Paris," he said. "Pack only what you can carry." Father's voice was firm.

"Can I say good-bye to Hans?" I asked.

"There is no time for that," he said.

I did not argue. My heart began to pound. Whatever was going on was different from anything that had ever happened before. I felt confused and decided it was clearly not safe to ask any questions. Besides, I didn't really want to hear the truth. Deep inside I was certain that whatever it was had to be terrible. Fredo, who was just eight years old then, also did as he was told, silently, following my example.

Things moved very fast, my parents packing, locking up things, whispering as they rushed past, but inside me everything turned to slow motion, as if glue had soaked through my skin.

We bundled up all we could fit into two large suitcases and two small rucksacks, and took a taxi to Oma Jenny's. Mother pleaded with her to go away with us, but she saw no reason to leave. Father explained it was dangerous for her to stay, because the Nazis had just marched into Vienna.

"Prague will be next, and soon," he warned, but Oma Jenny refused to change her mind.

"I'm an old lady," she protested. "Why would anyone bother with me? What would I do in another foreign country, at my age?"

"Well, then, let's not waste any more time," Father said, his voice harsh. "Let's go, quickly!"

Mother embraced her mother and cried. Oma Jenny reassured her. "I just know you'll be back soon, when all this blows over." Fredo and I got quick hugs as Father rushed us out the door.

I remember little about the train trip to France other than the long tunnel just before we reached Strasbourg. It seemed to go on forever. We had been traveling across Germany for several hours and my parents were very quiet. All four of us stayed in our seats and ate the sandwiches Mother had packed instead of going to the dining car, as the others in our compartment did. When a German soldier burst in without knocking and demanded to see our passports, I could feel Mother tremble next to me. I held my breath until he left and felt like crying, but held back the tears. After that my whole body turned to stone.

Soon after the train emerged from the tunnel, it stopped at a railroad station. The signs along the way had all been in German. Now they were in French. Our parents rushed to gather up our belongings and eased us toward the exit.

"Is it over?" I heard Mother whisper to Father as we waited for the conductor to push open the door.

"Almost." The conductor stepped aside. He helped Father lower our suitcases to the platform and we jumped off. Then we waited and watched the train leave.

"Now it is over," Father said.

Mother started to cry. "I think we're safe now," she said, pulling Fredo and me close as Father looked away. I felt her shiver as she held us.

I wondered why Mother was still afraid. Father didn't seem to be. He appeared to have everything under control, but it had all happened too fast for me. I remember wondering about a lot of other things, too. Who were the Nazis and why did they march into Vienna, and why was Father afraid they might march into Prague, too, and if they did, what would that have to do with us? But I asked nothing. I didn't ask anything about Paris, either. I didn't ask where were we going to live, where Fredo and I would go to school, and what would happen when someone spoke to me in French and I didn't understand. I preferred to ask no questions and hear no answers. I wished I had stayed in Prague, with Oma Jenny.

We found a small restaurant near the station where Father ordered thick mushroom soup, fish, a long stick of crispy bread, and chocolate mousse for dessert. All of it in French. I was impressed and surprised. I had never heard him speak French before. But then, there had always been a lot of things about my father that seemed mysterious.

Later that night we boarded another train and continued on to Paris.

# · 2 ·

# *Revelation in France*

A week after we arrived in Paris, Father took Fredo and me to a crowded street carnival near our small hotel in Porte de Saint-Cloud. I was driving an electric bumper car in a tented rink when I suddenly lost sight of Father. I had last seen him standing next to a striped pole with Fredo, but when I got off I was all turned around. Everywhere I looked I saw children with their parents, rushing from ride to ride, eating cotton candy, laughing and chattering. It brought to reality my most immediate fear: to be in a strange place where no one knew me and where everyone spoke a language I could not understand. I had forgotten the name of our hotel. I wandered around in circles, feeling nauseated with panic. I wanted to scream but I knew it would do no good. When Father finally found me, I was sitting on a curb, in tears, certain I was lost for good. He scolded me for getting off on the wrong side of the rink. I wet my pants. After that, I kept a small notebook with me at all times and wrote down all sorts of important information, in case I ever got lost again.

Fredo and I were sent to a private boarding school in Plessis-Robinson, near Versailles. Because boys and girls were housed separately, we were never together. We had to take turns visiting our parents on alternating weekends because their hotel room was very small—so small that Mother had to cook on a hot plate on the commode in the bathroom.

I felt out of place at school and struggled to learn French to quiet the constant taunting by classmates, who assumed I was German. I mastered the language so quickly I was awarded a prize for an essay on the fables of La Fontaine: a gold-embossed copy of Rabelais's bawdy *Gargantua and Pantagruel*, inscribed with my name. Had my parents bothered to read it, they would certainly have taken it away from me.

When Fredo and I went to Paris for summer recess in July of 1939, our parents met us with their suitcases packed. "We're getting out of Paris," Father tersely announced. It reminded me of the way we had left Prague: sudden and rushed. I did not know why we had to leave, but this time I did not mind. We had not lived in Paris long enough for me to care whether we stayed or not.

We took the train north, to Normandy, and got off at the small coastal town of Riva Bella. Father left us at the station and went to find a place for us to stay. He returned with a taxi that took us to a gabled villa where he had rented the two back bedrooms. The windows had flower boxes and looked out on tall pine trees and rosebushes. The old lady who owned the house lived in front.

The house stood on a tree-lined street leading down to the beach. We went swimming every day, got brown in the sun, took long walks, picked berries and mushrooms in the woods surrounding the village, and pretended we were on vacation.

Early in the morning on the first day of September we were awakened by the town crier, an old man dressed in knee breeches and braided waistcoat. He pedaled through the village on a bicycle, ringing a large, loud bell. Everybody rushed to the main square to hear him read from a scroll. German tanks had rolled into Poland, he announced, and planes were bombing cities. People in the crowd began to cry. I did not understand why. Poland was a long way off, wasn't it? I did not know that France and Britain had agreed to go to Poland's defense if Germany attacked.

"That means we are at war," Father explained.

The next day he disappeared. I did not think anything of it because Father frequently traveled, but Mother seemed unusually upset. I overheard her cry at night and that bothered me more than the war everyone was so concerned about. It all seemed far away and unreal. I tried not to worry, but I had many questions, questions to which I was afraid to hear the answers.

When Father reappeared, about two weeks later, he sent Fredo and me outside into the garden. We could hear him and Mother talking loudly, sounding very agitated. "I wonder what is happening now?" I thought. Fredo kept looking at me with searching eyes, but I could only shrug in confusion. When Father called us back in, Mother was crying.

"We're becoming Lutheran," Father said. "Then we're becoming Catholic. That way, when someone asks what were we before, we can say Lutheran. After that we are moving to Spain."

"What is Lutheran?" I asked.

"It's a religion. Like Catholic. Almost everybody in Czechoslovakia and France and Spain is Catholic."

"Is that why we have to become Catholic?"

"No. It's because Hitler wants to get rid of the Jews. His soldiers just invaded Poland and started a war."

"Why does he want to get rid of the Jews?"

"Just because they are Jews."

"Are we Jews?"

"Yes. But it is not safe to be a Jew, so we will hide in Spain and tell everyone we are Catholic."

"Isn't that a lie, Father?" I asked.

"Tell your daughter I don't have time for stupid questions," Father said to Mother as he walked out to take care of business.

Finding out I was a Jew had no meaning for me beyond the fact that being Jewish was dangerous, which to my naive, myth-inspired mind felt heroic, even thrilling, rather than frightening. I wanted to be a Jew. Lying about it felt wrong.

A few days later we took the train back to Paris and rented a room in a small pension. Father was gone most of the time, but Mother took Fredo and me shopping every day, to buy underwear, shoes, and canned food. We also bought bigger suitcases, to carry it all. I wondered how far it was to Spain.

One night my parents took Fredo to a barbershop for a haircut. I stayed alone to take a bath. While I was in the tub, all the sirens in Paris went off, and so did the lights. No bombs fell—in fact, nothing happened at all and the lights soon came on again—but I stayed in the cold tub, frozen with fear, until Mother pulled me out. Now I had a taste of what danger was all about. Being a hero assumed a new dimension, and I wondered if I was cut out to be one.

I remember little about the religious instruction classes that we attended along with several other people going through an abreviated conversion process. The Lutheran minister was very unpleasant and seemed in a great hurry to be done with us. The Catholic priest was kind and patient. He let me ask a lot of questions. One day I requested to talk to him alone.

"I think what we are doing is wrong. Father says we're Jews but he says Hitler wants to get rid of the Jews and I don't know why. I just know that if we're Jews, we shouldn't pretend we're something else. Father says we have to become Catholic or Hitler will get rid of us, too. But I don't want to say I'm Catholic when I'm really a Jew. It's a lie." I started to cry. The priest put his arm around me.

"Your father is right. You must obey him. But remember, Jesus was a Jew. He will understand."

I wasn't at all sure Jesus, or anyone else, for that matter, would ever understand. I thought about Joan of Arc, Jan Hus, and Saint John of Nepomuc. *They* certainly would never understand. *They* were not afraid to die for what was right. *They* never lied to save their lives. I didn't know what Jews believed or even what they were, but if I was a Jew, the right thing to do was to stay a Jew and not hide it or lie about it, *no matter what.*

We were baptized twice. It didn't seem to bother my parents or Fredo, but I felt like a coward and a criminal. Whatever else being a Jew was all about, I knew they were special, persecuted for being who they were, just like the heroes and saints I had read about. By lying, by denying I was one of them, I knew I had forever forfeited the right to call myself a Jew.

# · 3 ·

# *Refuge in Spain*

The train going south, from Paris to the Spanish border, had two passenger cars and two locomotives, one on each end, facing opposite directions. The train had just passed through Cerbère, the last town on the French side, when it stopped next to a narrow strip of concrete. The conductor rushed from compartment to compartment, shouting and gesturing at us.

"Allez, allez, vite! Tous dehors—dépêchez-vous, dépêchez-vous!" (Let's go, let's go, quick! Everyone out, hurry, hurry!)

We had been traveling all night. I had dozed off, and at first I did not know where I was and forgot where we were going. Then I remembered.

Everyone quickly gathered up belongings, shouldered rucksacks, balanced bundles on heads, pushed suitcases toward exits, and spilled down onto the platform. There were about twenty of us, including a little baby and an old man with a cane.

Except for our group, the station was deserted. Someone started counting heads. All seemed present and accounted for. Still, several of our fellow travelers became agitated.

"Someone was supposed to meet us," a woman wailed. "Where is he?"

"They promised he would be here," another shouted. "Maybe we got off at the wrong place."

"Non, non, pas ici! Là-bas, voyez!" (No, no, not here! Down there, look!)

A man pointed down the track. Looking south about two hundred meters we could see a yellow banner drawn across a barrier blocking the tracks. It spelled ESPAÑA in large black letters. Struggling with our cumbersome baggage, we all stumbled toward the sign.

Halfway there we heard our train start up again, behind us. We stopped and watched it take off, back the way it had come. As it disappeared around a bend, all that remained was a wisp of gray smoke.

I thought, "If we wanted to change our minds and turn back, *tant pis* [too bad]—it's too late now." We continued on toward the barrier.

A young soldier, with an odd triangular patent-leather hat and a rifle slung over his shoulder, stood leaning against the door of a dilapidated guardhouse just beyond the barrier. A man wearing a shabby suit and a black beret was with him. A truck, covered with a torn canvas top, was parked nearby. Beyond, the village of Port-Bou spread out before us: rows of what once had been neat little whitewashed, red-tiled houses. Many were now in ruins; the burnt-out remnants of a church steeple stood on a hill etched against wild, dark clouds. The ocean was so close we could hear the rhythm of the surf.

The man with the beret waved to us, but remained where he was. The young guardsman, rifle ready now, walked toward us.

"Documentos!" he ordered.

As everyone scrambled to pull out their entrance visas, I leaned against the banner-draped barrier and looked around. There was something special about the place. I did not know what made it special, but I could feel it. It made me dizzy. The air was soft and, now that the sun had come out of the clouds, the light was so intense I felt its warmth seep right through my skin. Everything felt strangely familiar, as though I had been there before. I sensed the tension in everyone else, the nervous whispering, the shuffling of papers, the jockeying of belongings into place, but I felt far removed from it, as though I had just entered a world where nothing bad could touch me. Why? I didn't know or care. I was just happy to feel it, to accept it as real, unaware that "magical thinking" had kicked in again to rescue me from being overwhelmed by uncertainty.

Mother and Father were right behind Fredo and me, their hands gripping our shoulders. The soldier went from person to person, collecting documents. He examined each set of papers carefully, ripped out a page, and returned the rest.

We were last. When he came to us, he looked down and smiled at me. I smiled back. He turned abruptly and went back to the guardhouse. When he came out, his hat, turned upside down, was filled with green grapes. He walked directly to me, and held out the hat.

"Son para ti, mona. Toma, toma." (They are for you, pretty one. Take, take.)

"Merci beaucoup." I had understood his gesture but had forgotten for a moment that I was no longer in France. I suppose being singled out in front of everybody should have surprised me, but it didn't: what was happening just seemed to be a natural part of the strange magic I felt. I took off the kerchief around my neck and held it for the soldier so he could pour the grapes into it.

Just then the barrier across the tracks went up, its gold and black banner fluttering in the breeze, sounding like a flock of birds suddenly rising in flight. Everyone rushed to the other side. We were in Spain.

For two years we lived with Señora Carron in her spacious flat on the top floor of an old apartment building in Barcelona, which emerged unscathed from the Fascist bombardments during the Spanish Civil War. A handsome widow with aristocratic bearing, Señora Carron was the mother of a Catalan poet who had fled to the United States shortly before Franco's troops entered Barcelona. Her personal contribution to the Republican cause, she told us, had been to keep a pot of olive oil bubbling on the stove and pour it down on any of Franco's soldiers unlucky enough to be passing below her balcony.

"My aim was not so bad, sometimes," she murmured with a bitter smile, as she reminisced about her war experiences.

Her maid, Pilar, was a tiny, wiry woman still mourning her husband and youngest son, who had died just two months apart, fighting on opposite sides in the war. Pilar taught me to cook fish in the Catalan style—in olive oil with garlic and almonds, which were among the few foods one could find in stores. She also taught me to play castanets and to speak the outlawed Catalan language, which sounded like French. Sometimes she took me to church on Sundays and holy days, explaining that Señora Carron had stopped attending services when the Spanish Civil War broke out.

Fredo and I walked each school day to the Lycée Français de Barcelone, which was housed in an elegant former palace and whose student body consisted of many foreigners, including children of diplomats. Although I cannot remember one friend from school with whom I spent time outside school, I do remember one teacher, who took a special interest in me. A Spaniard who had fought in the Civil War on Franco's side, he seemed to enjoy answering my questions about Spain. My unfamiliarity with Catholicism must have been obvious, because during the many hours we spent together, he took great pains to show me a rather idealized view of his faith, stressing its mystical, spiritual side: the miracles, the forgiveness through confession, and the martyrdom of Jesus to redeem humankind.

He told me about the glorious days when Spain ruled the world and Queen Isabella and King Ferdinand sent Christopher Columbus on his voyages to bring Jesus' word to the pagan Indians.

After school we sometimes visited a nearby church, where he showed me statues of saints whose lives he had told me about, and explained the meaning of the Mass and other rituals. He made it all sound fascinating and beautiful, and I was drawn to the clearly drawn dos and don'ts by which Catholics lived. Today I need only to close my eyes to see this teacher: slight and fair skinned, with a lovely full mustache and dark, intense eyes, but his name escapes me.

He, however, was not the only one for whom I developed an emotional attatchment while I attended the Lycée Français. The other was a fellow student, and I still remember his name fifty years later: François Bally. A tall, blond, and blue-eyed Swiss, François resembled the prince in one of my favorite fairy tales. For three months I secretly followed him home, after school, just to be near him. He never noticed.

As in Prague, I spent my free time roaming the neighborhood streets, looking into shop windows, eavesdropping on conversations, reading plaques on public buildings and on the bases of statues. Among my favorite haunts was the Casa Milá (commonly referred to as the Pedrera, or Stone Quarry) the massive and strange-looking apartment building with undulating granite walls, wildly twisted wrought-iron balconies, and asymmetrical windows. Back then it meant nothing to me that it was designed at the turn of the century by the famous modernist architect Antonio Gaudí. For me, it became a fairyland playground. Many times I sneaked past the doorman and climbed up the Pedrera's circular staircase, illuminated by stained-glass skylights, all the way to the roof. While up there, high above the city, among multicolored cracked-crockery-encrusted chimney pots resembling giant medieval knights in armor, I played secret, solitary fantasy games, undisturbed by reality.

For my parents, life was not so easy. They worked long hours, making gloves, and they always seemed preoccupied. Receiving mail became an obsession with them. Sometimes packages came from Uncle Milos in America. Then we had chocolate, sugar, flour, and canned sausage and condensed milk to share with Señora Carron and Pilar. Letters from Oma Jenny had stopped soon after we arrived in France, but Mother kept writing, blaming unreliable mail service and hoping that at least some of our letters would reach her.

What little food could be bought was rigidly rationed. Even two small potatoes required hours of standing in line. Eggs were nonexistent. So were meat and butter. Instead of bread, Fredo and I carried a slice of almond-paste loaf, called *turrón*, in our lunch bags.

We took many snapshots and sent them to Oma Jenny in Prague. One that I remember showed the four of us, smiling broadly, in the Plaza Cataluña, with tall palm trees and hundreds of pigeons all around us, except for one sitting on my shoulder. Before sending it off, Mother wrote on the back, "Geht's uns schlecht? Ein Dreck geht's uns schlecht! Wir leben unter den Palmen!" (Are we doing badly? Like hell we are! We are living under palm trees!) The photo came back, months later, stamped OCCUPANT UNKNOWN. We did not find out till much later that Oma Jenny had been taken to the Theresienstadt concentration camp, where she died.

My parents and Fredo kept mostly to themselves. Except for work and school, they made no attempt to socialize. I don't remember meeting or being aware of any other refugees the whole time we were in Spain. We certainly did not associate with any foreigners. But I was neither lonely nor bored. I explored all there was to hear, see, taste, and smell. I remember guitars echoing down narrow alleys, hands clapping out flamenco rhythms, and the sweet, sad sounds of the *sardana*. Pilar described how, before the war, musicians used to sit on little folding chairs in front of the cathedral in the Gothic Quarter to play their music on ancient reed instruments, while circles of espadrilled dancers, holding hands, danced the *sardana* with tiny intricate hopping steps, which Pilar tried to teach me. Once Franco had come to power, he punished strongly the anti-Fascist Catalans by outlawing *sardana* dancing as well as all other public manifestations of "Catalan Separatism," but the music could not be silenced.

Also, it was hard to resist the majestic pageantry of Catholic ritual. Holy Week processions were particularly compelling. Crowds of the faithful followed behind lavishly gowned and bejeweled statues of the Virgin Mary, snaking slowly through the streets. Bloody crucified Cristos were carried by long-shrouded *penitentes* peering out from eye slits in their pointed hood masks. Flower-wreathed first communicants, looking like child brides in their long white dresses, threw flower petals in the path of priests carrying gleaming monstrances containing the sacred host or the bone-fragment relics of a saint. At Easter services the air was thick with the heady scent of incense and the ethereal soprano voices of choirboys singing High Mass. It was intoxicating and I yearned to be part of it.

We spent the summer vacation of my twelfth year in the tiny fishing village of Tamaríu, on the Costa Brava, north of Barcelona, where we rented a small cottage. Father and Fredo spent most of the time fishing out on the bay. Mother usually lay on a blanket beneath an umbrella on the crescent-shaped beach, writing letters or reading. I preferred to roam and explore the secluded coves and inlets of the wild coast, glad to be alone. I had a secret spot in the hollow of a rock where I read, wrote poetry, drew pictures of gulls in flight, and thought about the future. I dreamed of living the life of a missionary nun and dying a martyr's death in some exotic and dangerous land.

In the midst of my girlish reveries, everything abruptly changed once again. Uncle Milos finally succeeded in obtaining our entrance visas to the United States, and in April of 1941 we left for America. As a precaution, we told everyone that we were merely going to visit friends and relatives in New York. Again we left behind everything we had, including my dream of remaining in Spain until I was old enough to live out my heroic destiny.

# · 4 ·

# A New Life
# in the New World

We boarded the SS *Magellanes* in Bilbao, on Spain's north Atlantic coast. After picking up another group of refugees in Lisbon, we set out to sea and spent the next twenty-seven days on a stormy Atlantic. Nearly everyone was seasick, bruised, and bloodied as the ship pitched and bucked, buffeted by violent waves. Chained-down chairs and tables ripped loose and flew through the air in the salons and dining rooms of the musty old cruise ship, which had been pressed into service long past her retirement and overloaded with twice her normal three-hundred-passenger capacity. Two days out of Nassau the churning seas calmed. We put in for repairs in Havana for a week before docking at last in New York, where Uncle Milos awaited us. He had visited us occasionally in Prague, laden with expensive gifts for everyone, but we had not seen him for a very long time.

As soon as we cleared customs and immigration inspection, Uncle Milos instructed his chauffeur to drive us to Rockefeller Center, for lunch. Here we were, just off the ship after so many days at sea, eating delicious food in an elegant outdoor café, surrounded by skyscrapers I had seen only in photographs while watching skaters go round and round on an artificial ice rink on a balmy spring day! It all felt like a dream.

Later that week Uncle Milos took Fredo and me to a fancy department store and outfitted us with new clothes, down to socks and underwear. Before we had time to settle in, a Catholic refugee organization contacted my family. After assessing our parents' financial status, they offered to send Fredo and me to Catholic boarding schools in New England, on special scholarships. Our parents accepted. A week later, I went off to Marycliff Academy in Arlington Heights, Massachusetts, and Fredo left for Mount Saint Charles Academy in Woonsocket, Rhode Island. Unencumbered by our presence, our parents moved into a small apartment and began to rebuild their lives in New York.

Fredo's school turned out to be a very poor choice for him, and he hated it. His pervasive sense of isolation was due not only to the language barrier but to the fact that he had no interest in religion. Moreover, the school emphasized sports, about which he knew nothing and for which he had no aptitude. With so much about him to set him apart from the rest, he soon became the victim of routine beatings at the hands of bullies who dominated the resident student body. Those in charge, members of a well-known Catholic teaching order, did not intervene. When Fredo pleaded with Father to allow him to leave school and live at home, he was told to stop acting like a sissy. After that he kept his misery to himself and endured the abuse until he graduated from high school.

My own experience was very different. Marycliff was a small

girls' school set on lovely grounds, with pleasant double rooms on three floors, a huge dining room, and a beautiful chapel. Most of the boarders went home on weekends. That first year I almost never did. My parents wanted me to master English as quickly as possible. There were two other foreign students at Marycliff, who also frequently spent their weekends there: Mabel, who came from France, and Sonia, like me, from Prague. We called ourselves the Three Musketeeresses. Despite the fact that each of us was fluent in at least two languages, the three of us did not have any one in common: they both spoke English, which I did not. I spoke Czech and German, which Mabel did not, French, which Sonia did not, and Spanish, which was Greek to both of the other two. This made for some very convoluted conversations and a lot of laughter.

I spent much of that first summer at Marycliff perched in a fork of branches in a wonderfully fertile cherry tree, spitting pits in all directions while Sister Larosee sat below, shooting phrases at me to which I was expected to respond in perfect English. I felt I was in paradise. When school started in the fall of 1941, I was fluent enough to be promoted from third grade, where I had been placed for two months on my arrival, to high school freshman. A few months later, in December, Japan attacked Pearl Harbor and finally pulled the United States into the war. During the following school year, September 1942 to June 1943, I completed my sophomore and junior years simultaneously. When I began my third year at Marycliff, at fifteen, I found myself the only senior boarder at school. I was sixteen when I graduated on D Day, June 6, 1944.

Despite the war, from which I kept myself aloof, much of my three-year stay at Marycliff was pure joy. I was happy. I had fun. I felt secure. I became a typical teenager. I risked expulsion more than once, joining others in such escapades as climbing down from upper-floor windows on rickety trellises to sneak out at night to meet friends, and raiding the huge convent refrigerator when hunger got the better of our resolve to fast during religious retreats. I discovered American boys were more fun and certainly more accessible than the Swiss boy I had worshiped from afar in Barcelona. They looked upon me as different from anyone else they had ever met and vied for my favors. I often felt on exhibit, like some exotic plant, but soon got over my embarrassment when they corrected my fractured English. One thing was certain: I felt special, and I loved all the extra attention.

Like so many other bobby-soxers, I fell under "Frankie" Sinatra's spell, and thought nothing of waiting in line for hours at the Paramount Theater in Manhattan to get tickets to his concerts when I was home visiting my parents. But it was Uncle Milos who broadened my experience, by bringing me into his private classical music world. He had been a child prodigy and was still a fine pianist. Unlike my father, who felt like a failure compared to his successful younger brother, and rarely complimented Fredo or me, mainly concerning himself with strict and often erratic discipline, Uncle Milos was loving and solicitous, as well as demonstrative and outgoing. He became my ideal hero-father surrogate.

Uncle Milos was charismatic, full of prodigious energy and with a voracious interest in theater, literature, art, and politics. One example of his energy was his tenacious battle to secure our United States visas, but only later did I learn that he had also arranged admissions for thirty other refugees by personally guaranteeing their financial support for several years.

Milos looked just like Picasso, with a temperament to match. He collected fine paintings and lived a glamorous life in an elegant East Side brownstone. Our love of music became a strong bond between us. His Sunday-afternoon musicales occasionally included piano duets with such luminaries as Leonard Bernstein and Artur Rubinstein, who performed with him on twin baby grands, and recitals by singers like Paul Robeson and Risë Stevens, all of whom were his friends. But my favorite times with Uncle Milos happened when just he and I had what he called "our secret dates."

He would call me at Marycliff on a Friday morning, announcing, "Be ready at four. We're going to Tanglewood." At precisely four he would appear at the front desk, telling the startled nun in charge, "I have come to rescue my niece." And off we would drive to the Berkshire Hills in western Massachusetts in his huge black Packard convertible to spend two days lying under oak trees near the Boston Symphony's music tent, listening to all the rehearsals while he critiqued the performances. Often we attended as many as four or even five concerts a weekend, which always included a visit backstage to meet the artists.

While one part of me lived the normal life of a teenage boarding school student, the rest of me struggled with an increasingly compelling pull into a spiritual realm I had never before had the opportunity to explore. At Marycliff I was able to participate in all the Catholic rituals I had watched, wistfully, as an outsider in Spain. In an environment where Mass and vesper services were part of our daily routine, and sacred texts were read during meals, I became more and more caught up in the mystique of Catholicism, and I eagerly responded to what seemed to be natural, logical solutions to all my inner conflicts. There was hope. If Jesus died for my sins, was not forgiveness attainable after all? Could everything that happened have all along been part of God's plan to bring me to Him?

I kept my past to myself. I loved the peaceful times in chapel and welcomed the frequent retreats with long stretches of total silence for writing, prayer, and meditation. I joined the choir and learned to sing Gregorian chant. To explain my unfamiliarity with Catholic prayers and rituals (when to genuflect, sit, or stand, when and how to respond to the priest, and so on), I told everyone I had converted from Lutheran Protestantism. Nobody ever suspected the truth. I never forgot it.

As a "convert," I was given special religious instruction by Father Hannegan, the school chaplain. A mixture of his broken French and my growing English fluency enabled us to discuss about as much philosophy and theology as a young teenager could handle. Under the stress of such intimacy, cracks in my story quickly appeared. I finally entrusted him with "the truth." He was supportive and compassionate and remained my dear friend until we both left Marycliff after my graduation in June of 1944: he to enter a Trappist monastery and I to live with my family in New York while attending college.

Recently, when Mother was liquidating the large Upper West Side Manhattan apartment where she had lived for more than forty years, she came across a bulging cardboard box. It was taped tightly shut, with "Private!! Do not open!!" hand printed all over it. Assuming the box was mine, she sent it to me along with the beautiful carved chest in which she found it.

What spilled out, when I cut open the tapes, were yellowed mementos of my years at Marycliff. I discovered gilded "holy pictures" and bookmarks depicting Jesus and the saints that I had received from nuns and fellow students for birthdays and holy days. There were letters from nuns and priests, encouraging me to persevere in my faith. Old notebooks were filled with detailed accounts of retreat lectures and vocational pep talks. At the bottom were poems. Dozens of poems. Poems I had written, poems into which I had poured my soul, lyrical poems about love and loneliness. But most were poems about God, prayers for grace to help my parents "find the true faith," and pleas for strength to hold on to my resolve to devote my life to Jesus as a missionary nun, despite the temptations of the "wicked world"!

Here are two examples:

> *I laugh and play when I go out*
> *I'm thrilled when I go dancing*
> *I know I like boys' company*
> *And enjoy a li'l romancing.*
> *But Jesus, dear, amidst it all*
> *Don't be afraid to lose me:*
> *I won't forget Thy gracious call*
> *Won't let the world confuse me.*

•

*Oh, dearest Lord, please hear my plea*
*And grant that some day I may see*
*My family gathered at Thy feet*
*No more afraid Thy glance to meet.*
*And, Jesus, soon I'll gladly part*
*With home, for Thine is my whole heart*
*In foreign lands Thy Name I'll teach*
*And may it every nation reach!*

As I read the poems, I felt oddly embarrassed by their intensity and intimacy, as though I had violated someone else's most private domain. Could that really have been me, more than four decades ago, when I was only fourteen, fifteen years old? I had forgotten how desperately I needed to believe, to belong, how deeply I felt about everything then, and what a struggle it was to contain all the opposites at war with one another inside me.

I still marvel at how patiently and good-naturedly my parents put up with my missionary zeal. Whenever I came home to the apartment, where most of our neighbors were Jews, I flaunted a large cross on a chain around my neck. On more than one occasion I noticed how Mother would press back into the elevator, as far from me as possible, whenever someone she knew got on. I felt brave and self-righteous and looked for opportunities to draw my family into religious discussions. They missed the seriousness of my efforts. "Look, sweetheart," Mother would say in a patronizing, bemused tone, "this is a phase. You'll outgrow all this foolishness."

Although my parents tried to persuade me to go to the coed Pratt Institute of Art, which had accepted me, I chose instead to attend Manhattanville College, a nearby girls' school run by the Sacred Heart order of nuns, which had awarded me a full four-year scholarship. Surrounded by the Kennedy clan's daughters, among those of other prominent Catholic families, I was intensely aware that I was not part of their crowd, nor of any other, for that matter. I seldom socialized with my classmates, and when I did, I felt uncomfortable and kept the real me hidden away.

Living at home while attending Manhattanville soon took its predictable toll. Far removed from the insulated life at Marycliff, where I was steeped in such a single-minded and protected atmosphere, everything felt conflicted. I was split between two antithetical worlds and spent the next three years growing increasingly uncertain about my Catholic faith.

Meanwhile, the war, which had seemed so far away at Marycliff, screamed out at me from radios and newspaper headlines at every street corner. Stories of the extermination camp horrors could no longer be dismissed as mere rumors, and Jewish refugees were struggling to reach a safe haven in Palestine.

The shame over my apostasy, not out of conviction but as an act of cowardice, hung over me like a dark cloud. I still saw myself as an impostor. My guilt had little to do with being a Jew or a Catholic, per se. "Honor" and "standing up for the truth" were the real issues. My early childhood heroes had taught me that one suffers gladly for the truth and does not lie, even to save one's life. Taking the easy way out while so many others died remained as simplistically unforgivable as ever.

In between weekend visits from George, a young navy man I had met in Atlantic City the summer I graduated, I attended religious retreats and kept up a secret correspondence with the mother superior of the Maryknoll (foreign missionary order) novitiate I planned to enter after graduation. I hoped *that* would settle the issue once and for all.

All the while, I fought a losing battle trying to bolster my weakening resolve. Questions I asked the Manhattanville faculty were given rigid and arbitrary answers: any challenge to Church dogma and practice was frowned upon as disruptive and branded a sign of failing faith. Since no one suspected my Jewish background, Jews were ridiculed and spoken of with derision in my presence. Some of the jokes and racial slurs were so ugly I should have protested. Instead, I stayed silent, ashamed, not knowing how to respond. Respond as what? A Jew? As the fraud and coward I knew I was, I felt

I had no credibility, no right to challenge anyone on *any* issue. What right did *I* have taking a stand? My silence only compounded my shame.

Toward the end of my junior year at Manhattanville, the anesthetic effect of my flight into Catholicism finally wore off. What had once made sense, what had felt healing and reassuring, now felt irrelevant and empty. In falling out of the Catholic Church's safe, warm womb, I had lost my purpose in life. Now nothing fit. Suddenly I had to face the difference between what Jesus taught and how his teachings were twisted by his followers to incite crusades, inquisitions, and pogroms. There was no refuge in the Church for me anymore, and no forgiveness. The scaffolding I had erected to support my shaky identity was falling away, leaving me with nothing solid to hold onto. Who was I really? Catholicism no longer worked for me, and I had no doubt that being a Jew had long ceased to be an option. Once again I felt I belonged nowhere.

When the war ended, George was not ready to rescue me from my isolation with an offer of marriage and returned to his home in the Midwest. At the ripe age of nineteen, I felt everything meaningful in my life had evaporated.

In that state of despondency I met a Jewish boy as removed from his religious roots as I, who wanted to marry me. He was five years older than I, quiet and unassuming. I was not in love with him, but, with his even-tempered nature, I envisioned a blessedly placid and uneventful life together, providing me a secure, serene haven, far removed from all the turmoil that had consumed me for so long. He was leaving to attend graduate school in California and I was eager to get away from New York. All I wanted was some semblance of peace. I agreed to marry him.

Not quite ready to let go of all my ties with the Church, I applied to New York's Auxiliary Bishop Donoghue for a dispensation to allow a priest to marry us. Instead, I was given a two-hour lecture detailing the pitfalls likely to befall a good Catholic girl marrying into a Jewish family: disrespect, immorality, blasphemy, sexual abuse. That finally broke the spell, shattering what little illusion I still had about the Catholic Church. We were married by a judge.

My husband joined an army internship program that allowed him to pursue his doctoral studies in psychology while assigned to major army hospitals. During the first few years of our marriage, I threw myself into caring for our two children, Peter and Debbie, while free-lancing as a jewelry and fashion designer. Outwardly, all seemed to be going well, but had I bothered to look inside, I would have found life empty.

We lived far from any relatives and, because the army kept moving us from post to post, we were torn from fragile connections with others again and again. There was little to feed me spiritually or emotionally, but I did not take time to notice. Instead, I lost myself in a whirlwind of activity.

My husband made very few demands on me. He seemed to be satisfied as long as dinner was served on time and his uniforms were properly pressed. His involvement with the family was peripheral and he kept himself aloof even from our children. I tried to draw him in, but his studies always came first and provided a convenient excuse to distance himself from all of us. After a while, his non-participation ceased to matter.

In 1958 my husband quit the army. We returned to southern California, bought a home, and fell back into much the same routine as before. His graduate school studies were replaced by years of analytic training. I resumed my free-lance designing work and volunteered teaching art at the children's school. We occasionally attended services at various safely non-sectarian Unitarian congregations, so our children developed nebulous religious and ethnic identities.

One day, eleven-year-old Debbie asked me an unexpected question.

"All my friends go to Sunday school. How come I can't go?"

"Because our church does not have one."

"But I want to go. Can we find me one with a Sunday school?"

57

"Why don't you try going with some of your friends and see if there is one you like. Maybe we can arrange for you to go."

Debbie spent several weekends attending services and religious instruction classes with various friends. One day she announced, "I have found a Sunday school I want to go to, only it should really be called a Saturday school, because that's when they have their services. Can I go?"

At first I did not understand. Then it dawned on me: she had chosen a Jewish congregation! I felt a shiver and suddenly I was back in September of 1939, in Normandy, when I found out we were Jews. My daughter was exactly the same age as I was then, and the coincidence felt too significant to ignore.

"I've never told you this, but your grandmother and grandfather on both sides of our family are Jews." As I said it, I knew how clumsy and evasive it sounded. Since my daughter had never been exposed to anti-Jewish propaganda, her response was predictably simple in its logic.

"Well, if *they* are Jews, that makes *us* Jews, too, doesn't it?"

Only then did I tell her what had happened to me when *I* was her age and why I thought I had lost the right to ever call myself a Jew. In the telling, many memories I had blocked out for years began to stir. At the same time, I felt as though a hand was being held out to me, welcoming me home. Could God have chosen my daughter to bring me back, to show me I was forgiven? Could my exile really be over at last?

When I first walked into a synagogue, it felt strange. I experienced neither the awe nor the majestic presence of God that had always swept over me when I entered a Catholic church. It was easy enough to say, "I am a Jew." But inside, I still felt like an interloper, an intruder in a place where I did not belong. How would I ever justify to anyone my survival by fraud, my years as a Catholic? Who would help me connect to roots I had never grown, to claim a birthright that I had denied? What if I never fit in? And if I did, what if it ended up meaningless? I felt alone with my doubts, certain no one would understand. All I could do was acquaint myself as best I could with the heritage to which my newly assumed identity now allowed me access.

I attended classes on various aspects of Judaism and began to read armfuls of books. But when I try now to remember what books I read, what subjects I studied, nothing comes to mind. It is all a blur, as though everything happened so fast or felt so strange I was unable to absorb it.

In reality, though I did not know it, my psychic system was breaking down. I was unable to sleep. I continued to work but found it increasingly stressful. I withdrew more and more inside the black cave that had become my safest refuge. Every time I was tempted to reach out to something or someone for help, to ask for anything, to seek even the smallest comfort, a voice inside me screamed, "Shut up, you're supposed to be dead!"

After a while I found it hard to get up in the morning and face a new day. I spent hours weeping without a clue to the source of my tears. My husband, unable to comfort me or to understand what was troubling me, kept urging me to see a therapist, but I could see no point to it. What would I tell him? "I have a nice husband, two wonderful children, and a successful career. We have a lovely house and enough money to live comfortably. I don't know what's wrong with me and why I wish I were dead"?

Just before Christmas 1960 we were invited to a party where one of the guests was introduced to me as a Jungian analyst. "What is the difference between Jungian and Freudian analysis?" I asked. "Jung makes room for the spiritual side of the psyche" was his response. That hit a nerve. The next day I called for an appointment.

It took me a long time to open up. I felt confused and unable to justify my despair. As I slowly began to peel back the layers of my past, I found myself wallowing in a bottomless pit. In addition to all the old issues about my conflicted identity and my guilt over being alive, new and more immediate issues soon emerged. These primarily concerned my inability to find joy in anything and the conviction that I was fated to be unhappy forever. The sterility of my marriage became less and less tolerable as I allowed my long-repressed true feelings to emerge. Instead of improving, I sank more deeply into the pit.

Bouts of depression became more frequent. Therapy turned more and more intense. Dreams poured out at the rate of four and five a night. Decoding these symbolic messages from my unconscious became my new religion and the analyst my substitute for God. I spent hours devouring everything Jung had ever written, plowing through his dozen or more massive Bollingen Series books in an attempt to understand and quiet the earthquake in my soul. Reading clarified things intellectually, but emotionally and spiritually I felt adrift, more convinced than ever that everything was hopeless.

In the spring of 1964, Uncle Milos came for a visit. He was by then in his sixties, and I hadn't seen him for a long time, but our special relationship was still there and I could open my heart to him, though not completely. Without going into great detail, I told him how depressed I felt. As we spoke, I felt certain that, if I could just get back to Spain, all of my pain and despair would disappear. Although it had been a quarter century since I left, Spain obviously still carried a special symbolic meaning for me.

"I wish I could leave everything behind and move to Spain," I blurted out.

"You don't have to go that far," he answered. "How about going for just a few weeks?" He wrote me a check and three weeks later I was on my way back to Spain.

I went alone, choosing to go by sea instead of flying, to give myself time to reflect, to get ready for what I knew would be a very emotional experience. Before I left and on board ship I took time to read as much as I could about the history of Spain relating to the places I would visit in addition to Barcelona, but hardly enough to make me an expert. I did, however, learn considerably more about the great influence Jews and Moors had on Spanish culture, and details of the persecution both suffered at the hands of the Catholic Church, facts my gentle teacher years ago had carefully avoided sharing with me.

The SS *Saturnia* was destined for southern Spain, where I had never been before. We docked at Málaga, on the Costa del Sol. The heady feeling that enveloped me the day I crossed the border in Port-Bou, so long ago, was there again when I left the ship.

The ancient Málaga Alcazaba (fort) perched on a hill in the heart of the city offered me my first glimpse of Moorish architecture, and I promptly fell in love with its graceful elegance. In Seville I walked the streets of the old Jewish quarter, with its flower-filled patios and tiny tree-shaded plazas, and climbed to the top of the Giralda tower of the huge Gothic cathedral built in its midst. I was astounded by the opulence I found in the treasure chamber of the Church of the Macarena, the Virgin Protector of bullfighters, where her lavishly bejeweled and gold-encrusted gowns are kept on display. Conscious of the many beggars I encountered everywhere I went, I whispered to the local woman next to me, "This would feed a lot of hungry mouths." "Yes," she replied, "but *this* feeds our souls."

As I approached the Alhambra in Granada, I was overwhelmed by the breathtaking sight of its massive red walls rising from a deep gorge against the snow-capped Sierra Nevada range behind it. I spent hours wandering through this Arabic fortress-palace, which was the last stronghold of Spain's Moorish rulers before they finally surrendered to the Catholic Monarchs in 1492. I was awestruck by the splendor of the many fountains and patios, as well as by the exquisite lacelike filigree walls and ceilings embedded with colored glass fragments that gave it its jewel-like ambience.

Inside Córdoba's enormous Mesquita (mosque), I threaded my way through the maze of alabaster columns supporting hundreds of arches striped in rust and ocher. I shared my Arab guide's outrage at the full-size Catholic cathedral that had been inflicted into the core of the building after the expulsion of the Moors, a vulgar insult to its architectual and spiritual integrity. I was, however, delighted to discover in a small plaza a charming bronze bust of Maimonides, the Golden Age's most honored Jewish scholar and medieval Córdoba's most illustrious son.

Although Toledo is primarily known today as the place where dozens of El Greco's paintings are on display in his beautifully restored medieval home, what moved me to tears was the sight of the Hebrew inscriptions etched into the walls of two lovely old synagogues bearing the incongruous names Santa María la Blanca and El Tránsito. These buildings were consecrated as Catholic churches after the Jews converted or were driven out and, although still the property of the Toledo archdiocese, they are now designated as national monuments.

I saved Barcelona for last. As I approached the city at dusk, driving from the airport past long-loved landmarks, surges of nostalgia caught in my throat.

The next morning I walked up the Paséo de Gracia in search of Gaudí's Pedrera, on whose roof I had played my solitary fantasy games as a child. Now it was one stop on a guided tourist tour of that great architect's local masterpieces. I waited until everyone else had left and took a nostalgic turn among the tile-encrusted chimneys still reminiscent of giant-sized knights in armor.

Later, I walked the few blocks to Calle Gerona and saw the old apartment building where we had lived with Señora Carron and Pilar. From there I had no trouble retracing my steps to the corner, a short distance away, where the Lycée Français was located. I found the graceful mansion a bit weathered, and smaller than I remembered, but a quarter century after my student days it was still alive with children's voices.

In the days that followed, I strolled through the cobblestoned streets of the Gothic Quarter and browsed through its many antiques shops, rare book stores, art galleries, and pottery bazaars. Everywhere I looked, something reminded me of the past.

I ate in little restaurants and sampled an endless variety of Catalan dishes, mixtures of fish, sausage, chicken, mushrooms, lamb, and rice flavored with garlic, saffron, and olive oil. More than once I found myself drifting back to the days, so long ago, when I watched Pilar transform her meager ingredients into culinary magic.

From the top of one of the serpentine spires of Gaudí's monumental still-unfinished Sagrada Familia Cathedral (Expiatory Temple of the Holy Family), I got a bird's-eye view of the entire city, clear down to the statue of Christopher Columbus, perched high on its column in the harbor, and the Mediterranean Sea beyond. My heart was full to bursting every waking moment, aching with long-forgotten dreams. But when the day of my departure arrived, I was ready to return home.

Spain served as a lovely distraction, and for a while I felt better. As the magic wore off, however, my depression returned. It came in waves, becoming ever more unfocused, without concrete content, and dissolved into an amorphous, wordless abyss. It wrapped itself around me, dense and dark, screening out the sun, blocking out sound, clogging every pore, making every breath an effort, every movement an ordeal.

Between the worst bouts of depression, I managed to function—working, taking care of the children and the house. During those periods of relative calm, I looked upon what was happening to me as my own failure, something I should have been able to control, so I tried my best to hide its severity from my family, friends, even my therapist. When I was caught in its black grip, all I was aware of was an all-pervasive *no* to everything except utter hopelessness.

It took years of intensive effort for the depression to become manageable. It was an uphill battle for every step gained. Today, the memory of those days has mercifully receded into the background, but it took a long time for me to learn to look at life with some measure of self-acceptance and optimism. Along the way, there were subtle signs of change, showing I was gaining insight, courage, and the resolve needed to set myself free from my self-imposed prison.

One such sign came in the form of two dreams, two years apart. In the first, I saw myself emerging from the sea (the unconscious), walking toward a massive wall surrounding an ancient city. Above the wall I could see the steeple of a church with a cross, the minaret of a mosque with a crescent, and the dome of a synagogue with a Star of David: I recognized the place as Jerusalem. As I walked toward the wall, the city kept receding, and I grew afraid that I might never be allowed to enter inside. Here the dream ended and I awoke in tears.

The second dream was identical to the first, except that this time the wall had a wide-open crack from top to bottom. As I walked toward it, I knew that I would eventually reach the city inside. Awake, I recognized this as a sign presaging the end of my exile and the redemption of my identity as a woman and a Jew. These two dreams led me back to my center, to my own reality, to the crucial issues that had taken me into therapy in the first place.

Things changed faster after that. When my children were ready to leave home, my husband and I finally divorced. I sold our home and bought a small townhouse I could handle alone. I gave up my designing job and entered graduate school, where I earned a master's degree in psychology. After two more years of internship and countless hours of supervised clinical work, I received my Marriage, Family, and Child Therapist's license, with a specialty in art therapy. My practice soon flourished and I developed a social life, but there was still one thing I had to do.

During this hectic period of personal growth, when recently activated parts of my extrovert self were claiming priority, I avoided the issue of my Jewish identity, although my two dreams proved I was working on it from within. As I grew more comfortable with the new me, I began to reach out. Little by little, very tentatively,

I began to look for ways to reconnect to the roots from which I had cut myself off for so long. I started attending services at various outreach Jewish congregations, most of which held Shabbat and Holy Day observances in Protestant churches because they had no synagogues of their own.

It was at one of these innovative services that I first learned the meaning of the Kol Nidre, the traditional prayer of Yom Kippur, the Jews' Day of Atonement. Because Jews so often were forced to make spiritual compromises under the threat of death, this ancient Aramaic prayer asked that God disregard any vows made during the past year that concerned their relationship to Him: vows of baptism and conversion, vows of denial, or vows of allegiance made on the crucifix. In the eleventh century, as more and more Jews were forcibly baptized and made to live as Christians, the Kol Nidre's wording was changed to apply to such vows made in the future as well as those made in the past.

It was of great comfort to me to learn that Jewish tradition, unlike Catholicism, not only acknowledged circumstances under which one might be forced to make compromises that went against one's conscience but provided an instrument specifically designed to bring about God's forgiveness. I felt this prayer could have been written for me.

By late 1988 I was finally ready to do what I knew I had to do: return to Spain to begin my quest for what I left behind there as a child. Spain was where the Jewish people had such a rich and varied history. Spain was where I first felt the full impact of my Jewish identity, as different from that of everyone else around me, without knowing anything about it except that it was *mine*. Spain was where I first learned to hide that Jewish identity, because it was too dangerous to embrace openly. Spain was also the place where other Jews had fled, *as Jews*, despite the danger. I had to return to Spain to speak to them and to find out what magical strength had sustained them during those terrible years. I knew that if I was ever to find my own connection to my lost Jewish self, Spain is where I would find it.

The fact that I would be exploring events that might make Spain and its people look heroic was met with mistrust, even outright hostility, by the local Jewish communities to which I turned for support. Jews of Spanish ancestry (Sephardim) basically dismissed the project as an "Ashkenazic issue," while the Central and Eastern European Jews wanted nothing to do with "anti-Semitic Spain," which had been allied with Hitler.

A high official of a major Jewish organization wrote, "I must tell you honestly that Spain is not on anybody's 'best' list. They are not taking in any Jews at this time, they welcomed Arafat, and they vote against Israel in the United Nations." I replied, "The fact that thousands of Jews are alive today because they were granted asylum in Spain during the Holocaust deserves to be told and remembered." That letter remains unanswered.

My own mother, still alert and feisty at eighty-five, never spoke about our life in Spain. By the time she was thirty-six years old, Spain was the third country to which we had been forced to flee, leaving everything behind. Her mother died in a concentration camp while we were in Spain. The Holocaust and our escape from it was something she clearly wanted to forget.

I visited Mother in New York in December 1988, days before my first research trip to Spain. Her lack of enthusiasm for my project came across loud and clear. "Who will still be alive, fifty years later? Who wants to remember? Why would anyone want to talk about that terrible time? Don't you remember what it was like? At the movies, when the newsreels showed Hitler's troops marching and his planes bombing, everybody jumped up, gave the Nazi salute, and cheered. We were scared all the time, and you want to make Spain look good?" I left for Spain without her blessing.

I did not intend to discuss my project with Mother again. She, however, brought up the issue the following year, in a most unexpected way. But before that happened, even after I had met with many people willing to talk about the experiences she believed everyone would want to forget, I felt sad and disloyal and wondered vaguely if she might not turn out to be right, after all.

One special event that confirmed my resolve to proceed with my quest was a symposium I attended in Los Angeles in November of 1988, "Shadows of the Holocaust," commemorating the fiftieth anniversary of Kristallnacht, the night when broken glass from vandalized synagogues, and from Jewish businesses and homes littered the streets of Germany, marking the beginning of the Holocaust.

Pierre Sauvage was the keynote speaker. His award-winning film, *Weapons of the Spirit,* tells the story of the five thousand villagers of Le Chambon sur Lignon (members of a Huguenot Protestant minority in Catholic France) who sheltered five thousand Jews in a "Conspiracy of Goodness," right under the nose of the Nazi war criminal Klaus Barbie, the infamous "Butcher of Lyons." The villagers of Le Chambon hid Sauvage's parents, and he himself was born there shortly before the end of the war.

Sauvage explained that his father, a prominent French journalist, had died just the week before. In an intensely personal way he described his painful and distant relationship with this man, who, after leaving Le Chambon, buried his past and never spoke to his son about what happened to his family during the war.

"I did not find out I was a Jew until I was eighteen years old and on my way to study in Paris, where I was to live with a cousin who had survived years in Auschwitz. Just before I left, my parents sat me down and told me I was Jewish or that *they* were Jewish, or that we were *born* Jewish, I don't remember which. The rest of the family, those who survived, had gone along with the deception: the conspiracy of silence worked. I never caught on. Perhaps they felt they had to remain in hiding all those years."

Sauvage's father's final request was to have no memorial, no funeral, to be cremated and have his ashes scattered. Obviously distressed, Sauvage concluded, "If I respected my father's wishes I wouldn't be a Jew, I wouldn't be the father of two Jews, and I would most certainly not be here with you today. We cannot assume as a given that, because of our love for our parents, because of our worry over what they went through, we have to be content to merely be dutiful children. We must not deny the pain, the guilt, the rage that must still be buried in many of us, regardless of whether we have the good fortune to still have our parents or not."

For me, Sauvage's words felt like a mandate to follow through with my resolve to retrieve something I lost even before it was mine to lose. It gave me the impetus to find out more about the place, the people, and the events that had so deeply affected my own life as well as those of so many others and about which so few seemed to know anything. It gave me the courage to go ahead with my quest, despite Mother's opposition.

A year after my first research trip to Spain I spent a few days with Mother in New York while working in the archives of the American Jewish Joint Distribution Committee, the agency that helped rescue, feed, clothe, house, and sustain so many refugees in Spain and elsewhere during the war years.

On my last night I was packing for my early-morning flight home to Los Angeles when my mother casually asked, "So, how is that project of yours coming along?"

I realized then how much I had wanted to tell her about what had happened in the year since I began my work, since we last were together. Facts poured out, names, places, events, as I described some of the more touching interviews. When I stopped, my mother remained silent for a long time.

"I wept when we had to leave Spain," she said at last. "I really hoped we could stay, but our visas finally came through, and you know Father."

"But I thought you hated it in Spain! You said you hated it!"

"I hated the fear, but I loved Spain." Again silence. "The Germans were everywhere. You could see them in the streets, with their Nazi uniforms and swastikas." Her voice grew faint and I could see her remember how it felt. "You were still a child, so how could you know what that meant? Any day they could have turned us over to them. You never knew when, you never could feel safe. But the Spanish people were different, they were wonderful." I saw the expression on her face soften. "Do you know how Father and I survived in Spain? We had to do something to make a living, to keep a roof over our heads and put food on the table, because what little we had with us, when we left Paris, was gone very quickly." For a moment she paused, lost in thought. "Remember the gloves?"

"You mean the gloves you made, the gloves for the stores?" Yes, I remembered the boxes with glove parts piled on the floor in the apartment we shared with Señora Carron and Pilar, Mother and Father cutting leather from cardboard patterns on the round dining table, women coming and going, picking up and delivering bundles of home labor. "Yes, I remember."

"Did I ever tell you how Father and I got started in the glove business?" I shook my head. "Well, this is how it happened. I made up three left gloves out of leather scrap bottoms and crocheted tops. Then I took those three gloves to the head of the Martí-Martí department store, the biggest one in Barcelona at that time. I right away asked to see Señor Martí-Martí himself. You should have seen how he loved those gloves! He gave me such a big order I got scared. Several dozen! I told him, 'Señor Martí-Martí, we are refugees, we have no money to buy leather.' So, you know what he did? He sat down and wrote a note and said to take it to his leather supplier. It said, 'Give them whatever they need.' Such a *Mensch*, that Señor Martí-Martí! Did he ask were we Jews? Did he care? He must have known, but no questions. He didn't ask for a credit statement like you would need here. Imagine, how he treated us, *foreigners*, without even a work permit! He just trusted us, just like that, and he believed we could produce, with no proof. Not like Paris, where nobody cared and nobody helped and we could not earn a single franc and Uncle Milos had to keep sending money so we could eat. Yes, the Spaniards knew we were refugees, but they were wonderful to us. We had it good living with Señora Carron and Pilar and I cried when we had to leave."

I listened, stunned, careful to hide my tears, afraid that if I showed any emotion she would take it all back. I wanted to whip out my recorder and tape a real, official interview with her, but I did not dare. It all felt too fragile, this rare connection with her on something so vital to the both of us. I was determined to write it all down before she could shove it back into the black hole where she had kept so many painful memories hidden for so long.

Flying back to Los Angeles the next morning I remembered speaking with Nina Mitrani, a Polish Jewess living in Barcelona, who was the first refugee I had interviewed a year before. After protesting that she could remember nothing, she proceeded to release a torrent of minutely detailed memories, including her lonely and dangerous climb over the Pyrenees Mountains as an eighteen-year-old bride, searching for her husband, who had preceded her into Spain.

"For someone who said she could remember nothing, you told your story as though it happened yesterday," I told her when she had finished.

"Yes, it felt like it all happened yesterday," Nina replied, "but to someone else."

I realized then, and again while listening to my mother, that some of us must bury our memories in order to go on living, while others are compelled to retrieve them in order to bring meaning into our lives.

# PART TWO

# THE RESCUED

# · 5 ·

# *The Unlikely Haven of Spain*

In 1940, France fell under Hitler's brutal onslaught and many refugees who had sought shelter there after fleeing from Austria, Czechoslovakia, Poland, Germany, and other occupied or threatened areas found themselves trapped in a narrow strip of land in southern France euphemistically called the Free Zone. While the Germans occupied the rest of France, the south was placed under the control of a Fascist puppet regime with headquarters in Vichy. Vichy France, which included the major port city of Marseilles, was headed by a revered French World War I hero, Marshal Henri-Philippe Pétain, who agreed to cooperate with the Nazis in return for a cruel semblance of self-rule and the promised repatriation of French prisoners of war.

The Gestapo, with widespread collaboration by the French population, openly controlled everything, including the strictly enforced Nazi racial policies. This meant Jews had to find a way out of France. Spain became the unlikely destination of thousands who had nowhere else to go and who were willing to brave any danger to escape certain deportation to concentration camps or worse, should they fall into German hands.

The absurdity of those desperate years is best symbolized by the paradox of refugees fleeing the Nazis' Final Solution by seeking asylum in a country where no Jews had been allowed to live openly, as Jews, for over four centuries. When I met with Dr. Isidro Gonzalez Garcia, a professor of history at Universidad Autonoma de Madrid and the author of many books on the relationship between Spain and the Jews, I asked him if any Jews had attempted to return to Spain before that unexpected and unlikely influx, and what might have motivated so many to seek asylum there under such dangerous circumstances.

"The first Jews to reenter Spain, about three hundred families, began to trickle back in the late 1800s when serious anti-Semitic uprisings and pogroms spread from Russia to Yugoslavia, Romania, and other Balkan countries. Because most of the Jews living there were Sephardim, whose ancestors settled in that area after their expulsion from Spain in 1492, Spanish diplomats stationed in those countries interceded on their behalf, securing their admittance to Spain. This was the first such effort by a Spanish government since the Jews were expelled."

Although this intercession made Spain look good to the rest of Europe, the Spanish government's motives were not entirely altruistic: the government hoped that those Jews, who still spoke Spanish, might establish commercial connections for Spain in other Mediterranean countries.

The return of those few Jews did not go unnoticed. The pros and cons of their presence were widely discussed in the Spanish press; people expressed opinions and took sides. Suddenly, after four hundred years, Spain had a "Jewish problem," like the rest of Eu-

rope. Liberals spoke about the need for reconciliation with the expelled Jews, while the intolerant and absolutist conservatives ar-
gued that if Jews were allowed to come back in great numbers, it
would result in a social destabilization. They were also opposed to
religious freedom, afraid that the presence of Jews would create religious division and undermine the power of the Catholic Church.

At the start of the 1900s, two Spanish diplomats emerged as
champions of the Jews: Dr. Angel Pulido and Salvador de Madariaga.
Both had close contacts with Jewish communities all over Europe
and both stressed the value of connections with Jews to promote
Spanish interests abroad. Pulido was the first to suggest a rapprochement with Jews and defended them as a matter of conscience,
but his efforts polarized the government and ultimately failed.

When the persecution of Jews intensified in Germany after
Hitler came to power in 1933, de Madariaga, then Spain's ambassador to the League of Nations, protested their mistreatment before the League and pleaded for the protection of all minorities in
the name of the Spanish Republic.

Then a curious thing happened. Although de Madariaga de-
cried the persecution of Jews and defended them in the League of
Nations, he opposed their readmittance to Spain. Why? There was
huge unemployment in Spain, and he feared that such an influx
might create great social upheaval. Also, he felt sure it would reac-
tivate anti-Semitism from the right-wing factions, which represented a powerful minority in Spain's liberal government.

During this same period, around 1935, the Germans had already
begun trying to "clean house" to get rid of their Jews, but had not
yet formulated their extermination policy. So when the Nazis heard
de Madariaga urge the League of Nations to help rescue and save
the persecuted Jews, the Nazis proposed to the government of Spain
that they should accept all the Jews they, the Germans, did not
want. In effect, the Germans said, "Here, take ours!" Spain's response, for all intents and purposes, was "No, thanks."

Thus, although Spain defended and championed Jews in the

international political arena, when it came right down to actually accepting them in their midst, they backed down, afraid that the presence of the Jews would create insurmountable problems. This resulted in a double standard: the Spanish people's conscience led them to want to help the Jews, but their internal economic and social problems kept the doors closed to them.

Then, in 1936, after years of obscurity and isolation, Spain became the focus of world attention when a small uprising against the Spanish Republic (which had ousted the monarchy only five years before) turned the country into an international battleground. The challenge to Spain's duly elected government by an obscure young officer in North Africa, Francisco Franco, precipitated the civil war that split the country in two and polarized the nations of the world into Left and Right, Fascist and Democratic camps. Foreign troops and bomber squads went to support "their side" in an ominous prelude to the tragedy that, in 1939, plunged Western civilization into darkness for six long years. Many believe the first shot of World War II actually rang out three years before, in Spain.

The outbreak of the Spanish Civil War forced Spain to deal with more pressing issues than the "Jewish Problem," which now receded into the background. Ironically, the Jews themselves found their own loyalties split: those in Spanish North Africa, mostly of Spanish descent, tended to support Franco's anti-Republican Nationalist insurgents, while the majority of those elsewhere considered themselves liberal and supported the anti-Franco Loyalist side. The International Brigades, from Russia, England, the United States, and other countries, were full of Jews supporting the Republic. Hitler and Mussolini rushed to Franco's aid and used Spain as a testing ground for sophisticated new weapons with which they planned to crush the Allies later.

World War II started in September 1939, less than six months after the Spanish Civil War ended. As information about the treatment of Jews became common knowledge and war activity intensified from 1940 through 1942, so did concern and discussions in

Spain about the fate of the Jews. Laws regulating their admittance were written and mostly ignored, but the fact remains that until 1942 Spain was closely tied to Franco's Fascist allies and it was extremely difficult for Jews to gain legal entry.

Then, in 1942–43, the tide of war turned and took on a dramatic new direction. The Axis powers sustained enormous casualties in Sicily and the Germans began to lose. It is at this point that Franco, demonstrating his shrewd political know-how, quietly got rid of his hard-line foreign minister, Ramón Serrano Suñer (his own brother-in-law, renowned for his Nazi sympathies), and replaced him with Count Francisco de Jordana y Sousa, who opposed Spain's ties to Hitler.

"Franco himself never said anything about Jews," admitted Professor Gonzalez. "He was once asked by an English journalist if he thought there was a Jewish problem in Spain. 'There is no Jewish problem,' he replied, 'because Spain has no Jews.' But, when the Axis began to lose the war, he found a way to quietly shift diplomatic policy from one supporting anti-Semitism to one more sympathetic to Jews. No official policy change was ever announced, but from then on the Spanish government simply closed its eyes and ears to what individual diplomats chose to do."

In Madrid, the American ambassador Carlton Hayes immediately found it easier to work with the Spanish authorities, and Spanish diplomats in Hungary, Bulgaria, Greece, and Romania were able to use their influence to facilitate the rescue of Jews as conditions became more dangerous for them in those countries, providing them with permits to enter Spain in increasing numbers.

Gonzalez also brought up an example that "showed a certain hypocrisy on the part of the Allies": their infamous Bermuda Conference.

By April 1943 the extermination policy of the Nazis was well known to President Roosevelt and the rest of the world. To confront this growing problem, a conference was convened in Bermuda by representatives of the allied nations. The primary issue to be discussed was the creation of a containment camp near Casablanca, in North Africa, so that Jews passing through Spain with nowhere else to go would have a safe place to stay until they could make other arrangements. Such a camp would enable Spain to absorb many more Jews, who would otherwise not be let in.

Although most of the participants originally appeared to favor establishing the camp, support for it quickly eroded. According to Gonzalez, the French and English opposed the plan because approving it "would make it appear that the Allies' primary war objective was to save the Jews." They feared that world opinion would turn against them if it looked as though they "favored the Jews." Also, the British were against the establishment of Palestine, and did not want an additional influx of Jews into that area.

The American chiefs of staff, including General Dwight D. Eisenhower and Admiral William Leahy, also refused to accept the proposal. In *Spain, the Jews, and Franco*, Professor Haim Avni, a historian at the University of Jerusalem, quotes President Roosevelt, to whom the final decision was left: "I know in fact that there is plenty of room in North Africa, but I raise the question of sending large numbers of Jews there. That would be extremely unwise" (May 14, 1943). In the end, the proposal was scuttled.

Professor Gonzalez concluded: "More could have been done to save Jews by the Allies themselves, but it wasn't. I have the entire transcript of the Bermuda Conference. All of those there knew about the crematoria. 'We know they are dying,' they said. They also knew the Germans were looking for a way out, to simply be rid of the Jews, but the participants were so concerned with public opinion, what might appear to be an overemphasis on helping Jews in the overall picture of the war, that very little was done. It was at this point, 1943–44, that the influx of Jews into Spain intensified."

Resisting all pressure from Hitler to participate actively unless he was guaranteed a large part of North Africa in return, Franco kept Spain out of World War II, but no one knew how long it would last.

Desperation, as anyone faced with limited choices in life-threatening situations quickly discovers, dictates drastic decisions. Thus, those squeezed by the advancing German armies into the narrow corridor between southernmost France and the Pyrenees were left with two options: stay and risk capture by the Nazis or brave an uncertain fate in Spain.

Thousands chose the latter. Almost all who did, survived. Most stayed a while, then went elsewhere. Some are still alive fifty years later. Their stories of bravery and determination exemplify the spirit that has helped so many Jews to survive centuries of persecution, in constant danger and deprivation, with their humanity intact.

What were Franco's motives for granting shelter to masses of Jewish refugees when Spain was struggling to recover from years of devastating civil strife that left its economy and public services in a shambles? Were Franco's ancestors converted Jews, as many believe, and would that be enough of an explanation? We may never know the full truth.

Some facts, however, are common knowledge: Franco had a reputation for brutal repression of the enemies of his regime. Free speech and other civil rights were almost nonexistent during his long tenure, which he touted as "thirty-six years of peace." Opposition was not tolerated, and thousands of dissenters disappeared into prisons, never to be seen again. The Catholic Church wielded great power as the official state religion, relegating all other faiths—Protestant, Islamic, as well as Jewish—to illegal status.

Nevertheless, it is equally true that, during Franco's rule, thousands of Jews survived because they were given asylum in Spain and in Spanish embassies in occupied countries. These facts, although amply documented, are considered by many too controversial and contradictory to be true and have remained lost in conjecture. The voices of those who speak to us from the following pages should do much to set the record straight in a very personal way: *they were there*.

# ·6·

# *Barcelona Again*

As I approached Barcelona at dusk in late December 1988, my excitement rose with each mile that brought me closer to the city I have loved so long.

I settled into my room at the Residencia Colón, in the old Gothic Quarter. Leaning out from the balcony and looking to the far right, I could see a wedge of the Cathedral Square, where *sardanas* dancers were once more free to perform their traditional Catalan Sunday-morning ritual now that Franco was dead. This evening, however, it was filled with hundreds of Christmas shoppers browsing through row after row of booths displaying tree trimmings, crèche figures, wreaths, candles, and all manner of handmade holiday gifts. The filigreed cathedral spires, lit from within, resembled gold lace cones. Spotlights illuminated the graceful Gothic arches, and the stained-glass windows cast a muted multicolored glow. Christmas music and carillons enhanced the festive atmosphere.

The city had grown but had not lost its soul. Barcelona had preserved its unique charm: in the old quarter, crowded cobblestoned streets, fragrant with the scent of flowers and fresh-baked bread, flowed onto intimate, tree-shaded plazas where benches, clustered around sparkling fountains, invited the weary to pause for a moment of rest. Fine-featured women, with flawless skin, linked arms, chattering animatedly as they walked. Dark and brooding Gypsies in long skirts and fringed shawls held babies wrapped in dirty blankets, sqatting on sidewalks and begging alms. Middle-aged men took time to cast appreciative glances and whisper *piropos* (traditional, elaborately poetic compliments) to pretty girls passing by. Foreign sailors bargained for souvenir trinkets in harbor shops. Teachers led the way as uniformed schoolchildren followed single file, holding onto knotted ropes to keep from getting lost. Street musicians and mimes competed for audiences among newsstands, bird stalls, and flower booths along the wide center strip of the tree-lined Ramblas (main boulevards). Sidewalk cafés and *tapa* bars overflowed with tourists and shoppers sipping sherry or lingering over thick, sweet espresso while nibbling on baby snails, pickled octopus, fried sardines, *serrano* ham, roasted almonds, and ripe olives. Thousands of pigeons still grew fat and fearless in the Plaza Catalunya (as it is spelled in Catalan), providing a lively backdrop for photographers, as they had when I was a child.

Just as I had no connection to the Jewish community of Prague as a child, I never explored Barcelona's Jewish past until I returned fifty years later. That city's Jews have a long and illustrious history. Their community flourished for eight hundred years before thousands of its members were slaughtered and all its synagogues destroyed by Christian zealots on Ash Wednesday, in 1391. Montjuïc (Mountain of the Jews), which overlooks the city, was once the home of many of Barcelona's Jews. The cemetery spilling down its slopes served the Jewish community until its devastation. All that remains now are a few tombstones kept in a special room devoted to Jewish artifacts in the Historical Museum.

Below, in the city's heart, many of the narrow streets of the Call (Jewish Quarter in Catalan) still bear the names of some former inhabitants. Walking through the bustling maze of shops and eateries one cannot help but feel their presence and imagine what life must have been like for them during the many centuries they lived there, before those few who survived the great massacre were finally exiled.

In 1954, twenty-six years before the right to free and open worship was finally granted to all religions in Spain, the first synagogue in Spain since 1492 was quietly established in Barcelona. Because it was considered illegal, the tiny Jewish community took great care to keep its activities as secret as possible.

More than five thousand Jews now live in the city. Not all are active in their community. Those who are, including a small minority of middle-European Ashkenazim within a great majority of Sephardim, jointly own and support Barcelona's Jewish Center, housed in a three-story building on a quiet side street in a middle-class, mostly commercial neighborhood. Although a Sephardic rabbi serves both factions, the membership maintains two sanctuaries, on two different floors of their building, and has separate prayer services. All other functions and responsibilities are shared.

Security at the center is strict. Doors are electronically controlled and monitored by strategically placed surveillance video cameras. All who wish to enter must first identify themselves, as a precaution against terrorists. The building houses not only both synagogues but also a library, several meeting rooms for holy-day celebrations, a suite of offices, and classrooms where children and adults study Hebrew, the Torah, the Talmud, and Jewish history. The center also operates an excellent school, the Liceo Sefardi, for children from kindergarten through high school, and a summer camp in the countryside that attracts children from all over Spain and France. A kosher butchershop is located nearby, as are other Jewish-owned businesses. Many of the members of the community live within walking distance of the center, and it is there I met with several of those who told me their stories.

# · 7 ·

# Nina's Story: "Never Go Up, Only Down"

Although Nina Mitrani was the first Jewish refugee I contacted in Barcelona, she was not one of those with whom I had a prearranged appointment. I was concerned about her reaction to my sudden intrusion into her life, and wondered if she would consent to see me. I was, after all, a stranger.

When I called Nina, I briefly explained the purpose of my visit and told her a mutual friend in Madrid had suggested I contact her. Her response was not very encouraging: "I am not sure how much I can remember," she protested, "I have not thought or spoken about any of this since it all happened, fifty years ago. I am sorry, but I doubt I will be of much help to you." Only when I added, quickly, that my family also came to Barcelona from France during the war, and that we might actually have been in the same place at the same time, did she consent, reluctantly, to meet with me.

A full-figured and handsome woman with soft reddish hair and a ready smile, Nina looks younger than her sixty-five years. Despite her earlier hesitation, once she began to speak, her story unfolded with surprising ease. I chose to include it here because, aside from graphically showing the dangers facing those who dared brave the forbidding trek over the Pyrenees and the single-minded resolve needed to survive it, her story provides a unique glimpse into the role played by the Spanish clergy and local police in aiding Jewish refugees.

"The year was 1942 and the Nazis had already begun rounding up Jews and sending them to camps. I was living in Paris at the time, with my parents, my brother, and my two sisters. We had fled there from Poland the year before. I was not quite eighteen years old. The Germans were everywhere. My husband, Tito, who is Italian, fled to Spain without me, just four days after we were married, and I was to follow as soon as I had the proper papers."

As an Italian citizen, Tito had no problem obtaining a Spanish entry visa quickly. It never occurred to him that Nina would have trouble following him, because he believed she, too, was now an Italian, by marriage. But, although Tito was able to obtain a Spanish *entrance* visa for Nina, the Vichy French refused to give her an *exit* visa. To them she remained a Jew, and Jews were not allowed to leave.

Nina stayed hidden in Paris, a day here, a day there, while the rest of her family went south to the Free Zone, which was not yet occupied by the Germans. Like Tito, her parents left her behind, secure in their belief that she would have no problem getting into Spain. But Nina had no proof of Italian citizenship, and obtaining an Italian passport proved more difficult than anyone anticipated. She remained alone in Paris a whole year, waiting for the Italian papers, which never arrived.

When the Germans finally invaded the rest of France and there was no more Free Zone, Nina's parents went into hiding in Saint-

Giron, a small town in the Pyrenees near Andorra. Nina made up her mind to flee to Spain with or without papers, but was not willing to leave France without saying good-bye to her parents first.

"In the meantime, Tito was in Spain, waiting for me. Although he had friends there, I did not know exactly where he was because we could not receive or send mail. Times were terrible, but at eighteen, none of this was the tragedy for me it seemed to be for everyone else; I knew I had my whole life ahead of me."

Nina found Saint-Giron was not as tiny as she had imagined. It had six thousand inhabitants. There was a café in the center, owned by people sympathetic to the hundreds of refugees who congregated there every day. Most had attempted to cross over into Spain at least once, and had been caught by the French police and forced to return. The café was a very popular place, even though it was also frequented by Germans. Upstairs there were three or four guest rooms. It was in one of those rooms that the owners kept Nina's family hidden for one and a half years. They brought them food and news of what was happening outside.

Nina found her family in Saint-Giron but remained determined to go to Spain to be with her husband. She managed to get false identity papers, including a forged passport, and spent her time gathering information about ways to get out of France and into Spain. Several people urged her to see the Italian consul in Perpignan, closer to the Spanish border.

"I knew the Italian people, in general, were very good with their Jews, but at first I did not want to have anything to do with Italian officials, because they were allied with the Germans politically. I decided to look up this particular consul only because he had a reputation for helping Jews. I said good-bye to my family one more time and went to Perpignan.

"The consul's name was Otto Lenghi. I told him, 'I am Italian by marriage, but the truth is, I am also a Jew.' When he heard that I was Jewish, tears filled his eyes. 'You poor child, what will you do here? Come, I will take you home to my wife and sons.'"

The Lenghis were very helpful to Nina, who described the consul's wife as "an enchanting woman." She told Nina her husband was a Jew who had converted when he married her (a French Christian), but that all his family had remained Jews. The Lenghis introduced Nina to a *passeur*, a smuggler, who was a bandit and a friend of the Germans.

"I found out that this man often boasted, 'I will never let Jews and Poles enter my house or cross the border,' but fortunately he had no idea I was both a Jew and a Polak. He thought I was French or Italian. People said that during the war this man killed a lot of people and he was under a death sentence in Spain for murder. He had no politics, this man, and I was afraid to go with him, but I was running out of options. Also, the Lenghis told me, 'Nothing will happen to you because he knows you have no money and he has no clue that you are Jewish. You have blond hair, you don't look like a Jew, and he knows your husband is Italian. He is doing it only to show off how clever he is, to impress us.'"

Despite the danger, and still without French exit papers, Nina decided to risk it. The *passeur* told her to take the train from Perpignan to the border, to Banyuls-sur-Mer, and to wait there for his wife, who would take her to a hut they had up in the mountains. He warned her that because so many refugees were trying to cross over, the border would be heavily guarded.

"When I arrived at Banyuls, the station was filled with Germans and police asking for papers. I had my forged passport in my purse, but my legal passport was hidden in a small suitcase. The fact was that showing *either* passport would have gotten me into trouble. My *false* passport claimed I was French, but said I was born in Warsaw, which instantly looked suspicious. My *legal* passport had a big red 'J' printed across the front, showing I was a Jew. But that was not all. The worst part was that I had left the Spanish entrance visa Tito had gotten for me inside *that* passport, in my suitcase! Things were so complicated, so rushed and confusing, how could anyone be sure to always think of all the necessary details? I knew

I had to come up with something, fast, but I was terrified and didn't know what to do.

"Sitting next to me, in the train, was an old woman with a small child. When the train stopped, I took the child's hand and got off with them. The old woman could of course see something was going on, but she said nothing. We looked like a French family, a grandmother with a daughter and a granddaughter. I was very lucky. No one stopped me."

Nina had no trouble finding the smuggler's wife, who was waiting to take her into the mountains. She hardly spoke to Nina and just ordered her to follow. They started climbing up, up, up, for six or seven hours. It was January, but luckily there was no snow. Nina kept nothing of value in her small suitcase, except a few extra clothes and her Spanish entrance visa.

They walked and climbed so long Nina thought she could not take another step. When they finally got to the hut, halfway up the mountain, the woman's husband, who was supposed to meet them, was not yet there. They were met by the couple's twenty-year-old daughter instead. The hut was very primitive, with a dirt floor and only a couple of cots. Nina was told to lie down and rest, because there was a lot more climbing ahead for them. The two women warned her to be quiet, since there were two or three German outposts close by.

"At four in the morning voices awoke me. It was the husband. I suddenly became terrified. It now occurred to me how crazy I was to do what I was doing. That man was a murderer! He could kill me and no one would stop him or even find out about it.

"He came in and said, 'Get up. My daughter will take you over the border.' I breathed a sigh of relief, knowing he would not be going along. They gave me a piece of bread and sausage for the road. The daughter took along a small bottle of water. As we began our climb I could see she knew her job well, keeping out of the Germans' way as much as possible. Still, we saw them and they saw us.

They made no trouble and called 'Hola, hola,' because they assumed I was one of the girl's friends."

During a particularly hard climb, the girl guide urged Nina to toss her suitcase down the mountain, because it was dangerous to carry anything that would call attention to them. That meant Nina would no longer have any papers, no passports, nothing to identify her, not even the Spanish entrance visa. But the girl convinced her it was better that way: once Nina got into Spain, she'd be safe, and if they were stopped on the French side, she would just introduce Nina as her girlfriend.

"The going got harder and harder the higher we climbed. We finally came to a narrow pass and the girl pointed down and said, 'Look, that is Spain, down there. I cannot take you any farther, but just keep going right, right, right, and you will make it. Never go up, only down.' After that I was on my own.

"I don't remember much about the next three days. I did not know the way, but I just kept going right and down. I came to a river. It was too deep to cross but I kept hearing the girl saying 'never go up, only down,' so I followed the river down till I came to a cow path where I could wade across.

"Early in the morning of the third day, I saw a house with smoke coming out of the chimney. I was too exhausted to keep going, so I just walked into the house. The people in it were very startled to see me. They were also very afraid, because helping refugees was strictly forbidden. It was most dangerous for them to have me there, being so close to the border."

Many others, besides Jews, were trapped in southern France, trying to escape from the Germans: Communists, and political and religious dissidents, many of them Christians. When the Vichy French regime was installed by the Germans, all Frenchmen of military age trying to flee were returned as deserters. When the Germans finally occupied the rest of France, Franco made an agreement with Hitler that no political refugees fleeing the Nazis would be allowed to hide in Spain, so everyone was afraid to get caught. But this law was not meant to keep out Jews. Two months after Nina got to Spain, her brother tried to cross over.

"He was caught and turned back, because he was French and assumed to be either a deserter or an enemy of the Franco regime. No one even bothered to ask whether he was a Jew or not. But if you were lucky enough *not* to get caught at the border and managed to get deeper inside Spain, they let you stay. They put you in prison or into a camp and kept you there until someone claimed responsibility for you. It is true, however, that many were caught at the border and turned back, because most were French, not because they were Jews."

At first the people in the house told Nina she could not stay. When they saw how exhausted she was, they gave her a blanket so she could rest, but they made her stay outside, away from the house, in case the border guards came by. Since she had arrived early in the morning, they agreed to let her sleep all day, but told her she had to leave by nightfall.

"I don't know why, but I wasn't afraid. Maybe because by now I was far enough inside Spain and believed the Germans could no longer take me back. I was just so happy to be there! Not once, climbing over the mountain, did I think to be afraid of wild animals, even when I was all alone. I just wanted to get into Spain and past the guards without being caught.

"By the time the people in that house told me I had to leave, I had at least had some sleep, but I had not eaten in three days, and was starving. Like the girl guide, they too told me I had to 'keep to the right.' So I took a path and began to walk. I walked for hours. Eight hours after leaving the farmhouse I came to Raboz, a very tiny and very ancient little mountain village. All the children I met there ran after me, thinking I was a madwoman, because everything I wore was torn, my coat, my stockings, and shoes. My legs were all bloody, and I did not speak to anyone."

That village had a small hotel and restaurant, like the one in

Saint-Giron, where everybody came to drink and meet and talk. It was run by a Spanish woman of French origin, from near the border. She happened to be looking into the street when Nina passed by.

"I must have been a sight! She ran out and spoke to me in French. I told her I was a refugee and that I was alone. She could hardly believe that. No one believed that I could have come down the mountains alone, and she said, 'Oh, ma pauvre petite!' (You poor child!) She took me in and put me up at her place. She was so kind to me, that woman. She washed me and fed me soup and put me to bed. She washed my clothes and said I could sleep as long as I wanted. She said that she expected the chief of police and the town *padre* to be at the café that night and that she would plead with them to let me stay and sleep. 'Otherwise they will take you off to jail right away,' she warned me."

The woman kept her word. That night she spoke to the police chief and the priest. "You can't take her away tonight," she told them. "Tonight she sleeps in a warm bed with sheets. The child needs rest. Tomorrow you can take her to Figueras" (a town thirty miles away, where there was a large and modern jail).

"Well, she convinced them to let me stay. Next day I spoke with them, the Spanish police chief and the priest. Not in Spanish, in French. They were very helpful. They did nothing to me. Nothing. They explained that what I had to do was go to Figueras and give myself up. The priest said, 'When you get to the Figueras jail, ask for the jail priest. He is my friend and teacher. Tell him I am sending you to him.' And so they let me rest for three days. On the third day the police chief came for me and picked up another refugee, a Frenchman who claimed to be Canadian, and delivered us both to the police commission in Figueras. That was the procedure for anyone coming into Spain illegally."

At the commission Nina met about thirty or thirty-five other refugees, who had been caught crossing over the mountains. All claimed they were Canadians or Germans. Nina soon found out that all of them were French, but all had destroyed their papers, because as Frenchmen they would have been automatically returned to France. Nina was one of only two women brought in.

"They left us there all day, with the police screaming like crazy, the whole time. All of us were starving. One man pleaded for some food, and the policeman hit him twice. None of us got any food all day."

When the commissioner finally came into the room where all the refugees were waiting to be processed, the young Frenchman who had come with Nina from Raboz whispered, "Remember, I am *Canadian*." Nina understood why he needed her to say that, and agreed to corroborate his alibi. The young man added he had family in Madrid who would help get him out of jail, if he could only convince the authorities to let him stay.

Nina and the young man spent hours talking together, waiting their turn to be called. Nina was summoned first. The commissioner took her into another room.

"We spoke in French. Everyone spoke French, because they were so close to the border. He asked why I had come to Spain and I told him I had an Italian husband in San Sebastián. I explained that the French had refused to let me leave because I was Jewish, so I had to come illegally. He said, 'All right, I will let you go. You can leave and sleep at the hotel in town tonight.' I thought, 'What a relief not to have to go to jail!' But the commissioner was not done with me. He said, 'Good. You are going to the hotel. But first you will tell me what that young Frenchman you were talking with told you.' I told him I knew nothing about him, except that he was a Canadian, not French, and beyond that he was a stranger to me. He said, 'I am told you spent a long time talking with him.' When I insisted that I knew nothing more about him, he started to scream at me. He screamed for a whole hour. Finally he said, 'You are going to jail, like the rest! Go! Get out of here!' So, at two-thirty A.M. they took us all to jail. Without food, without anything."

Nina never found out what happened to the young Frenchman. The prison in Figueras turned out to be brand-new and clean, with a section for men and another for women, and a patio in the middle between the two sections. When Nina got there, the other women all looked at her in awe. They told her she was the first woman who was not in tears when she arrived there.

"They did not understand that I was so very happy just to be in Spain. I knew I was going to get out of that prison. I was so young, so optimistic! I had wanted to get to Spain and I had made it! I felt it was a miracle, but a miracle I had earned. Another part to my luck, my miracle, was that it was January and there was no snow. Days were warm and sunny. Nights were cold, but not cold enough to kill: that year the severe cold had come earlier. You see, luck was with me all the way! Nobody believed I came alone. Everyone wanted to know who brought me, who helped me, who showed me the way. 'But I came alone,' I insisted. 'Impossible,' they said, because so many men and women trying to cross had died. The cemetery was full of those who were found dead."

When Nina arrived at the prison, everyone was fainting from hunger. When the prison cooks made soup and bread, they had not figured on all the additional refugee prisoners, so there was no food for the new arrivals. But Nina had some money, one hundred pesetas (the equivalent of two thousand today). The innkeeper who had taken her in at Raboz had given it to her, folded up into a tiny square and stuck onto her body under an adhesive bandage. Although the prison guards had taken off all Nina's clothes several times to search her, they never discovered it. She knew that with that money she would find a way to get some food somehow.

"Next day I saw the prison priest walk by and asked to speak to him. I said, 'Listen, the *padre* in Raboz told me to contact you. He said to tell you that he is sending me to you, and that I could trust you. I am not a Catholic. I am here as a refugee, as you already know, but I am also a Jew.' Although he was a very old man, he was very interested in conditions outside Spain. He asked me a lot of questions: 'What is the situation? What is happening to the Jews?' I answered as well as I could. Then I told him I was starving, that

I had not eaten in over three days, not since Raboz, and I would surely be dead if they had not fed me there. I told him I had smuggled in one hundred pesetas and was afraid the guards would punish me if they found out and confiscate the money. I asked if he could give me a voucher for it so I could buy bread and milk at the prison *cantina* and feed all those of us fainting from hunger.

"He asked me, 'Tell me the truth: is that really all the money you have?' When I swore that was all I had, he laughed and said, 'One hundred pesetas is nothing. Keep the money. But I will arrange something. In a few minutes another priest will call you and say that someone has left some money for you as a gift, to buy food at the *cantina*.' After he left, everything happened just as he promised. Every day, for the next ten days, two or three of us went to the *cantina* and bought food and everybody ate."

As soon as Nina arrived in the Figueras prison she wrote to her husband's friends in San Sebastián, who would know his whereabouts. They notified Tito, but because Nina did not specify where she was being held, he had to go from prison to prison until he finally found the right one. He showed the prison chief duplicates of all of Nina's papers, including a proper visa, and demanded to know why she was in prison. They explained that the papers meant nothing and the visa carried no weight because Nina had entered Spain illegally. "That is the only reason she is in prison. But don't worry," the chief assured Tito, "there is an organization here called the Joint (American Jewish Joint Distribution Committee). They get illegals like your wife released from jail. I will notify them, but it will take a few days for them to get here."

When the Joint's people arrived, all seventy refugees were released. It turned out all were Jews.

Asked if the Joint had paid off anyone to get them freed, Nina replied she doubted it. "Money was given to refugees once they were out. Money for them to live on. They put them up in hotels. They gave them food. Whatever they needed. They kept them there for months. I myself did not ask for help at that time because I did not need anything. I had Tito."

So, after almost a year and a half, Tito and Nina were together at last. "I had not cried all those months of waiting, but when I saw him I cried for a long time. I had forgotten what it was like to be with him, but I never gave up hope."

Tito took Nina to San Sebastián, where he had stayed with friends during the many months it had taken her to get to Spain. At first all they wanted to do was be together, to talk, to make up for all the time they had lost. They still had a little money left from before, and San Sebastián was a small town where everything was very cheap.

"But when you have very little money, even cheap is too expensive. We stayed in a tiny hotel for six months. The owners were a lovely Spanish Christian couple, very generous. They let us stay with them even though they knew we were Jews and illegal, and we paid them almost no rent. They helped us so much, and we would have liked to stay, but eventually we had to leave to make money somehow, somewhere. We remained close and wrote to each other until very recently, when the old couple finally died."

Nina and Tito decided to go to Barcelona and immediately went for help to the Joint, a refugee assistance agency set up by American Jews. Although illegal refugees were not allowed to work, no one seemed too concerned about enforcing this law. Even though the Joint provided the essentials for survival, most of those who could work tried to find ways to supplement that small stipend. Nina soon found work as a nurse, because she had worked for the Red Cross in France before the war, while Tito was hired to give French and Hebrew lessons in a college.

"Everybody had wonderful relations with the Joint. They helped all the refugees who came to them. They gave everybody money, not much, but enough to subsist. They got them passports, papers (mostly forged), jobs, permits, whatever was needed. For a long time, the Joint was the only organization helping Jews in Barcelona. They took care of, and rescued many, many Jews, helped them stay a while and to go to other places eventually, like Canada, South America, and even Israel."

When asked about Franco's role in helping Jews get to Spain, Nina responded, "There are those who say that Franco personally interceded for Jews during the war. This is true, but it did not happen until much later. I heard that Franco's diplomats got Jews released from concentration camps, mostly Jews of Spanish origin. Franco, himself, helped some Sephardic Jews after the war. I personally know that is so, because, after the Six-Day War in the Middle East, a ship came to Barcelona from Alexandria, full of Egyptian Jews.

"But during the early part of the war Franco was a Fascist, a great friend of Hitler and of the Italians, and he did not lift a finger to help the Jews. After 1943, things changed. Franco was afraid Hitler was not going to win the war. He was no fool, Franco. But I cannot forget that for a long time this was a Fascist country. When officials came into the prisons and gave the Nazi salute, those who did not salute back had their hair cut off. While I was at Figueras prison we had to sing Spanish anthems and salute like a Nazi every morning when they came in. I did not want to do it, but the others all whispered, 'Do it, raise your hand, raise your hand, or they will cut off your hair.' So I did it, but I gave only the most minimal salute.

"Tito and I have been living in Spain as Jews for nearly fifty years. Like everywhere else, sometimes things are good, sometimes bad. Now it is good, but we miss our children. They were born here, but they live in Israel now.

"In Spain anti-Jewishness is learned early, in the schools. Not so much now, but before, almost everything was anti-Jewish. At Easter time, everyone said the Jews killed Christ. In San Sebastián, which was a much smaller and more backward city than Barcelona, I awoke one Easter morning and heard a terrible racket outside.

When I asked what they were doing, they said, 'Killing Jews!' They were of course not really doing that, it was just a traditional pretend-game played by children that time of year, a commemoration of the past, but it was frightening. That is why my children are in Israel, not here. They said, 'We don't want our children to go through what you went through.'

"So why do we remain here? Because that is how life evolved. My parents survived the war in France and stayed there, but my husband's family followed us to Spain. My husband began to work here, and now we are established, have many friends, and live very well. We love Barcelona. People suffered a lot here during the Civil War. Catalans were mostly against Franco, and the people here understood the suffering of refugees well, because they, themselves, were treated so badly by Franco's people. They did not care whether the refugees were Jews or not, they never even asked. All that mattered was that they were refugees: *that* they could connect with. The word 'refugee' opened doors.

"When Tito and I first arrived in Barcelona I was very thin and anemic. I went to see a doctor and when I wanted to pay him he asked, 'Are you a refugee?' When I told him yes, he said, 'For refugees, no charge.' He treated me, gave me prescriptions, medications, all free. Yes, Spanish politics was awful, but the Spanish people themselves were wonderful to us. Despite how hard things were for them during the war, they were generous and treated us incredibly well."

A break in Nina's story occurred here and I thought we were finished, when a big smile suddenly appeared on her face. "There is one thing I forgot that I must tell you about. Remember when I was coming down the mountains, before I got into Raboz? Well, some distance from the village I suddenly ran into three Spanish Guardias Civil. Before I could hide, they stopped me and asked where I was going. I told them I was an Italian refugee, coming from France, but that I had no papers. They said I had to go back to France. I should have been terrified, because the *one* thing I had feared most had happened. But I was not afraid. I was hungry. I was exhausted, I was hurting, but I was not afraid. I just sat down on the ground and said, 'I am not moving. I am not going back.'

"First they looked at one another, not sure what to do with me. I must have looked a fright, after spending three days climbing in those mountains. They talked among themselves for a while. Finally they said I could pass, but first I had to give each one of them a kiss! I was considering doing what they asked when suddenly there was a shot, maybe a hunter, or someone getting killed somewhere nearby. It must have scared them, because without another word they just ran off, leaving me there. I was able to go on and I didn't even have to kiss them!"

Nina looked triumphant now, and finally seemed ready to stop.

For a moment I lost sight of the effort it must have taken for Nina to dredge up all the terrible details of her life during the war. "For someone who said she could remember nothing, you didn't do too badly," I told her. Now Nina's eyes drifted off into some faraway place. Her big smile was gone. "Yes, when I think about those times," she said, after a long pause, "about all those people and all those events, it feels as though it all happened yesterday . . . but to someone else."

I could do nothing but express my gratitude to her for sharing her story with me.

# · 8 ·

# Hilde and Peter:
# Mother and Son

Peter Blau and I have been friends for years. "You must meet my mother," Peter often said. "She is just the way you describe yours, full of vim and vinegar!" When I finally did meet Hilde, I had to agree with Peter. The resemblance between our two mothers is remarkable and not just skin deep. Both women were born in Vienna and speak English with the same soft accent. Neither looked the least bit stereotypically "Jewish," with their blond hair, blue eyes, little turned-up noses, and remarkably youthful, creamy-fair complexions. Though both are well into their eighties, each is still active and often "difficult."

Not until I mentioned the subject of my quest did I find out that Peter and I also shared something else: sanctuary in Spain during World War II. I hadn't known that Peter, about nine years younger than I, had braved the difficult trek over the Pyrenees with his mother at the young age of only two and a half. When Peter told me about it I was stunned. How could we have known each other so long without ever sharing our histories? It brought home once more how deeply buried many of us have kept that part of our lives, for different reasons, but hidden away nevertheless.

Hilde's and Peter's experiences offer a rather personal look at conditions under which "illegal" adults and children were kept apart, in Spanish prisons and orphanages, and what life was like for them among the local Spanish people after they were finally released.

What led to Hilde's decision to flee to Spain is as important as what happened to her and Peter once they got there, because it dramatically points up the contrast between the atmosphere of active persecution and life-threatening danger they left behind and the relative comfort and safety so many of us found in Spain, despite all expectations to the contrary.

As soon as Hilde began telling her story, it struck me how much she sounded like Nina. Like her, she seemed oddly detached, as though she were speaking about someone else, someone to whom she had no emotional connection. With a deceptively casual indifference, Hilde rushed past the dramatic signposts of her life without so much as a moment's pause for reflection, and without losing that defiant smile on her face.

For a long time Peter just allowed his mother to talk while he listened in silence.

"We were living in Vienna. My mother, my husband, and Peter. Right after the Anschluss in 1938, my husband was taken to Dachau. Peter was one and a half years old then. I was twenty-eight. I did not know what to do, but I felt I had to do something. Leaving Peter behind with a nursemaid, I went first to Aachen and then hired a guide to take me over the mountains into Belgium, to Antwerp. I had first cousins there who were diamond merchants.

I got an apartment and started working to get my husband released from Dachau."

Although Hilde kept writing encouraging letters to her husband, telling him she would get him out, she failed to secure his release. Not one to give up easily, she flew to Munich, where she took a room in a hotel near Dachau.

"I told the hotel owners right away, 'I am Jewish.' To my surprise, they did not react badly. In fact, they treated me quite well, gave me a nice room and all. Next day I went to a park near the camp and overheard people talking about the Jews held there. From the way they talked, I assumed they had seen them. I asked one of the women, 'How did they look?' hoping to get some information about conditions in the camp. 'Terrible, terrible,' she answered. 'They had horns!'"

An important piece of information Hilde picked up was that all the prisoners in Dachau were about to be moved to Buchenwald. She rushed to the railway station just in time to see the long line of prisoners being herded into trains, on their way to the camp that very moment. She tried to find her husband, but it was too late.

"I did not give up. I now went to Weimar and took a hotel room there. This time I hired a lawyer. I gave him a picture of my child for my husband and told him to see what he could do to free him. The authorities allowed him to see my husband and give him our baby's picture, but refused to let me in. The lawyer took my money but was unable to do more than that. The Nazis still refused to free my husband. I tried all kinds of ways to help him, but could get no further than the lawyer. It was a dead end.

"So, after all that, I decided to go back to Vienna. You should have seen me then. I was very pretty. I looked like a typical Aryan girl, blond and blue-eyed, and I was afraid of nothing. Next day I marched right into Gestapo headquarters and asked to see the chief. 'I want you to release my husband from Buchenwald,' I told him. He looked me over. 'But surely you are not Jewish, *gnädige Frau* [dear lady]?' he said. 'One hundred percent!' I shot back. Was I afraid? No, I was not afraid."

Her bravado got her nowhere, but as she was leaving, Hilde ran into a man who recognized her as someone he had known since she was a young girl. He was sitting downstairs at Gestapo headquarters, handing out passes to the hundreds of people wanting to see the officials upstairs. "Too bad I missed you going up," he told her. "As you can see, it normally takes many hours to get in. Next time, let me know before you come here so I can arrange to make things easier for you."

"I cannot tell you how much time and money I spent trying to get results! I had to pay bribes to all kinds of Gestapo people who promised to get my husband released. I bought visas for many different places for us to go to. I even bought boat tickets to Shanghai. I wanted to be prepared to leave as soon as he got out. I went to Gestapo headquarters every day, pleading for his release."

During this time Hilde was also sending packages to the United States, because that is where she eventually intended to end up. One package, containing a fur coat, was intercepted by the Nazis. Hilde had given her mother's address on it as sender, and because it was illegal for Jews to ship valuables out of the country, the Gestapo went looking for her mother and arrested her.

Of course Hilde told the Gestapo *she* had sent the package, not her mother. But that did not get her mother released until Hilde's friend at Gestapo headquarters interceded on her behalf. After that incident, it was clearly no longer safe for her to stay in Vienna.

In the meantime, all her efforts to get her husband released finally paid off. But, although she knew he was already on his way back to Vienna, Hilde felt she could not afford to wait for him. By that time, staying in Vienna even one extra day had become much too dangerous for her. "I left as quickly as possible, returning first to Aachen, and climbing once again over the mountains to Antwerp. From there I got all kinds of false papers for my family back in Vienna, hired guides, and finally was able to send for my mother, husband, and child. They all got to Antwerp safely, just in time for the German blitz on Belgium. When the Germans occupied Belgium, we decided to try to flee to Paris."

Getting the necessary papers to get into France proved to be no problem for Hilde's mother, because she had a "stateless passport." Hilde and her husband, with their German-Austrian ones, ran into much greater difficulties. Unwilling to leave alone, Hilde's mother decided to stay in Belgium with her family.

"One day the Germans staged a huge bombardment, one of the worst of the whole war. They even hit all the hospitals. This was the time of the great [Allied] flight from Dunkirk. We hid in the cellar, with buckets of water and towels. In the morning everything was saturated with gunpowder. We went upstairs to our apartment and found the Germans had flown low through the streets, machine-gunning right into the houses, left and right. The rooms were full of shells, everything was shattered."

Here Peter broke in. "I remember that. The cellar, the bombs exploding, the terrible noise, nuns praying, wet towels covering my nose to keep out the odor of phosphorus, smelling like rotten eggs . . ."

Hilde interrupted him in mid-sentence: "When we came upstairs, everything was shot to pieces. I looked out the broken window and saw the Germans strutting down the streets, taking over the city. We fled to Antwerp, but soon the Germans marched in there, too."

They decided to stay in Antwerp, but Hilde's husband was arrested again and sent to Saint-Cyprien, a concentration camp in southern France.

"I got him released again," she said and laughed. "I just learned how to get it done. I had a lot of practice by then. We stayed in Antwerp for two years, right with the Nazis, until 1941. Then we went to Marseilles. My mother got the flu and died there She was young, only sixty-three. After she died we went to Paris, where I had a brother who was in hiding at a doctor's house. As soon as we arrived in Paris, a policeman informed us that there would be a roundup of all Jews the next day."

Without so much as taking a breath, Hilde went on with her marathon account. "My brother decided to leave Paris and escape south before the roundup. I had Peter with me when I took him to the station. As my brother was getting on the train he said, 'How can I take off and just leave you here? Come with me!' All I had with me was my son and a handbag with money and jewelry. I didn't think twice. I simply got on the train and left with my brother."

As I listened I marveled at the casualness with which Hilde enumerated the many places to which she had to flee, hardly allowing a moment to reflect on the enormous effort and ingenuity required to accomplish each move. If she was rushing through the details because it was too hard for her to dwell on those events, her demeanor gave no clue of any discomfort.

"I left everything behind, including my husband. There was no time to think things through, everything happened too fast. You learned to trust your instincts."

The next day, during the Paris roundup, Hilde's husband was picked up by the Nazis and once again taken to a camp. One day when the guards were taking count, he hid under his bunk. When everyone left for their work details, he managed to escape and went to a café, where he overheard some people discussing their plans to flee to Switzerland. Taking advantage of this opportunity, he threatened to turn them in to the police if they did not take him along. Seeing he meant business, they gave in to his demand. All of them made it into Switzerland, where Hilde's husband remained until 1946.

Meantime, Hilde, her brother, and little Peter went as far south as the train would take them and ended up in a small town near the Spanish border. "We rented a room at a hotel full of other refugees, all hoping to get into Spain. We heard that several people in town had experience guiding others over the mountains. My brother and I decided to hire one of them, and try to make it into

Spain too. I was determined to get to America, and Spain was the best way to get there. No, I was not worried about Franco. *Anything* was better than staying in France.

"Peter was by then about two and a half years old. We spent three days crossing over the mountains. There were about eight or ten of us, altogether. It was dry and warm. We ate figs and apples from the trees. My brother carried Peter. At one point, Peter wandered off and we all took turns looking to find him. We brought along nothing, no luggage whatsoever, afraid we would be stopped if we looked suspicious. All we wanted was to get out of reach of the Germans."

After a while they could see lights in the distance. France was all blacked out, so they knew that had to be Spain.

"We made it, but just when we thought we were safe, Spanish guards appeared and took us all prisoner. We were interrogated at the police station in a small town inside the border. After that I was taken to a women's prison in Gerona. Peter was taken away by nuns and put in a Catholic hospice for orphaned children.

"They put me in with political prisoners, not with criminals. Every Sunday the orphanage nuns brought Peter to see me in prison, and for Peter this was heaven. Where he was staying he was always hungry. They never seemed to have enough food for him there. But when he came to the prison, he was pampered, given whipped cream, hot chocolate, bananas, pomegranates. God only knows where they got all that food! I, myself, was treated very well. I slept on a bed with white sheets, and whenever Peter came, the nuns in charge of the prison gave him food no one else got. One of the nuns was allowed to go into town to run errands. I gave her money and she bought me lipsticks and nail polish."

No one ever asked Hilde if she was a Jew. "I don't know if they knew or not. They put me in prison because I came into Spain illegally, and because I had no papers, not because I was a Jew. They did not know what else to do with me. There were hundreds of others like me. Most of those caught were put in with criminals, thieves, robbers. Me, they put in with the politicals because I learned Spanish so fast and they wanted to use me to help out in the prison office.

"There were hundreds of refugees in that prison, most all of them Jews caught trying to escape from Hitler. I saw so many children, hundreds of them, brought in by nuns and priests, to visit their mothers in prison, crying for Mama! It was so sad, but I wasn't worried about Peter, because I knew he was well taken care of."

Peter winced noticeably when Hilde said that and shook his head. "I was very fearful all the time," he said. "I missed my mother. I was not yet three. The priests at the Catholic institution scared me. All I remember is black. I looked forward all week long to Sunday, when I could visit my mother. They let me right into the cell. I saw all the fruit, the clean bed; I hated to leave and cried every time I had to go. Where I lived I stayed in a long dorm with two rows of beds. I remember always being hungry. Sometimes I sneaked into the kitchen at night to steal food from the refrigerator. Once I got caught. They beat me, they humiliated me in front of everyone.

"All the other children were orphans, spoke only Spanish. We were all treated the same, and none of us had enough food. I picked up the language fast, but I had no friends, never felt I fit in. We would play in the yard and catch flies. We'd tear off their wings and eat the bodies, not because we were hungry but because it was a game. All the kids did it and I did it too. I went along with it because I wanted to belong, but I never really did.

"I was scared all the time. I thought about death and dying a lot, all the time, even though I never really saw anyone die. I think they probably tried their best at the institution, but it was a very cold place, no special treatment, no nurturing at all. All I knew was I just wanted to be with my mother."

While Peter spoke, Hilde's face showed no trace of emotion. She had remembered it *her* way, and she was determined that nobody was going to change that, not even her son. Peter's version of the facts might as well have happened to a stranger. Without a comment, she resumed her story.

"One day a delegation from the HIAS [Hebrew Immigrant Aid Society] came to the prison. They offered the prison officials two dollars for each prisoner they agreed to release. Three months later we all got out. Hundreds of us were released."

They were taken to a small town nearby, Caldas de Malavella, and put up in unoccupied luxury hotels. Spanish guards supervised them. The HIAS paid two dollars a day for their keep. In those days, especially in Spain, that was a lot of money.

"We had lovely rooms, ate in the dining room. We were under guard, but they treated us like guests. Peter came with me, of course. The Spanish treated us very well. Sometimes they let me take the train to Gerona to visit the political prisoners with whom I had become friends in prison. After a while the authorities released us altogether and we were free to go wherever we wanted to. *Free.*"

Hilde took Peter to Barcelona and immediately went to the Joint, where she was given enough money to live in a small hotel full of other refugees, in the Plaza de Italia. After meeting her, Dr. Sammy Seguerra, who headed the Joint at that time, offered her a job working for him, so she was even able to earn extra money.

I asked Hilde what event stood out most in her memory of that time.

"I will never forget the moment I was released from prison and had to sing 'Arriba España!' (Hail, Spain!). Everyone had to give the Nazi salute for Franco. I did not mind. I had no bitterness toward Franco. He never hurt us. We were well treated. The guards came to the hotels where we were staying after hours, at night, and fraternized with us, even though we had to go to the police station every day, to sign our name. I never once had a bad time. To the contrary, I had a wonderful life. I went to nightclubs, I even had a Spanish boyfriend! My husband was in Switzerland, and I had not been happy with him for a long time. I really did not want to leave Spain."

Hilde stopped. I looked at Peter. "I knew about none of this," he said. Changing the subject before I had time to ask him anything, he added, "What I do remember is that when my mother was released from prison she rented a bike for me. I can still see myself riding my bike in a park, down a sloping hill, on a cement walkway, eating fruit, happy at last. I could speak Spanish as well as Catalan, I was allowed to do whatever I wanted. I was in heaven. I was part of Spanish life, I associated with Spanish children. I was really happy there."

Hilde continued. "We had no hunger, no deprivation. When we were living in Caldas de Malavella we were given tortillas [Spanish-style omelettes] to eat, with eggs and potatoes, waited on by waiters and waitresses. That was in 1942. My boyfriend and I went dancing in clubs in the quarter where all the prostitutes lived. It was so much fun!

"I never felt any anti-Semitism. Never. I was pretty then. Boys ran after me. Once the mother of one of the boys I dated came after me and said, 'You *estranjeras* [foreign girls], you come here and turn the heads of our boys and then run off and want nothing to do with them!' But this was actually a compliment, more a complaint that I was rejecting her son than a rejection of *me*. It had nothing to do with me being Jewish. Nothing derogatory was ever said."

When I asked Hilde how and when she and Peter got to America, she laughed.

"I was so lucky! Long before I got to Spain, when I was still in Vienna and while my husband was in Dachau, I applied for an American visa. At that time everyone seemed to have a relative or sponsor in the United States to help them get in. I had no one. So, I went to the American Embassy and asked to see a list of names of people in America. I looked up ten people with my maiden name, and ten with my then married name, Blau. I wrote a letter to each one, asking them to please sponsor me. Everyone of them responded, and one, a Mr. Blau, even went so far as to send an affidavit for me, my son, my husband, and my mother! The odd thing about all this was that Blau was actually not this man's real name. He hated the one he was born with and was determined to change it. One of his employers was named Blau, so that is what he chose for himself and that is the name under which he offered us the affidavits our family needed!

"I had been working for the Joint for two years when a children's convoy to the United States was organized. Peter was the very first child to be assigned to this convoy, probably because I worked for the Joint. When they took him to the ship, the Spanish authorities asked him to say something into a microphone, to be broadcast on radio. Peter of course spoke fluent Spanish by then. I did not hear him myself, but others, who did, told me he said, 'Mama, if you don't follow soon, I will break your face!' "

His sponsor, Mr. Blau of Washington, D.C., met Peter on arrival and took him into his home. He was very well-to-do and lived very luxuriously.

"They took me to this elegant home, with two maids," Peter recalled. "I had my own room. They had two sons, and they treated me like one of the family."

"After I got Mr. Blau's affidavits, before we left Vienna," Hilde resumed, "I shipped him a huge van, filled with all our furniture, lovely antiques with gold coins hidden in some of the drawers. There even was a grand piano, Persian rugs, jewelry. When I finally got to the US, some months after Peter did, Mr. Blau told me that all the things I had shipped him had arrived rotten and broken, and claimed there was nothing of value left to salvage. I was suspicious and angry, but never let on. He saved our lives, so I never made an issue of any of it."

Hilde fell silent. After a brief pause, Peter took up the narrative. "What is hard now is the sadness I feel for what my mother went through, how hard she fought to make us safe, to get my father out of camps, to get us to the States . . ."

Hilde quickly interrupted. "But I always try to remember the good times only. There was such a great deal of tragedy. I don't want to think about that. I try not to think about the time when my mother got sick, when I couldn't find a doctor, when I couldn't help her and she died . . ." Just this once, there was a slight crack in her voice.

Peter broke in. "But you were always resilient, never paralyzed . . ."

In their bond of mutual support, they took turns protecting each other from the pain of the past. I was deeply touched to observe this gentle conspiracy of love. It proved that, even fifty years after the fact, dwelling on the details of such a harsh reality might at times be too much for anyone to bear, even as strong, brave a woman as Hilde.

# ·9·

# *Leon's Odyssey*

Leon Nussbaum and his family are part of the thriving Toronto Jewish refugee community, most of whose members emigrated to Canada in the late 1940s and early 1950s. He is a rather short, stocky, and balding eighty-year-old man, but his vitality is striking. His eyes, clear and alive, are the eyes of a young man.

After suffering great hardships before and during his journey to safety in Spain, Leon often found himself treated with unexpected kindness. Although he admitted that some people near home, in Vienna, and in France also took considerable risks to help him, he was surprised and deeply touched at the length to which ordinary Spaniards, even those in the direst of circumstances, as well as government officials and police, were willing to extend themselves for refugees like himself, strangers who were dependent on their generosity for their very survival.

"Although most of my family perished in the Holocaust," he began, "this is a positive story, full of more good things than one would expect, even miracles. That is why I want the world to know about it.

"I come from a religious family, but my father was very modern. He was in the export-import business in Vienna, traveled frequently, and was very successful. Even before Hitler, he knew Jews were in danger. When Hitler annexed Austria in March 1938 and cheering masses welcomed him to Vienna, the first thing the SS did was to take over all the Jewish enterprises.

"At that time I was a young man of twenty-eight, already quite successful, running a knitting factory owned by a Jewish family. My brother, Joseph, and I lived with my parents in a comfortable second-floor apartment, right in the city. A married sister lived in Prague. My younger sister was in England.

"The day after Hitler arrived, SS men in full uniform burst into the place where I worked and asked who was in charge. When I presented myself, they demanded I hand over the keys to the factory. They assembled all the workers in one place, Jews on one side, Gentiles on the other. The SS officer in charge turned to the Gentiles, speaking only to them. 'What kind of grievances do you have against the Jews?' he asked.

"You must understand, all of us, owners and employees, were like one big family. We made no distinction between Jews and Gentiles. Most of us knew one another for a long time as friends and acquaintances. So, when the SS officer asked the Gentiles if any of them had any complaints against the Jews, there was only silence. Not one person had anything to say. These were my friends! Two women, Angela Simons and another one, whose name escapes me, had tears running down their cheeks. 'Why are you crying?' asked the SS man. 'You must have a grievance. Come, come, speak up!'

But, again, no one spoke. The SS got nowhere with any of them and finally gave up."

Before they left, the Germans said to Leon, "We are putting one of our own people in charge. From now on you have no rights here. You will ask permission for everything. You are not allowed to quit or work anywhere else. We need you here to keep this factory going. You will continue to run things, but you have no authority anymore. You work for us now."

Everything was supposed to look normal, as though nothing had changed. Everyone was expected to keep doing his or her job, but Leon had to work without pay. He had to come in early every morning and was not allowed to leave at night until he was dismissed.

"The SS sent a man to oversee the smooth functioning of the factory. He did nothing, but his presence was a constant reminder of what had happened. We were slaves now. We did what had to be done because we had no other choice. Two or three weeks passed, and then one day some businessmen showed up at our factory. They had me show them around and explain everything. One of these men seemed particularly interested and asked me a lot of questions. He was not from Vienna and lived in a province some distance away." Later this man pulled Leon aside.

"The person they put in charge here knows nothing about running this factory," he told Leon. "That is why I am talking to you. *You* know what you are doing, know how to run this factory." For hours he questioned Leon about a lot of very technical matters, and, of course, Leon had to answer because he knew the SS had sent the man. Finally he told Leon, "I like this company. The machinery is modern, the people work well. I am taking it over."

This man was Albert Kopf, whose father was a Nazi Gauleiter (district chief) in charge of a neighboring province. He announced that the whole factory would be moved to Altach, a small town near the Swiss border. Leon thought, My God, how can he expect this to be accomplished? We will have to transport everything all the way across Austria!

But Kopf was determined. He was very nice to Leon, very complimentary and full of encouragement, but Leon was not fooled by all the flattery. He knew Kopf acted that way only because he needed him. Kopf himself owned a lace-making plant in Altach, with outdated machinery. With Leon's knitting machines added to his own he would end up with a very nice combination, increasing the volume and variety of what he could produce. He knew Leon was the only one who could accomplish what he needed: move the factory and make it work.

" 'You are going to install the factory for me there. I will pay your round-trip rail fare. I will also pay for your room and board while you are there, for as long as it takes to make sure everything works. In addition, when you are finished, I will give you three thousand shillings and a letter that states you have my permission to leave Austria, if you want to leave.'

"We both knew he had no real authority or power to give me a thing, permission to leave, passport, safe passage, or anything else, but he assured me the letter would show those in charge that I was 'a good Jew,' and had dutifully discharged my obligations to the party. He implied that this alone would get me preferential treatment. I did not trust him, but I did hope his letter might carry some weight, might help me and my family get out of Austria. In any case, even if it did no good at all, I had no choice but to go along with the arrangement."

While the machinery was being moved, Leon stayed with strangers in Altach. He worked hard, and the job was completed in six weeks. The day he finished, he asked Kopf for his pay and the letter. "He looked straight at me with steely eyes. 'Jew, if you do not disappear immediately, I shall hand you over to the Gestapo!' Although I knew from the beginning I could not trust him, this came as a shock. 'You promised! What about my letter?' I asked. 'Go! I will send the letter later,' he screamed.

"Here I was, alone, in a strange town, far from home. Jews were not allowed in hotels. I no longer had a place to stay, but I still had my return train ticket, so I decided to go back home. Empty-handed."

The day Leon arrived in Vienna, the Gestapo was going from house to house, picking up all young Jews to deport them to labor camps. They had a list showing who lived where. "My brother, Joseph, had been forewarned, so we were prepared. When we saw the Gestapo truck stop in front of our place, Joseph and I escaped through a small window in a ground-floor washroom. We stayed hidden, nearby, close enough to see who was going in and out of our building. The Gestapo were not interested in Mother or Father, because they were too old, but they were determined to find Joseph and me. They poked with sticks under the beds, searching for us, sure we had to be somewhere. Finally, they gave up. After they left, taking with them all those they caught, we snuck back home. I telephoned a Gentile Czech friend, Alois Eck, who had worked with me at the factory, and explained what had just happened. I told him we had to get away, and asked if he could help.

"Alois arrived half an hour later, riding a motorcycle with a sidecar. Dressed in a brown uniform, with swastikas all over, he stormed into our building, up the stairs, and down the hall to our apartment, screaming, 'Where are the Jews!' All the neighbors swarmed into the hallway to look at and applaud the 'Nazi' who was doing such a good job. No one guessed he was an impostor. He burst into our apartment. 'Come on, let's go!' he screamed. 'Take him first,' I said, shoving my brother at him, knowing there was room for only one of us in his sidecar. I figured if he took Joseph first, he would return for me, his friend, but he might not be willing to take such added risk for my brother, who was a stranger to him. Alois grabbed Joseph by the scruff of the neck and threw him down the stairs. Then I heard the motorcycle roar off. Three quarters of an hour later Alois returned for me. 'You dirty Jew,' he bellowed, 'don't you know it is useless to try to escape?' With that he threw me down the stairs, as he had Joseph, pushed me into the sidecar, and took off. He brought me to his family home, some distance from Vienna, where Joseph was waiting for me with Alois's father and mother."

Alois's parents were understandably upset at suddenly finding themselves with two runaway Jews on their hands, and asked them to leave. Leon now approached Angela Simons, the Gentile co-worker who had cried when the Nazis came to take over the factory. Although she did not have enough space for the two brothers, her mother had a small room where she let them stay. She was very kind and generous to them, but after a few days it became obvious the situation was too dangerous. Someone was sure to see them, so they decided to take their chances and return home.

Of course all their "good neighbors" were surprised to see Leon and his brother, because none of the others had returned, once they had been taken away by the Gestapo. From then on both brothers lived in terror, wondering when someone would denounce them.

One day in December 1938 a Nazi knocked on Leon's door and said to his parents, "We like this apartment. You have ten days to vacate it." Although the family knew this sort of thing was happening to other Jews, everywhere, it still came as a shock. The reality was that if the Nazis wanted something, they took it.

"You can imagine the panic my parents felt. It was the middle of winter. When Father told the Nazi they needed time because they had no other place to go, he suggested they try settling down under one of the Danube's bridges. Father remembered hearing that one of the men at his synagogue was planning to emigrate to Israel with his family. Since Jews were no longer allowed to rent apartments, and this man had a small flat, Father went to him for help. The man agreed to take us in, temporarily and 'unofficially.'

"In the meantime, we began to make frantic efforts to obtain passports, to get out of Austria as quickly as possible. Ironically, the Germans at that time were eager to have Jews leave, just to be rid of us, but there was no quick way to cut through the red tape involved in getting passports."

After days of fruitless efforts, Leon went to see a travel agent he had used occasionally. Although he noticed a framed picture of Hitler over his desk, Leon asked him to help. The travel agent agreed to do what he could and in two days he had their passports ready. When Leon offered him money, he refused to take it.

Now that Leon and his family were free to leave, all they needed was a country that would let them in. In a very roundabout and risky way they finally obtained forged Belgian visas and arranged to leave by train.

"We made it across the border, but, while we were going through Belgian passport controls, our visas were immediately declared invalid. 'You must go back,' they told us. 'You cannot remain here.' We had to think fast. Since we had relatives in Antwerp, we asked for permission to contact them. One of them bribed a guard into letting us stay in Antwerp for ten days, to give us time to obtain valid visas. We never got the visas, but managed to stay hidden in Antwerp for eight months, from January 1939 until September." That is when World War II broke out officially.

Now there began a serious search by Belgian authorities for all "German nationals," which, since the Anschluss, also included Austrians. "You would assume that the big 'J' on our passports, showing we were Jews, proving we were on *their side, not* the Germans', would help, but it didn't. We were hunted, along with the rest, as spies and 'Fifth Columnists.' My parents hid with friends, Joseph escaped, but I was caught.

"Those they caught were put on cattle and freight trains and shipped off to France. The train I was on had been used to transport phosphorus. Foul-smelling phosphorus dust was everywhere, making us ill. We were packed in, sixty to a car, without food or water, for nearly twenty hours. We became so dehydrated, our tongues swelled up and we sucked on leather straps hanging from the walls to obtain a little moisture. When the train stopped and we got off, some of us could not even stand up, much less walk.

They beat us to get us moving, piled us into trucks, and transported us to Saint-Cyprien, a concentration camp far from the front, on the beach in southern France."

The camp held about four thousand prisoners, convicted criminals as well as anyone considered a threat to Allied security. Military police guarded the beach, but criminals were in charge of the twenty-odd barracks. Conditions were horrendous. Leon made up his mind to find a way out of that terrible place.

"One day I had a surprise: I ran into my uncle Ephraim, who had arrived at Saint-Cyprien shortly after I did. He told me that my father had also been caught, was seriously ill, and also somewhere in the same camp, in one of the other barracks. He also brought the sad news that my younger sister, who had been living safely in London, happened to be visiting the family when the war broke out and was captured with my mother. Both were sent to some camp. We never saw either of them again.

"One day after I had been in Saint-Cyprien for three months, Uncle Ephraim came to me and handed me twenty dollars. 'There is a capo [prisoner in charge of other prisoners] here who has been selling safe-conduct passes. I have been hiding this money. Take it to the capo and ask him to get three passes—for you, your father, and me.' The capo delivered the passes after a few days and we left the camp that very evening.

"Our safe-conduct passes said 'Destination: Luchon,' a small town close to the Spanish border. We decided we'd better go to Luchon before we got into trouble. Much of northern France was collapsing, but the southern third was still relatively safe. Once in Luchon, we contacted the HIAS, which helped so many other Jews with food and shelter. I myself was able to find work in a local coal mine to help support us."

A Turkish friend helped Leon get forged Turkish identity papers, a passport, and a birth certificate. "If you ever get into trouble anywhere," he advised him. "It may save your life." Leon tore up his legal Austrian papers and kept only the false ones.

He remained in Luchon with his uncle and father for one and a half years, from May 1940 to October 1941. When the Germans finally occupied the rest of France and arrived in Luchon, they decreed that only local people, natives of Luchon, were allowed to remain. All Jews were told to present themselves in the main square the next day with a piece of bread and a blanket. Leon refused to go, and was given shelter by a sympathetic French family named Novio, who agreed to hide him in a hayloft in their barn. Uncle Ephraim chose to obey the decree. Although Leon tried his best to talk him out of it, his uncle had made up his mind. Before he left, he gave Leon $12 in coins. "Sew them into the seam of your coat. You will need them." He was also able to procure a safe-conduct pass to Lyons for Leon's father. "I never understood why Uncle Ephraim did not get one for himself, too. He must have been tired of running. We never saw him alive again."

The weather now turned cold and raw. It began to snow. Hiding and running became more and more difficult. The Germans stepped up their hunt for Jews. They posted an announcement in the town square: "Some Jews have defied our decree and did not present themselves as ordered. Whoever is hiding or found to be helping to hide a Jew will be executed in the marketplace." Madame Novio told Leon she could no longer keep him. "My family is in danger now, and so are you." She offered to ask her son Laurance, who was in the Resistance, to help Leon.

"Laurance arrived the next night with a young man, a smuggler named Zamora. A Spaniard who had fled the Spanish Civil War, Zamora lived in Luchon, but his family was still in Spain. He supported them by smuggling people and medicine back and forth across the Spanish border, over the Pyrenees. Laurance said to Zamora, 'This is my friend Leon. Take him to Spain and bring back a note showing he arrived safely or you will not live.'

"Make sure Zamora takes you past Los Bordetes, all the way to Las Bordas," Laurance warned Leon. "If you get caught too close to the border, near Los Bordetes, the border guards will turn you back."

Zamora promised to take Leon over the mountains and said he would meet him early the next morning at the edge of the forest, on the outskirts of Luchon.

"Madame Novio prepared me well for my journey. She filled a backpack with a thermos of hot coffee, a bottle of wine, bread, cheese, and lard. She also gave me two pairs of heavy socks, sturdy military boots, and a Spanish-French dictionary small enough to fit in my trouser pockets. She was truly wonderful to me, a stranger to whom she owed nothing."

Meeting Zamora proved problematic. The main road out of town was guarded by the Gestapo, and the curfew, which began at five P.M., was still in effect when Leon was due to meet him. Leon started out before dawn, and as he approached the edge of town he could see the guards' cigarettes glow in the dark. He was afraid, but he also knew there was no turning back anymore, because he had run out of options.

"My heart was pounding as I walked right past them. No one stopped me. When I reached our rendezvous spot I was startled to find not one but *eight* people waiting: Zamora and seven strangers! They turned out to be three couples in their fifties, Jews from Paris on the run since the Germans invaded the Unoccupied Zone, and another smuggler. I felt outraged. The arrangements I had made were for *myself, alone!* How in the world would so many of us escape the attention of the Gestapo? These old people would surely hold us back and endanger our lives. Here was I, a young athlete, a soccer player in excellent physical condition, twenty-odd years younger than the others, expected to risk my neck while dragging them along! But, like it or not, the fact was we were stuck with one another."

They began their climb up the mountain, through dense pine forests, and much to Leon's surprise, the "old ones" did not do too badly. He did offer to carry the suitcase of a Mrs. Kurtz, one of the more frail-appearing members of the group, but all in all he had to admit they pulled their own weight rather well.

At one point Zamora warned them they were approaching one particular road that had bunkers every two hundred yards manned by Germans. That road had to be crossed in order to get to the other side of the mountain and the border beyond. He stressed the extreme danger, and the importance of everyone being "invisible" in that area. The other guide said he would climb up a tree and blow a whistle when the coast was clear. "Each time I give the signal, one of you must run across the road as fast as you can."

Leon refused to be the first to go. "These people will never make it across, what with the ice and snow," he protested. "One of them is bound to slip and fall, holler, and attract the Germans. I'll take my chances and wait here, hidden, until I am sure nothing will go wrong." Nothing went wrong. One by one they rushed across, no one fell, no one made a peep. Then it was Leon's turn. Finally all had passed that most dangerous spot.

While everyone knew the Germans patrolled that particular mountain road, nobody, not even Zamora, could foretell what would await them on the Spanish side of the border. It had been his custom to go only so far, to a shepherds' hut on the French side, where he would leave the contraband medicines or the people he was smuggling out and collect the money due him. Then he would return to France while others took over and continued into Spain. Beyond that point, he knew only that rules and regulations kept changing. From day to day no one knew what to expect.

The group kept climbing until there were no more trees. It was difficult to keep going up at an altitude of eight thousand feet. After twelve more hours of climbing Leon became worried. "Where is Spain?" he asked. Zamora pointed to the far horizon. "See those mountaintops, over there? Spain is on the other side."

"On hearing this, one of the older men, named Piaček, let out a moan: 'I refuse to go on. I want to die here.' With that he lay down on the ground and started to scream. Everyone froze in terror. Someone will hear us, that will be the end of us, I thought. Zamora remained calm. He squatted down next to Piaček and whispered, 'You want to die? Well, you'll suffer too much if we just leave you here. I'd better shoot you right now.' He pulled a gun from his belt and held it to Piaček's head. Miraculously, Piaček rediscovered his will to live very quickly and joined the rest of us on our climb with renewed vigor."

After several more hours they reached a spot from where they could see a small town. "Over there is Los Bordetes," Zamora pointed out. This was the town Laurance had warned Leon to avoid. To keep from getting caught he knew he had to get beyond there, to Las Bordas.

"Once you get to Los Bordetes," Zamora explained, "you'll be in Spain, but the Germans are guarding the town and it is very dangerous there." Despite the danger, all except Leon chose to risk going there anyway and left with their guide. Zamora remained with Leon.

"The two of us continued to climb for several more hours, till late that night. By noon the next day it had started to snow. After a while Zamora stopped. He was agitated, turning here, turning there. 'I cannot see the path anymore, because the snow has covered it up. I am lost. We are through. We are dead.' I was stunned. How can this be? I thought. This is my *guide*! He is *supposed to know the way*! We stopped for a few minutes, not knowing what to do or where to go, but the snow was falling so hard we knew we would get buried if we did not keep moving. So we went on climbing blindly, without direction, just to stay alive.

"All of a sudden my legs gave out, just collapsed under me. Yes, I, the great athlete, was flat on my behind, unable to move! 'Move your legs!' Zamora commanded. It was no use. My legs felt dead. 'I'll have to leave you here if you can't come along,' he said. 'I cannot afford to be caught in Spain.' With that he shrugged and faded into the snow. As I watched him disappear, you can well imagine what thoughts passed through my mind. I felt rage. And I felt helpless. After all I had gone through, was *this* where it would end? I wondered if the others had met a similar fate. Just then Zamora reappeared. 'I found a cave,' he announced. 'I am going to hide you there. Then I must leave.'

"With that he grabbed me by the shoulders and dragged me some distance to a small cave. He pushed me in and made sure I was well protected from the wind and snow. He demanded I hand over my coat. I refused. Then he asked for my wine and bread, and took that. I was left with my coat and the lard. He himself wore only a light jacket, boots, and a beret—no scarf, no real protection against the bitter cold. 'Don't move and don't fall asleep or you'll freeze. I shall try to save myself. If I succeed, I shall come back for you.'

"Once again I watched him disappear in the blizzard. Not ten minutes later I was up on my feet, fit and able to function again! Terror sometimes shocks you into quick cures. I screamed at the top of my voice, calling for Zamora to come back. But, by then he was far gone, and I had no choice but to get back into the cave. Not that I had the slightest hope of being rescued. I was certain I would die in that godforsaken place.

"I stayed in the cave for fifteen hours. I don't know what kept me alive. Hope died and revived again and again. I kept drifting off during the night, only to have violent nightmares wake me up. And then suddenly the sun came up on a magnificent morning. It was a magical, mystical experience, the sunshine gleaming like gold on pure-white snow, with me alone, the only person alive anywhere. I was sure I must be dreaming. The silence was deafening. My heart was pounding in my ears.

"I kept having all sorts of hallucinations, shadows moving, figures appearing and fading, not knowing what was real and what was not. I saw a black dot approaching. Just another mirage. But it kept moving. As it got closer I saw the dot was a human figure. Then there was a sharp whistle. I was sure it must be a German, looking for me. I pulled back into the cave and closed my eyes. When I heard footsteps close by I looked up and saw not a German soldier but a shepherd smiling down at me."

It turned out to be one of the men Zamora had talked into searching for Leon after stumbling upon their hiding place, hours after leaving him in his cave. Like Zamora, they were Spaniards, Republican refugees from Franco's regime, hunted as deserters and traitors by Franco's soldiers while daily risking their lives as smugglers. The whistle alerted the others that Leon had been found. When they appeared, Zamora was among them.

"When Zamora saw me he shouted my name and began to cry like a baby. He ran to me and kissed me. I hugged him back. 'Here, you have certainly earned your two thousand francs,' I said, handing him the money. He refused to accept any of it. 'You will need it where you are going,' he said. 'Just follow the footprints in the snow. Someone will meet you and show you the rest of the way. I must go now.' Before he left, I gave Zamora the note for Laurance, confirming that I had arrived safely in Spain. I watched him and his band of fellow smugglers disappear on their way back to France."

Within two hours Leon reached a shepherd's cabin, where he was expected. There he was fed bread, goat's milk, and cheese, and allowed to rest. When it was time to leave, the shepherd advised him to go down into the village and give himself up to the first soldier he encountered. "Don't try to be a hero," he warned Leon.

Leon thanked him, left, and did as he was told, although he was terrified that he would be turned over to the Germans. When they took him into the police station he was prepared for the worst and was determined to get it over with.

"'I must tell you, I am a Jew,' I said to the policeman in charge. He glared back at me, annoyed. 'What do you mean, you are a Jew? Do you expect preferential treatment for *that*?' Hearing that, I laughed out loud for the first time in a long time!"

That little town had a tiny jail, just big enough to hold seven or eight prisoners. When Leon arrived, there were forty to fifty people in it, Jewish refugees from all over. To his great surprise, the other six who had started off with him and Zamora were among them! "I had been so sure I was smarter and would end up safer, going *my* way, yet here we all were, back together, and none of the others had gone through *my* ordeal!"

Because so many were squeezed into such a little space, the Spanish authorities had to do something to be rid of the prisoners. They decided to take them to Zaragoza, a bigger town with a bigger jail. The problem was that in winter the direct roads were blocked, and Zaragoza was accessible only by a detour passing through French territory. How could they risk going back to France again, after what they all had gone through to get out?

"While we were trying to figure out a way to avoid going back through German-occupied territory, German soldiers stationed nearby found out about us. They came to the jail, and told the gendarmes they knew a large number of illegal escapees had been smuggled into Spain and were being held there. 'They are ours and we want them back!' one of them screamed. The mayor of the town refused to obey. 'We cannot deliver these people over to you. They are on Spanish soil and under *our* protection.' The Germans were not about to leave empty-handed. 'Well, at least let us have two or three,' they pleaded, 'because we have to bring back *somebody*.' The mayor asked for volunteers. Of course, there were none. All of us were terrified the Germans would simply choose three at random. But that did not happen. When nobody volunteered and the Germans saw the Spaniards would not cooperate, they left."

After getting through that crisis, everyone went back to worrying about getting to Zaragoza. When Leon explained to the Spaniards that it was too dangerous for them to go back through France, the police told them about a half-finished tunnel through the mountains. " 'It is all raw rock, and dangerous,' they warned, but all of us decided it was still better than going back across the border.

"The guards drove us to the tunnel entrance in a truck and led the way in. The first part was not too bad. From then on it was not just on foot, but on our knees. It was a mud hole filled with rocks and water running through. Political prisoners had been working on it under terrible conditions. Imagine forty to fifty of us, many old and infirm, crawling through all that.

"It was eight hundred meters to the other side. It took us hours and hours, but we were determined to make it. The end of the tunnel opened on a town named Puente de Suerte, which means Lucky Bridge. A perfect name! We started out in the dead of winter, in bitter cold. We were soaked through and half frozen when we suddenly emerged in a village bathed in bright sunshine.

"Although we arrived under police guard, it struck me that we were actually being protected from the Nazis by these Spaniards. As I thought about that, I wondered, could the roads on which we came *into Spain* possibly be the same roads other Jews took to get *out of Spain*, nearly five hundred years before, trying to escape persecution by the Inquisition?"

Puente de Suerte was a very small coal-mining town of just a few hundred inhabitants. When Leon and his companions arrived there, it was early evening. The guards took them to the marketplace, a typical Spanish plaza surrounded by buildings held up by an arcade housing shops. There were just two exits from the plaza, one on each side. That made it difficult to escape but easy for the guards to keep an eye on their charges. It also gave them time to figure out what to do with them.

"We were exhausted and looked terrible. Some of us stayed in the center of the plaza and just collapsed. Others drifted toward the arcades and began knocking on doors, asking for permission to spend the night indoors. While many managed to stay with townspeople that night, most were not clever or brave enough to make those kinds of arrangements.

"Around six o'clock I was leaning against one of the columns, trying to decide what to do, when a poorly dressed, weary-looking passerby stopped and asked what I was doing there. When he saw I did not understand Spanish, he repeated his question in French, and spoke it quite well. I told him I was a refugee running from the Nazis, that all of us were there under guard but had no idea where we were being taken next. He said, 'Come, follow me.' I figured, what did I have to lose, so I followed him out one of the exits. 'I am taking you home. My wife is waiting.'

"This man's name was González. He was a miner just getting off the day shift in the pit. Home was a small flat. 'We have a guest,' he announced to his wife. 'What do you mean, a guest?' she whispered. He repeated: 'He is *our* guest.' She tried again: 'Our Juanito is coming home from work at midnight. Where will we put our guest? We have no bed.' González answered, 'Our guest will sleep in Juanito's bed, and Juanito will sleep on the floor.' That ended the discussion. González explained, 'I know what it is to be a refugee. I had to flee to France during the war.'

"His wife made dinner: polenta, a cornmeal mush, and put a jar of black coffee in the center of the table. González got up on a chair and took a box down from a high shelf. He removed two tiny saccharin tablets and offered them to me. 'What about you?' I asked. '*You* take them, you are a guest. *We* take them only on holidays.' That's how poor they were! I protested, but they insisted. So I ate and drank what they offered, and it felt like the best meal I ever had because I had been starving. There were no restaurants, and no food to be found anywhere; we were lost people and until then no one seemed to care. Here was this poor, poor man, and he *did* care.

"Earlier, when González approached me under the arcade, I had noticed that he was wearing only cloth and rope espadrilles. During supper I asked him, 'How can you work in a mine, in the cold and damp of winter, without real shoes?' He smiled. 'I do have real shoes. One pair of leather shoes. My son and I take turns wearing them. When he gets to work, I give him the shoes and go home in my espadrilles. When he gets home, it will be my turn to wear the shoes again.' Listening to him I made a solemn silent vow: If I ever make any money, no matter where I am, I am going to send these people two thousand saccharin pills and two sets of leather boots!

"We talked a while more. 'You are welcome in my house if you want to stay on,' González said before he went to sleep. 'But you

127

must tell the police where you are or there will be trouble.' In the morning, I was awakened by loud knocks on the door. Two soldiers demanded to know if I was there. By then González had left for the mines. His wife tried to explain I was in bed, too sick to go with them. But they did not believe that story. They just pulled me out of bed and threw me on a truck."

Leon was taken to the prison in Zaragoza. "Such misery! It held mostly political prisoners, sick with TB and dysentery, lying on cold floors, on thin blankets. Because I was a different kind of prisoner I got better treatment. They gave me prison rations twice a day—*caldo*, a watery soup, and some bread, more of the same at night. God knows how the others survived."

After six weeks Leon was moved to Modelo Prison in Barcelona, where other illegal refugees were held. Those in charge did not know who the refugees were or where they came from. Most had no papers at all, or false ones. They were Polish, French, Austrian, German, but they all claimed to be American, British, or Canadian, even though they spoke not a word of English. They picked any nationality whose diplomats were most likely to help them. The prison officials simply contacted various embassies to come and claim their own nationals.

"When the Spanish jailers asked about my citizenship, I said I was a Turk. When the man from the Turkish Embassy came to see me he of course could tell immediately that I was no Turk. He kept talking to me in Turkish and saw I did not understand a word, but he never let on. He knew I was a Jew. But, although he did not betray me, he was unable to get me released.

"On arrival at Modelo, each prisoner had to declare all valuables, and was given a number. All our clothes were marked with that number before they were taken away to be deloused. Well, that's the end of my money, I thought. I was sure that if someone did not steal them first, Uncle Ephraim's coins would be discovered in my coat seam and confiscated, and that I would get punished for concealing them.

"As I expected, when my clothes were returned, the coins were gone. The next night one of the Spanish political prisoners approached me and asked me if I was number so and so. I knew *that was it*. I had been caught. There was no point denying it so I said yes, expecting the worst. He asked, 'Are you missing something?' 'No,' I lied, 'I am missing nothing.' 'Are you sure?' he insisted. There was something about the way he looked at me that made me admit the truth. 'Then these must belong to you.' With that he reached into his pocket and handed me the missing coins. He could have used them. Nobody would have known the difference if he had kept them. But he didn't.

"Conditions at Modelo were deplorable, but you must understand, I felt safe there. One of those in my cell was Mr. Kurtz, the man whose wife's suitcase I carried across the mountains. He was constantly complaining about his fate, having to be in prison, resenting that he could not be free. I kept telling him, 'What are you complaining about? I feel lucky, because, even in prison, I feel free because we're in Spain!'

"But Kurtz was one of the exceptions. Most of us were relieved just to be in a safe place, not running anymore. I no longer felt afraid. Gone were the terrible nightmares and hallucinations I had in that cave. All I knew was that here nobody cared if I was a Jew or not. Nobody even asked. Anywhere. All they cared about was that I was a refugee, and the only issue was whether I was a member of one of the International Brigades, which fought against Franco. Since I was not, I had nothing to fear.

"I was never afraid the Spaniards would turn us over to the Germans. Never. They *protected* us! Of course they did not want us to be a burden to them, they were so poor themselves. That is why they allowed the HIAS and the Joint to operate and help us. And that is why they called the foreign diplomats to get their people out of jail. But they did not betray us.

"Only men were kept in Modelo. The women stayed close by, but in outside housing, like small pensions. Except for having to keep in touch with the police, they were free. Anyone in prison who had someone on the outside to guarantee that he would cause no problems, that he was not a criminal and would not be a burden to the authorities, was released. Mostly it was the wives who claimed their men. Little by little almost everyboby was let out. Kurtz's wife eventually got him released too. Finally only one other man and I remained in prison. Our problem was we had no one outside to vouch for us."

When Kurtz left, he said to Leon, "You once did me a favor: you carried my wife's suitcase over the mountains. Now it is my turn: I will help you get out of here." He and his wife lived in a small pension. A young woman who worked for the Joint also lived at that same pension. She had no one and was all alone in Spain. One day Mrs. Kurtz approached her. "'There is a man in prison who has no one to vouch for him. He is a good man. Would you help get him out? All you need to do is present yourself as his bride.' 'How can you ask me to do this?' the girl protested. 'I don't even know him and certainly don't want to be responsible for a stranger.'"

At first she refused, but Kurtz's wife must have been very persuasive, because later the girl went to the police station and signed papers to "claim her fiancé." Although she was told that being a fiancée was not enough, that you had to be wife to get someone released, she would not take no for an answer.

"She went to the Barcelona chief of police, pleaded to have me liberated, paid twenty dollars, and got me out. We met the day I was released and eventually got to know each other rather well. Paula was twenty-one. I was thirty-two. I pursued her a long time, and seven years after we met we were married in Toronto. And we are still together!" Leon beamed. "All this came just from carrying Mrs. Kurtz's suitcase!

"I had arrived in Modelo Prison in January 1942 and was released in early March. The very first thing I did as soon as I was free was go to the beach. Next I went to the HIAS, and they gave me the most wonderful things! They put me up at the Pensión

Marti, right on the Ramblas. I had a private room, food, even a little money. I was taken care of."

At about this time the Russians finally broke the siege of Stalingrad. The tide of the war had turned and the Germans needed all their men. They recalled all the technicians they had left in Spain after the Civil War to help rebuild Spain. With the Germans gone, Spain suddenly needed qualified technical people to take their place. As an engineer, Leon had no difficulty getting a job, even though, officially, refugees were not allowed to work.

He was interviewed by the accountant of a big firm, the Franco-Hispano-Alemana Company, who assumed Leon was an anti-Franco Frenchman because he spoke only French, and promptly threw him out. Undeterred, Leon returned another day and this time asked to speak to the head of the company, Señor Pedro Rivas, a very influential industrialist and a former mayor of the city of Tarragona.

"I had a good interview and Señor Rivas asked for references. I told him I was a Turk and had no references. He was so desperate for someone to work, he said he would give me a ten-day trial period working in one of the sections that had come to a standstill. 'Show me what you can do, and if you do well, I'll keep you when the ten days are up.'

"I worked sixteen hours a day to prove myself and when my trial period was up the *gerente* [boss] said, 'You have a job, you are hired, but I still need references.' I told him again, 'I have no references. I can only show you what I can do. I am honest. I work hard. I have good skills. I will not disappoint you.' Rivas said, 'I don't know what you are hiding, or why, but I like you. I, myself, shall provide your references.' So, I had a good job. I also made a good friend. With my first paycheck I bought two pairs of heavy leather boots and two thousand saccharin tablets and sent them to González. He wrote to thank me.

"After a while most of the Spaniards working with me put two and two together. They knew I was a Jew, but it did not seem to matter to them. One of them was a man named Pedro Marcello.

A very good man, a section head. He knew I was a Jew but he obviously had never met anyone Jewish before. One day he invited me home for supper. When I got to his place he introduced me to his wife and two children. 'This is my friend Leon,' he said, and they all just stood there, staring at me. I got more and more uncomfortable, when his wife finally burst out, 'But he looks just like our own Juanito!' Their son! They had a hard time believing I could actually be a Jew and look like everyone else!"

After Leon was at work a while he set out to find out what had happened to his father. He heard his father had reached Lyons with the safe-conduct pass Uncle Ephraim had gotten for him while they were still in Luchon. A cousin told him he was being hidden by the nuns of a convent hospital, illegally and unofficially, as a "non-person," to keep the Germans from finding him. For a while Leon was able to get news about his father from that cousin, but when all the Jews in France were deported, the news reports stopped. His father could not write because he was not supposed to exist.

"I was paid an excellent salary and I wanted to help my father. I approached Señor Rivas, who had all sorts of international connections and who by then knew a lot about me, including the fact that I was a Jew. 'I need to send money to my father in France, but I don't know how to do it, because he is hiding as a "non-person," in a convent. Can you help me?'

"'How much do you want to send him?' he asked. 'A thousand pesetas,' I said. He said, 'Two thousand.' I corrected him. 'I have only one thousand, that is all.' 'I will contribute the other thousand,' Rivas said. Can you imagine that?"

With his international connections, Rivas had the money delivered to the hospital by diplomatic pouch. The first time he tried it, a problem developed. The money had been sent to the Spanish consul in Saint-Etienne, who asked his male secretary to deliver the envelope to the convent. He was told to hand it to the mother superior and say the name "Nussbaum," but she refused to accept it. "There is no such person here," she said, afraid to let a stranger know she was harboring a Jew. The secretary returned the envelope to the consulate, and a woman was sent out in his place. This time the nun accepted it. There were no more problems after that.

"I continued to send money to my father throughout the rest of the war, until after liberation. Each time I sent money, Rivas doubled it. When the war ended, I went to France and got my father out. I finally left Spain in 1946 and came to Canada. Rivas and I stayed in touch for years, until he died."

"It was all so long ago, but it is still so new, those people so strong in my heart. Aside from Rivas and González, the only one I heard from was Alois Eck, my Czech friend who rescued Joseph and me from the Gestapo with his motorcycle, by pretending to be a Nazi. Years later I heard that someone had denounced him, someone who was suspicious of what he had done that day. He was picked up by the Gestapo shortly after that incident and imprisoned. God only knows what they did to him there. All I know is that during one year and a half in prison he never once revealed a thing. This I heard from others. Then, around 1959, I heard from Alois himself. He had found out where I was and wrote to tell me that his own brother was very ill in Prague and he needed money to go there and help him. We spoke on the phone. He sounded like a broken man. It was very painful talking to him. Of course I sent him money. After that we lost touch again. I tried to find him, but he just disappeared.

"I wish I could have done more for him. He saved our lives. Joseph and I both survived, but he . . . Alois Eck . . . *he* is the real hero."

The positive story Leon had promised me proved to contain several dark chapters, which now and then dimmed the glow cast by all his triumphs over adversity and the generosity accorded him by others. But Leon's warmth, his optimism, and his faith in the basic goodness of man made it possible for him to focus primarily on the miracles that enabled him to survive.

# · 10 ·

# *Mendel and Ruchel Defy Danger*

Mendel and Ruchel Slucki live in southern California, where the climate reminds them of southern France, Spain, and Cuba, places where they sought shelter during their six-year-long struggle to escape the Holocaust.

Tiny in stature and well into their eighties, both exude an amazing alertness. Their English is colored with a charming mixture of syntax and accents from several languages, of which the most readily recognizable is Yiddish. They travel frequently, take classes, do volunteer work, participate in symposia on Jewish political and philosophical issues, and read voraciously.

Their memories are huge, but what was most striking about them was the way they related to each other: their devotion, the way they finished each other's sentences, their smiles of approval and agreement as they helped each other reconstruct their past left no doubt that the horrors they had survived together had served to strengthen the bond of love between them.

The Sluckis have known each other since their childhood in Warsaw. Ruchel and her family moved to Paris when she was a young girl in 1926, and Mendel followed two years later. They married in 1929. Mendel worked as a tailor and Ruchel as a furrier. Their first child, a boy, died of a strep throat infection at the age of fourteen months. Henry, their surviving son, was born a few years later, in 1934.

At that time, it was almost impossible for foreign Jews to become French citizens, but the government offered citizenship to any foreigner who agreed to join the French army for a minimum of three months, during peacetime, or for the duration of hostilities in case of war. When war broke out in 1939, Mendel was one of the first to volunteer. He was sent to a training camp near the Spanish border, while Ruchel remained in Paris with little Henry. Then Mendel was sent to the front at the Maginot Line.

"It was terrible. Out of thirty-five hundred men sent there from my unit, only five hundred returned. Most were killed or wounded, the rest were taken prisoner. One day, after our lines were bombed for hours, I came across the body of one of my best friends, or rather half his body on the ground and half up in a tree. When I saw this horror I fell to the ground and cried like a baby. I can tell you, after that, I have never laughed again as I used to before.

"I somehow managed to always stay ahead of the Germans. As the Nazis marched south, right on my heels, I passed many French soldiers just sitting by the side of the road, waiting to surrender. One of them called to me, 'Why are you running? Take it easy, the *boches* [Krauts] are just half a kilometer from here!' 'That's good enough for me,' I told him, and decided to make *that* my policy from then on: to always stay at least one half kilometer *ahead* of the Germans."

When the French defenses collapsed in the summer of 1940

and France was cut in two by the German occupation of the northern and central regions, Mendel was demobilized in Montauban, a small town near Toulouse, in the Vichy (unoccupied southern) Zone. By then, everyone in the Occupied Zone had been issued gas masks, and all Jews were given yellow patches with the word "Juif" (Jew), which they were forced to wear. Ruchel, who was in Paris with Henry the day the Germans marched in, wanted Mendel to return there, but he was determined to stay out of the Occupied Zone. So, in August 1940, Ruchel and Henry joined Mendel in Montauban, where other members of their family and many other refugees soon followed.

When the Sluckis settled in Montauban, they found not only Jews and other opponents of Fascism hiding from Hitler, but many Loyalist defectors of the defeated Spanish Republican army who had escaped from the Franco regime. This was a welcome surprise for them, because they had always been politically active in liberal causes and had been members of a group of supporters of the anti-Franco forces operating in Paris during the Spanish Civil War. In Montauban they easily made friends, both with the expatriate Spaniards and the local people. All the while they were making plans eventually to flee to Spain and from there to the United States.

"As soon as my family joined me in Montauban, I had to find a way to make a living. I was a good tailor and people always need clothes. All I lacked was permission to work. When I applied for the labor permit, I soon discovered there was an unwritten law that Jews should not be allowed to work. Anti-Semitism has always been present in France, especially in official circles. But no one ever came right out and admitted it. They let you know in hidden ways.

"When I asked how to get the permit, I was told I first needed to get a signature from a certain judge, then take it to someone in the Department of Services for Non-French Residents for his signature. On that one day I was sent back and forth several times between those two officials, each claiming he could do nothing until the other signed.

"I finally realized I was being led around by the nose and that neither one had any intention of helping me. When the judge shrugged and said, for the fifth time, that his hands were tied, I told him, 'Judge, I think someone is trying to make fun of me.' He became all flustered and said, 'Ce n'est pas moi!' [Not me!] And as sometimes happens when you have run out of patience, two words popped out of my mouth I would never dare say if I thought about consequences: '*Prove it!*' Imagine, a Jew saying this to a judge! His response was to grab me by the arm. 'We are going to see that other man,' he said, and out we went, across the town plaza, the Polish Jew and the French judge, in full view of everybody!

"When we arrived at the Non-French Residents Services office, the little man in charge acted very strange. He mumbled, he stuttered. 'But, Judge, this man is a . . . is a . . .' I finished the sentence for him: 'Yes, this man is a Jew!' Now that the truth was out, the man spoke up: 'You don't seem to realize we lost the war! The Germans control everything here. They make the rules. We have to obey.' I said, 'What do you mean, *you* lost the war! *I* was in the French army, *I* fought at the Maginot Line! *I* was demobilized right here in Montauban! I am a tailor. I have the right to work and support my family! And besides,' I added, 'I don't see any Germans here right now!'

"The judge turned to me and said, 'Let's go.' Outside, he continued, 'You have defended yourself very well, and I myself will send a petition to Vichy so that you will be allowed to work.' And that is what he did. It took four months, but I finally got my permit."

Soon after that happened, a local Frenchman got Mendel a permit to travel within a certain radius, covering quite a large area. As a Jew, he would never have been able to obtain such a permit. Since it applied only to himself, Mendel went to a doctor in town who'd befriended him and asked him to write a note stating he had a heart condition that made it dangerous for him to travel alone. The trick worked. Soon it was legal for both Mendel and Ruchel to travel almost anywhere they wanted to go.

Mendel easily established himself in town as a tailor, sewing for other refugees, local citizens, even government officials. The family lived a relatively comfortable life, and even traveled to nearby resorts for short vacations.

Henry, now in his fifties, who was enrolled in school at that time, remembers one incident in Montauban he would never forget. "When I was a child in France, my great hero was Marshal Pétain. One day it was announced that Pétain was going to visit Montauban, and, as was the custom, one or two of the top students in each class, of which I was one, were to be given the honor of meeting him. When I arrived at the gathering, my teacher came up to me and asked what I thought I was doing there. 'I'm here to meet Marshal Pétain,' I told her. 'Go back, you can't meet him. You're a Jew.' I will never forget my feeling of confusion and betrayal. Although I knew I was a Jew, I thought of myself primarily as French. I went home and asked my parents, 'What am I first, French or Jewish?' That was the first time I actually felt discrimination against me as a Jew.'"

Shortly after they arrived in Montauban, Ruchel's sister Miriam left her two children with the Sluckis while she herself returned to Paris, so Mendel rented a larger house in town to accommodate his extended family.

Because they were allowed to travel and had connections with officials, Mendel and Ruchel quickly acquired a reputation for helping other refugees. People running from the Germans, trying to get out of the Occupied Zone, as well as foreign Jews escaping from camps abandoned by the French, who had interned them as "illegals," all ended up in Montauban. They needed help with everything. Unlike Mendel, who was automatically given legal residence in Montauban as a demobilized soldier, these people were unable to live there legally or obtain ration books, because the labor department kept turning down their work permit applications.

"People knew to come to me for good clothes. They saw I had ways of getting better materials than usual because I had connections, from before. One day a customer came to me to make him a suit. This man turned out to be the minister of labor for the whole area. When I found out who he was, I asked him, 'Are you the one responsible for approving or disapproving work permit applications?' He said yes, he was. So, this was the man responsible for keeping so many refugees illegal, with no work permit, no residency, no legal status, and no food. He was a very tall man, and you can see how short I am, but I reached up and took him by the lapels and asked him, 'You know what people say about you? They say you are an anti-Semite!' I knew that, despite their reputation for it, French people do not like to be thought of as anti-Semitic. He acted shocked and protested, 'How can you accuse me of such a thing?' 'Many Jewish refugees have to live as "illegals,"' I pressed on, 'because you keep denying their work permits.' He seemed genuinely surprised. 'Mon Dieu, I had no idea!' With that he pulled out a bunch of his business cards and handed them to me. 'If you know any persons who need their application approved, just put your name on my cards and tell them to bring them to me.' After that we did not have any more problems with work permits."

One day a woman told Mendel that her husband had just been picked up by the Gestapo, and was in a camp nearby waiting to be deported to Germany. She pleaded with him to use his influence to get him released. By coincidence, Mendel was just making a coat for a high government official who happened to be the chief of Services for Non-French Residents.

"I made up an excuse to see this man at his office, pretending he needed an extra fitting, and told him about the problem. 'I like you should help this man get out of camp and off the deportation list,' I told him. He shook his head. 'If the man is already on the list and ready to leave, it is too late,' he said. 'Not even I can do anything anymore.' There had to be a way. Then I got an idea. 'What would you do if I told you that man robbed me?' I asked. He smiled and said, 'I would have to arrest him and bring him to Montauban to answer the charges.' 'Well,' I told him, 'I tell you this man robbed me. I want you should arrest him.' The official winked at me and whispered, 'Maybe you should sit on *my* side of the desk instead of me.'"

A few days later the woman's husband was brought before the official and charged with robbery. He was put in jail, but the false charges against him were soon dropped because there was no proof of a crime. He was released to his wife, and he escaped deportation, while that very day the others in the camp were sent to Germany. Ironically, that good deed later saved the Sluckis' lives.

In late summer of 1942, the Germans requested that the French supply them with fifty thousand workers for slave labor in German factories. Glad to have this opportunity to rid France of as many Jews as possible, Pierre Laval, the Vichy government's anti-Semitic collaborator premier, replied, "Why settle for fifty thousand French when we can send you one hundred fifty thousand Jews?"

The police in Montauban heard about this and let out the rumor that there would be a roundup of Jews on a certain day, so they could hide. A Catholic farm family hid the Sluckis for three days, until the emergency was over and it was safe for them to return to town, but of course no one knew when the next roundup would be called.

"Local residents were most helpful," Ruchel said. "When I went shopping in the grocery stores they let me buy whatever I needed, even without ration books, and at regular prices, instead of black market rates, because they knew we were refugees and that we had our own as well as my sister Miriam's two children living with us. They had compassion. It is important to remember that we survived because so many people were helping us, despite the danger to them."

Mendel added, "This area was not yet occupied by the Germans and it was a small city, about forty thousand people, and most of the French there were still human. We found out later that because of the police's advance warning, most of us were saved. Only fourteen were caught out of about four hundred fifty Jews."

Here Mendel, who had been talking almost nonstop for quite some time, stopped. Both his face, which had been so animated, and his voice, which had sounded so excited as he shared his story, now turned somber. He continued in a very subdued tone.

"I don't know if I should tell this. So much of what happened while we were in danger was good, people helping, taking care of each other. But I do not think back on everything with pride. Some of it makes me feel ashamed. I want to tell this story because it shows how Jews dealt with each other when injustice happened among us, even while we ourselves were victims of so much injustice from others.

"Once a man named Sam came to me, recommended by my sister-in-law Miriam. He told me he had escaped from a concentration camp in the Occupied Zone and had difficulties getting a residency permit in Montauban. Through one of my contacts, I was able to obtain the permit he needed. Soon he became not only my friend but also the friend of our relatives and other friends. He often joined us at dinner and for playing cards.

"One summer day we were playing cards outside, on the grass, because it was so hot. One of the men, Simon, took off his coat and put it on a chair inside the house. Later that evening, when everyone was gone, Simon called to tell me that twenty thousand francs and his ration card were gone from his jacket pocket. I asked was he sure, but he said yes, he knew exactly what he carried on his person. I was of course shocked. Who could have been the thief? All but two of the group were family, and they were good friends. I checked all around the room, hoping the money maybe fell out, but I found nothing. Later that same night my sister-in-law called to say that five thousand francs from her pocketbook was also missing!

"I knew the person who took the money had plenty of time to hide it by now, so there was little chance to catch the thief. I did nothing and said nothing to anyone about what happened. But I had a plan. We had another card game scheduled a few days later, so I decided to wait and deal with the problem then. Next time, when everyone was present, with my knees shaking, I closed the doors and told everyone, 'A crime has been committed. Money has been stolen. We must find out who is guilty. I want everyone should let himself be searched.'

"I had no idea how the others would feel about me asking this. Even if they said yes, if they agreed to be searched, why would the thief be stupid enough to still carry so much stolen money on him? On the other hand, I figured he might think it was safer to keep it on his person instead of giving some other thief a chance to steal it from a hiding place. Anyway, nobody said no; we had the search and found a bundle of money sewed into the lining of Sam's coat! Sam, the man I helped get residency papers, had eighty-five thousand in francs and two hundred in dollars on him!

"When I held it up, to show everybody, he was so afraid we would take away all his money he betrayed himself by saying, 'Sixty thousand francs of this is mine!' I was filled with disgust and shame. How could a Jew, a Jew who was helped by other Jews in time of danger, steal from them? I said to him, 'Sam, you have committed a criminal act. But circumstances make it important to keep this only among ourselves, not to involve outsiders. So, we will deal with this matter alone.'

"We locked Sam in a room while the rest of us deliberated how to deal with him. When we came to a decision we let him out and sat him down. I said to him, 'If we look upon what you did as a quick business venture that failed, we can assume now you did not make a profit. Since you were not successful, it will cost you the twenty-five thousand francs you stole. This money will be returned to Simon and Miriam, from whom you took it. But because you are also a criminal, you will have to pay a penalty of twenty-five thousand francs. This we will divide between all of us who had to bear the shadow of suspicion from your act. The rest you can keep. Now, what did you do with the ration card you stole from Simon?' He said, 'I was afraid to keep it so I tore it up.' I was even more sickened. 'How could you deprive one of your own of food at a time like this? You don't deserve to live among us.'

"I took the residency permit I had procured for him and tore it into pieces. Later that night we took him to the train station and made sure that he left town, knowing that without a residency card or travel permit he was now in the same position as when he came to Montauban. No worse, no better. We gave the extra twenty-five thousand francs we took from him to an organization that helped refugees in our area.

"I feel ashamed to tell you this story, ashamed that such a thing could happen among Jews, but I am glad that we did not let Sam's act go unpunished. We took care of it ourselves."

Mendel looked somber for a moment, then his face brightened once more. "Now I want to tell you something that happened that I am very proud of. I told you I had a permit to travel almost anywhere I wanted to go. On this particular day I was at the train station at Moulin, a town very close to the demarcation line between the occupied and unoccupied parts of France. I was waiting for my train to go back to Montauban when I noticed this woman with a small girl acting very nervous. You know, under the conditions we had to live with, you develop sharp instincts. I knew by looking at her that this woman was running. I took a chance and walked up to her. 'Do you speak Yiddish?' I asked. She looked scared and answered in Yiddish, 'Why do you want to know? What business of yours is it?' I said, 'If you have just come here from the Occupied Zone, you have to be very careful. If they catch you they will take you right back.' She began to protest, saying no, she did not come from up north, and nothing was going to happen and I should leave her alone. With that she walked away.

"A few minutes later her little girl came over to me, alone, and said, 'My mother wants to talk to you.' I told her to tell her mother to follow me. I walked to a place that was a little hidden and waited for the woman. How come it was all right for me to be there and not safe for her, she wanted to know. I explained I had a travel permit. After a few more questions she finally admitted she had just arrived from the Occupied Zone illegally. I told her, 'You must get away from here as quickly as possible. If you want, I will get you tickets to go to Montauban.' She offered to give me the money, but I did not want to take it. I did not want she should worry that I would steal the money or that I would denounce her, so I told her to stay where she was and I would get the tickets. 'You can pay me after. Watch me carefully. I will wait until just before our train is ready to pull out. Then I will signal you. As soon as I do, run as fast as you can and get on the train after me. That way no one can stop you before you get on.'

"With my travel permit for two I had no trouble getting tickets for her. I stood on the platform, waiting for the conductor to get on. Then I gave her the signal and she did just as I asked. On the train I put her and the child in a compartment and kept them there while I stood watch outside. When the control came I showed him my papers and told him that was my family in the compartment.

"We got to Montauban safely. I took her and her child home to Ruchel and we helped her get settled. If she had stayed in Moulin she would definitely have been sent back. This way she was safe. In 1961 Ruchel and I visited Paris and found the young girl, who now is the mother of a little girl of her own. We kissed and hugged and she cried. 'If it were not for Mendel,' she told everyone, 'I would not be here today.' I feel very proud I had the good sense to approach the mother when I did, that I helped her and her child survive."

From the first day they arrived in Montauban, Mendel tried to find a way to smuggle his family into Spain. Things in France were definitely not getting better. Trains were leaving daily for Germany, filled with Jews. When the rest of France was about to be occupied, the Sluckis first considered going to Switzerland, like some of their other relatives, but decided against it. They were afraid a little country like that, all surrounded and closed in by land, was likely to be taken over if the Germans won, forcing the Swiss to turn over their Jews to Hitler. Spain, on the other hand, even with

Franco, seemed a better choice: neutral, like Switzerland, but open, surrounded on three sides by water.

When the Germans finally invaded the rest of France in 1942, it was too dangerous for anyone attempting to escape to hesitate any longer. Ruchel's sister Miriam came back from Paris to pick up her children, hoping to get into Switzerland. Mendel, Ruchel, and Henry moved closer to the Spanish border, to Luchon. Even though they had no papers to enter Spain, they were determined to find someone to help them get there as soon as possible.

One day Ruchel met a woman who offered to introduce her to a couple of smugglers with experience crossing the Pyrenees. She left Mendel to take care of details while she and Henry returned to Montauban to liquidate everything, knowing they would need every franc they could raise to pay the guide who would take them into Spain. While at Montauban, Ruchel took a quick trip to Toulouse, to exchange some francs into pesetas because Spanish smugglers had to be paid in their own currency. The man who traded in the francs for pesetas was a young Spaniard, an anti-Franco refugee. He explained he had family in Barcelona but, because it was dangerous for Spaniards to receive mail from France, he had been afraid to write to them. "If you ever get to Barcelona," he told Ruchel, "please give my mother this note. She does not know I am alive." Later, Mendel wrote the mother's address on another piece of paper, rolled the boy's note and the address into two tiny scrolls, and hid one in each pant pocket for safekeeping.

Meanwhile, the woman arranging the smuggling operation asked Mendel for ten thousand francs up front. Cautious and practical, he told her he would give her only one thousand of it as a deposit, promising to pay the rest after the smugglers confirmed their plans. Agreements were reached at last, but as their departure date drew close, Ruchel and Henry had not yet returned from Montauban. Then, just when they were due back, an order was passed, temporarily forbidding civilian use of trains that were needed to carry

Germans south to occupy the rest of France. So, there was Mendel, ready at last to leave for Spain, with Ruchel and Henry still stuck in Montauban! There was nothing for him to do but wait.

One day Mendel and a friend who knew all about his escape plans met in a café. "Those are the men your woman hired to take you into Spain," the friend said, pointing to another table. Mendel went over to introduce himself. "I am one of the three people you will be taking into Spain."

"Take you to Spain?" one of them asked. "Oh, no. That is much too dangerous. We are only supposed to take you to the border. From there you will have to make other arrangements."

Surprised and angry, Mendel was also relieved he had not paid the go-between all the money up front. This woman happened to be a barmaid in that very café, so he confronted her right then and there. "You lied to me about the arrangements. I want back the money I gave you." She hissed, "You will pay me the ten thousand francs you promised me or I will denounce you to the police." Mendel shot back, "If you do, I will turn *you* in!"

One of the other refugees in the café quickly gave the woman one thousand francs just to shut her up before the loud exchange attracted police attention and everybody got into trouble. She grabbed the money and that was the end of it. But now Mendel had to make all new arrangements.

When Ruchel and Henry finally returned to Luchon, Mendel was still searching for a way to get them out of France. One day he met two men who were in the business of arranging people-smuggling. "How much do you charge to get someone into Spain?" Mendel asked. "Fifty thousand francs a person," one of the smuggle brokers answered. "Well," said the other one, "I want all three should go for the price of one, because *this* is the man who saved my nephew from being deported to Germany." This indeed turned out to be the uncle of the man whom Mendel had falsely accused of being a robber to save him from being shipped to a concentration camp!

Fifty thousand francs would have been enough for all the Sluckis to live on without working for three years. Although they did not have anywhere near that kind of money, they agreed to the arrangements anyway. "We decided to worry how to pay later," admitted Mendel. The men told them two smugglers would take them over the mountains on foot and from there by car to Barcelona.

When the Sluckis went to meet their guides, a small misunderstanding over the exact location caused them to miss one another. Once again, new arrangements had to be made. Three days later they were finally set to meet with another guide, who agreed to get them to the border. The two go-betweens described the guide and carefully spelled out the procedure the Sluckis were to follow. "'You will all be taking a train together and then change buses twice. Follow the guide but do not talk to him until you get out of town, no matter what,' they warned us. 'Pretend you do not know each other.'

"We found the right place, identified the guide, and made no contact, just as we were told. We took the train and switched buses twice, together. While on the second bus, our guide suddenly got off without us. We tried to get off too, but the bus driver blocked the exit and forced us to go on alone. As you can imagine, we were terrified. We did not know what to expect next. After a while, the bus stopped. The driver told us to get out and drove off. We were left alone, in the middle of nowhere, on a deserted road. It was about nine-thirty at night, cold and pitch dark.

"Suddenly two young men appeared from the shadows. Without a word, they grabbed our bags and ordered us to follow them up a hill. We did as we were told. We were afraid not to, although I was sure they were bandits, ready to rob and kill us. 'Your guide left you on the bus because he was too tired to continue,' one of them said at last. 'He asked us to take you from here to the Spanish border.' What a relief to have an explanation, to have some hope again!

"We continued climbing until after two in the morning. Finally, we reached a shack where we were allowed to rest. It had no electricity, and water had to be pumped from a well outside. When we entered, an old woman screamed at our guides, 'Why did you bring more refugees? Don't you remember what happened to last week's group? The German patrol caught them!' I realized instantly that the group we had accidentally missed earlier was the group caught by the German border patrol, and got a strong feeling that someone was watching over us, keeping us safe."

Ruchel wrapped Henry in warm clothes and put him to sleep on a dirty bed in the shack. She and Mendel slept on the floor. Before dawn three Spanish smugglers arrived at the shack, carrying silk stockings and other luxury items fresh from a run into Spain. The Sluckis rehashed all details of the arrangements with the guides and the smugglers. The French guides would get one half the amount agreed upon, twenty-five thousand francs, and the Spanish smugglers would receive the other half, in pesetas, after safe arrival inside Spain.

"Next morning all of us began a long and steep climb up the snowy mountains. In addition to the contraband, the smugglers brought along food: a leg of lamb, a big loaf of bread, and a bottle of red wine. At noon we stopped to rest and eat. When we were done, the two French guides said, 'We have brought you to the Spanish border. Our part is over. Now we want our money.' As we said our good-byes, after paying them their share, I thought about the ironic destiny of the Jewish people. Nearly five hundred years before, our ancestors had crossed this spot from Spain into France to save their lives. Now, here we were, crossing from France into Spain for the same reason. That is the way Jewish people have survived for centuries.

"We continued on, with the three Spanish smugglers leading the way. The weather was beautiful, but very cold. Everywhere we looked there was only ice and snow. The Spaniards were well equipped, wearing snowshoes and heavy jackets. They had an ice pick with which they made holes for us to step into, to make walking more secure as we followed them in a line. For a while, the lead guide carried Henry under his arm, like a sack of potatoes. Ruchel came next, followed by the second guide. Then came I, and last came the third Spaniard. We got to a frozen waterfall where we had to pass over a very narrow ledge. When I tried to crawl across, I slipped. If the guide behind me had not caught me by my coat collar and pulled me up, I would have ended up frozen in a deep crevasse.

"Later that afternoon one of the guides went ahead to see if the road was clear for us to continue. The rest of us stopped to lie down and rest. When the guide returned, he warned us that a border patrol house was just ahead. As we approached it we had to crouch down below window level so no one would see us. All this time little Henry was as good as gold, kept up with us, walking without a peep. Later he said he thought it was all an exciting adventure, and that he felt very safe with us and the guides to protect him."

By the fourth evening the group was already well inside Spain, and more likely to run into Spanish patrols. That night they arrived at a shepherds' cabin on top of a mountain. It had no windows and only a dirt floor, and smoke poured out the open door from a fire inside. The shack was full of other refugees, trying to keep warm. The smoke was thick enough to choke a person, so everyone kept going in and out, to catch a breath of fresh air, despite the cold and wind.

Soon after the Slucki party settled in, another guide brought in his charge, a Mr. Cohen, the head of the Jewish community in Toulouse. Mr. Cohen complained loudly that he had foolishly paid his guide the full amount in advance, to take him over the mountains and to have a car ready to take him to Barcelona. Now this guide informed him he was not able to provide the car as promised! Mr. Cohen was clearly very upset, because he knew he was stuck with his bad bargain.

The Sluckis offered to help him find a solution, and Mr. Cohen promised to pay fifty thousand francs if someone could find a car big enough for all of them. One of the guides agreed to see what he could do and set off for the village below. Hours later, when he had not returned, all began to worry if they would ever see him again. When he finally showed up he had with him a man and a mule! The car was at the bottom of the mountain, he explained. He also informed them the driver was asking for seventy thousand francs, instead of the fifty thousand he had been offered.

"I became very angry. 'Isn't it strange,' I screamed at the driver, 'that you, who accuse *us* of being money-hungry Jews, claim to have no interest in money, yet *here you are*, extorting money from us when we need it to save our lives! We offered you all we have and it is still not enough for you!' One of the smugglers got scared, because I was yelling out my disgust so loud. 'Be careful, your voice is echoing all over the mountains, they will arrest you!' I was so outraged I replied, 'If I go, you go too.' Afraid that all of us would be caught, Mr. Cohen offered to pay half the price asked, even though there were three of us and only one of him. He settled on sixty thousand francs total."

They were finally ready to leave the mountaintop. Henry was put on the mule, with Mr. Cohen's suitcases behind him, and the rest walked alongside all the way into the village. The guide led them to the back entrance of an inn, because the police and border guards were eating supper inside. The innkeeper brought them food and took them to their rooms in the rear of the inn. All went to sleep, exhausted.

"The smugglers woke us up in the middle of the night and told us the car was ready. Their job was done. We paid them the money they were owed and wished one another well. The driver waited out in the car, and asked to be paid before starting out. As before, I agreed to give him only a part of it, with the rest to be paid when we were safe in Barcelona."

The car was old and noisy, but it worked. After an hour, the driver announced there was a police guard post up ahead, and asked everyone to duck down. He raced the engine, hard, then turned off the motor and coasted past the police post without any noise to call attention to himself or his cargo. The next few hours were relatively uneventful.

"We had been traveling for some time when a highway policeman suddenly appeared right in front of us, blocking the way. I was sure we were finished. He demanded to see the driver's permits, and asked what we were carrying in our baggage to make sure we were not smuggling contraband, or black market items, such as meat, bread, oil, sugar, or other foodstuffs. We told him we had only 'ropa' [clothes]. With that he waved us on. I was sure that if it were not four in the morning, and not so dark, he would have demanded to see our papers, which of course we did not have, and we would all have been thrown in jail.

"A few hours later, just outside Laredo, we were stopped again. As before, the driver was asked to show his papers, but this time it was light out and we were sure the policeman would ask us for *our* papers, too. We expected the worst, but, after examining the driver's permits, he waved us on. Just as the engine started up again, he changed his mind and started to bang on the rear window. The driver raced away, pretending not to notice. We were all quiet a long time after that. My heart pounded against my chest as I wondered how often we could be so lucky."

They still had a three-hour drive to Barcelona when they came to the outskirts of a little town, Montserrat. Mendel asked the driver if he knew a hotel in Barcelona where they would not be required to show papers. The driver did not answer right away, but when they got into Montserrat he stopped the car and told the three adults to get out. "Walk down the main street," he told them, "and I will meet you at the other end of town, about half a kilometer away." At first his suggestion sounded suspicious, but on second thought they decided the plan made sense. After being stopped twice, it was clearly safer for the driver not to have three adults in the car with him. Besides, he was still owed the rest of his money, so nobody believed they had cause to worry. Mendel, Ruchel, and Mr. Cohen got out and watched the car drive off with their luggage and little Henry in the backseat.

Montserrat was full of police. Something must have happened earlier, because there was a lot of commotion, with men in uniform everywhere. As they walked among them, the Sluckis and Mr. Cohen tried to be as unobtrusive as possible, but Mendel got very nervous and suggested they walk on a parallel street, where they would be less noticeable. Ruchel refused. "If we don't follow the driver's instructions to the letter we might lose Henry," she said, so they did it her way.

The Sluckis and Mr. Cohen had walked for ten more minutes when, halfway down the street, they saw little Henry sitting on the sidewalk curb, with all their belongings next to him. The car and driver were nowhere in sight.

"He said he was going to get gasoline," the boy explained, looking not the least bit worried.

It did not take a genius to understand what had happened. When Mendel asked the driver to find a hotel that did not require papers, the driver must have realized his charges were illegals. After that he was too scared to go on. It must have been very dangerous for him, but Mendel conceded he had been pretty clever. He got rid of the adults first, then the child and the baggage. Then he left, without even bothering to collect the rest of his money.

"We still had most of it, thank God, which was a good thing because here we were, in this strange town, full of military police, with no one to take us to Barcelona. But we reminded ourselves how lucky it was that Ruchel had insisted we should stay on the main street. We could have lost our son!"

Going to Barcelona by train was too risky without papers. They knew they had to find another car to take them the rest of the way. When a gas station attendant agreed to help them, the last thing they expected was to be offered a 1941 American car complete with driver!

"I was amazed that, as we drove down the road, people kept saluting us! They probably thought we were important government officials. Who else would drive such a car? As we approached Barcelona, I once again asked the driver to take us to a hotel where no legal documents would be required. The one he took us to was much too expensive for Ruchel and me, but Mr. Cohen said yes, he could afford it. He told the driver to find another place for us and then come back to get paid."

Ruchel spoke up: "We did not know what to do next. We were almost all out of money. Then I remembered the two notes the young Spaniard in Toulouse had asked me to bring to his mother in case we ever got to Barcelona. Well, here we were, in Barcelona at last, and since we knew no one else, Mendel asked the driver to take us to the address on one of the two little pieces of paper he had carried rolled up in the bottom of his pant pocket all this time.

"When we arrived at the address, we found a very rich-looking place. Marble walls, fancy carpets, gold mirrors and paintings in the lobby, a doorman, and even an elevator! We were afraid to go in, so messy and dirty after our long journey. I suggested Mendel should go up alone, but he took along the driver."

Mendel continued, "When I rang the bell upstairs, a woman answered. I handed her the note from the boy. She burst into tears when she read it, threw her arms around me, and said, 'Oh, thank God! Come in, come in!' When the driver told her there was a woman and a child waiting downstairs, she sent her daughter to bring up Ruchel and Henry."

"This woman explained we had brought her the first sign that her son was alive since the end of the Civil War, when he fled to France," added Ruchel. "Here we were, refugees ourselves, bringing this poor woman the most precious news a mother can hear. Although her name has disappeared from both of our memories, Mendel and I always think of her with great affection. She could not do enough for us. She had two daughters and offered us their room to stay in. She spoke French, and from the simple meal she cooked for us we could tell that she, herself, had very little. There was only an oil lamp, no electricity. She told us that her husband had been a high government official in the Republican administration, before the Civil War. When Franco came to power, all the old money became worthless and people had to change it into new currency. Because of their former position, as enemies of the Franco regime, she was afraid to go and trade in the old money, so her family became penniless overnight. Somehow she and her daughters were able to hold onto their apartment, taking in laundry from rich people and doing housework. Still, even in her sad circumstances, she was willing to share with us the little she had.

"A few days after we arrived in her house a family friend came to visit. When he found out we were staying with her, he pulled Mendel aside. 'You cannot stay here,' he told him. 'These people have nothing, they can barely manage to stay alive. Come to my house, I have room for you.' So we told the lady we would see her as soon as we were settled and went with her friend. This man, Ramón, gave us a room in his home and fed us for several days, without asking anything from us. He, himself, was in hiding from Franco's police, after fighting on the wrong side in the Civil War. He lived in secret, with false identity papers, and made a living as a truck driver. He called the Joint for us so we could get assistance.

"The Joint helped us right away. They gave us money to live on, and asked us to come back the next week for more money. This was not enough to live on for all of us, but before spending any of it we went back to the woman who took us in and offered to share that money with her. She refused to accept it. 'We, my daughters and I, are still richer than you, because we have a roof over our heads,' she said. Before we left, I put half the money in a dish on the dining-room table. We felt so very lucky to have met such good people upon arriving in Barcelona, and were very grateful to her."

Mendel added, "These Spaniards never asked if we were Jews, but they let us know they knew. In fact, that lady told us she felt

Spaniards owed the Jewish people a debt because of what they did to Jews during the Inquisition."

With the money the Joint gave them, the Sluckis were able to rent a room with a family right in town, and began to feel like normal people, living a normal life. Henry went to a French Catholic school in the neighborhood. One day a teacher fell into conversation with him during lunch and asked where he lived. "When Henry told her we all lived in one room with only one bed, with a strange family, the teacher said she knew of an apartment they might be able to rent. She gave Henry the address and that is how we happened to move into a lovely two-room flat.

"Refugees usually ran into each other in the Joint office or in the Plaza de Cataluña, on weekends. We recognized one another by overhearing us talk in Yiddish or French. Some of us were friends from before. Others met in Spain. I guess maybe there were five thousand foreign Jews in Barcelona alone, while I was there. I don't know how many others were in Miranda de Ebro [a detention camp for illegal male refugees] and Madrid. We had no knowledge of any local Jews, if there were any."

Soon after the Sluckis arrived in Barcelona, the Joint informed them that Mrs. Roosevelt was arranging to bring one thousand refugee children to stay with private families in the United States. Since the Vichy government refused to let any Jewish children leave France, the United States visas were being offered by the HIAS to children living in Spain, Portugal, or any other country that allowed them to leave. As it turned out, only five hundred of those visas were actually used, and, of those, not all were taken by Jewish children. The Sluckis were asked if they were interested in sending Henry. They turned down the offer. Ruchel explained, "We felt safe for the first time in a long time, and a separation from our child was something we could not even think about after what almost happened in Montserrat."

Mendel took up the narrative: "By 1943 a rumor went around

that all male refugees between eighteen and forty-two were going to be interned to prevent them from joining their own countries' armed forces to fight against the Axis. Since I was only thirty-seven I decided to grow a beard to look older. When I went to the police and they asked my age, I lied and told them I was forty-three. The policeman looked at me funny and asked if I had any documents to prove my age. I told him I threw them away because I did not want to have any identification on me crossing over the Pyrenees in case the French caught us. He then asked me a lot of questions, like, how old was I when I was married and when my son was born, and in what year did certain events happen, and I had to give him the right answers to fit the age I gave him. I was terrified I would say something wrong and get caught, so I had to think fast not to make a mistake. The policeman said he knew I was not forty-three, but because I answered all the questions right he had to give me residence papers anyway."

Several weeks after the first children's transport left for the States, another one was formed, and the Sluckis were again asked if they wanted to let Henry go. This time they went so far as to register him, but when departure time arrived, they were unable to let him go. They compromised by going to the railroad station to see off the other children.

"It was one of the most emotional scenes we have ever had to watch," recalled Ruchel, "parents saying good-bye to their children, weeping, frightened, not knowing when or if they would ever see each other again. Mendel and I decided we would never again let ourselves witness anything like this.

"Then when a third group of children was being formed, in late 1943, we registered Henry again. Why? Because by then we heard another rumor: that a refugee camp was being set up in North Africa and that all of us in Spain would be sent there. We did not want Henry to go to a camp and miss an opportunity to live with a family in America. We could not be so selfish. How we agonized over this! We finally asked the Joint if they could arrange to have Henry stay with relatives instead of strangers in the US. The Joint agreed to try to do as we asked if we provided them with a written statement from my uncle in the US stating he was willing and able to accept Henry to live with him. The Joint also promised to reunite us after the war.

"We immediately wrote to my uncle, telling him Henry was coming, but there was no guarantee this would work. First, we did not know his wife, and how she would feel about having a small boy to take care of, for God knows how long. Even if all went well, we had no clue about their financial situation, and we could not even count on the mail getting through to them with the war conditions. Besides, there was no way all this could be arranged fast enough, before the transport left. We decided to go ahead and risk sending Henry anyway, without knowing who would take him when he arrived in America.

"We will never forget the day Henry had to leave, September 15, 1943. He was still a little boy, just over nine years old, but very brave and well mannered. During the trolley ride to the railroad station, Mendel and I spoke to him about how he should behave living with people he did not know, and without having us near. We told him to always listen politely and do what he was asked to do, even if he did not agree with it. We wanted him to know it was important to always try to be pleasant and agreeable, to make things easier on everybody. Years later, a parent himself by now, Henry told us he still remembered our advice to him on that terrible day.

"When we arrived at the station platform, with the train already waiting, we met the leader of the group. He told us to say our good-byes before Henry boarded. I will never forget a moment of that pain. Henry kept telling us not to cry while tears were running down his own face. When the train pulled out he was at the window, waving as we ran alongside, until he disappeared. Even today I can still feel the agony of that separation."

Mendel continued: "Several weeks after Henry left we were notified by both the Joint and the HIAS that our son was accepted by

Ruchel's uncle, Nathan Gura, and was living with him and his wife, Jenny, in New York. Soon this was confirmed when we started getting letters from Henry himself, and we felt easier about having him so far away. They treated our son like one of the family.

"Meantime, all the time we were in Spain, other relatives who had emigrated to Mexico kept telling us they were trying to get us visas to join them there. Then, about nine months after Henry left, we got a call from the Cuban consulate in Barcelona, informing us they were authorized to give us transit visas to Cuba because there were Mexican visas waiting for us in Havana! They asked us to come with our passports so they could finish up all the paperwork."

The problem was, the Sluckis *had* no passports. The HIAS intervened on their behalf at the Polish Embassy in Lisbon and helped them obtain Polish passports. The HIAS also paid for their passage and made all their travel arrangements. So, on March 29, 1944, Mendel and Ruchel finally left Spain, on the SS *Magellanes* (the very ship my family and I had traveled on!), and reached Havana on April 23. They rushed to the Mexican Embassy, only to be informed by the consul that their Mexican visas had expired and that they would have to be interned in a detention camp while the Cuban authorities figured out what to do with them!

Exasperated, Mendel created a huge commotion at the consulate, but it still took five days for him and Ruchel to be released. In the end they never did make it to Mexico. Because of the war, the Cuban government allowed them to stay in Havana.

"Finally, in 1946, two and a half years after we said good-bye to our son, we were reunited in New York. To this day, that is the happiest moment of our lives."

Mendel became very pensive here, and when he went on he spoke more slowly, choosing his words carefully.

"We have never forgotten how lucky we were to have survived the Holocaust, to have been helped by so many people along the way, in France and in Spain, where people put their own lives in danger to save us. The guides, even though they were paid, took many chances for us, to bring us to safety. We will always be grateful to them. We will never forget what the Joint and the HIAS did for us, and especially the Spanish authorities, who closed their eyes to many regulations and left us in peace for two and a half years, until others were ready to let us in. Now we feel blessed to live here in this country for so many years. Yes, we have been very lucky.

"Another thing we must never forget is why all this happened. We must remember that what the Nazis wanted was to destroy the whole Jewish people, everywhere. Survival became every Jew's daily concern for twelve long years. While we were forced to learn how to survive, we also learned to take care of each other. We must keep remembering how important it is to take care of one another. Those of us who lived through it could not have survived that horror without looking out for each other.

"Not everyone in our family had our good fortune. Because we will hold their memories in our hearts forever, I want to name those who did not survive, who perished in concentration camps at Auschwitz, Treblinka, and Chelmno:

"Ruchel's parents, Moshe-Ber and Chaya Gitel Gura.

"Ruchel's sister, Ita Gura, and her six-month-old baby.

"Ruchel's uncles and aunts, Itzrak and Gisha Leah Gura and their son, Bernard, and Abraham and Miriam Baum and their daughter, Margaret.

"My sister, Hasia Slucki, and her six-month-old baby.

"My sister-in-law, Gitel Slucki, and her two sons, Shmuel and Haim."

Just before we said good-bye, Mendel added a footnote: "Someone once asked me, 'Mendel, what would you do, where would you go if, God forbid, we were faced with another Holocaust?' I did not hesitate a moment. 'Go back to Spain,' I said. That is where we felt the safest. We encountered no anti-Semitism. Yes, we would go back to Spain."

# PART THREE

# THE RESCUERS

# ·11·

# *The Conscience of a Few*

The general public, even the majority of well-informed and so-phisticated Jews, know little or nothing about the rescue of Jewish refugees in Spain during World War II. When they hear about it, most refuse to believe it actually happened or doubt that a signif-icant number of Jews would have been involved. How *could* it be true? Franco and Hitler were allies. After Franco won the Civil War, German troops were all over Spain, making sure the Spaniards toed the Fascist party line. What's more, the Catholic Church, which had refused to intervene on behalf of Jews and remained silent when Hitler began to persecute them, supported Franco's revolt and was firmly entrenched as Spain's official state religion. With Spain's public image so closely linked to the Inquisition and the ex-pulsion of their *own Sephardic* Jews, why would anyone expect

Spaniards to help *foreign Ashkenazic* Jews, especially at a time when other nations seemed notoriously unsympathetic and mostly ignored their desperate pleas for help?

There are indications that many Spaniards carry a certain collective guilt over their treatment of Jews five hundred years ago, but it is doubtful that Spain's rescue efforts during the Holocaust can be ascribed to that fact alone. The reasons are far more complex, far more amorphous, and may never be clear enough to allow any firm conclusions to be drawn. There are, however, clues that shed some light on the psychological and political climate in Spain when the fate of European Jews became known to the Spanish leaders.

Evidence shows that despite Spain's alliance with the Axis, the efforts of a few men of broad moral principles touched the conscience of some of those in power deeply enough to affect their actions. Professor Luis Suarez Fernandez, a historian and author of several books on Franco and Spain's relationship with Jews, elaborated on this issue when we met in Madrid.

Although information about confiscation of property, curtailment of civil rights, and other injustices and harassments imposed on Jews was brought to the attention of Spanish authorities by the French ambassador to Madrid as early as 1940, not until 1942 did the fact that Jews were being persecuted in Germany and Nazi-occupied countries arouse any significant attention in Spain. While Franco's recently appointed liberal foreign minister, Conde de Jordana, managed to resist great pressure from Hitler to enact similar anti-Jewish measures in Spain, he was unable to get sufficient support from his colleagues to actively help the persecuted Jews.

In the meantime, anti-Semitism was being whipped into high gear by a German propaganda agency headed by Hans Lazar, who bombarded Spaniards with vicious anti-Jewish pamphlets and placards.

Then an event occurred that finally brought about a change in the Spanish consciousness. In 1942 a group of Spanish doctors went to Poland and met with the Nazi Gauleiter Frankel of Warsaw. As-

suming he was speaking with others of his own orientation, Frankel
went into considerable detail about Germany's plan to exterminate
Jews. At that time the Final Solution by use of gas chambers had
not yet been worked out, so he disclosed that the plan was to con-
fine Jews in places where conditions were so terrible, sanitation so
poor, and nourishment so inadequate that life could not be sustained and the Jews would quickly die.

On their return, the doctors gave this information to Admiral
Carrero Blanco, one of Franco's closest confidants. He, in turn, told
Franco. "Franco's immediate reaction is not known," admitted Professor Suarez, "but it is a significant and well known fact that, from
that time on, the Germans kept a large contingent of the Gestapo
in Spain because Hitler could no longer rely on Franco's full support." It is also important to note that this coincides with the time
when the Spanish border with France was opened to facilitate the
entry of Jews into Spain.

A few months later, Foreign Minister Jordana told Franco about
an urgent request he had received from the Spanish ambassadors
in Athens, Budapest, Sofia, and Bucharest: a plea for authority to
give Spanish citizenship to the Jews in those cities (mostly of Spanish ancestry) to keep them from being deported to concentration
camps. Heinrich Himmler, Hitler's Gestapo chief, found out about
this request and urged Franco to say no, but since Spain was officially a neutral country, Adolf Eichmann agreed to give Spain until the end of March 1943 to get all "their" Jews out of Greece,
Hungary, Bulgaria, and Romania, or they would all be sent to concentration camps. This is when the "repatriation of Spanish Jews"
began.

Professor Suarez claims that the Spanish people were afraid that
this influx of Jews would be used by Hitler as a pretext for invad-
ing Spain. "Many more Jews would have been allowed to enter this
country if that fear had not been there. But, although only Sephardim
had official sanction, Jewish refugees kept coming. Evidence shows
that no one ever bothered to ask whether the refugees let in were

Ashkenazic or Sephardic Jews, or even if they were Jews at all."

Professor Suarez recounted the story of one of the great but almost unknown champions of Hungary's endangered Jews, who happened to be a Spaniard. This young man's efforts on their behalf were as heroic as those of Raoul Wallenberg, who was working in Budapest at the same time. "Angel Sanz Briz was the secretary of the Spanish Embassy at the time when Hungary's Jews were being sent to German slave labor camps in huge numbers. When he saw what was happening, he repeatedly went to the spot where the Jews were being loaded into trucks by the Gestapo and stopped them, saying, 'These are *my* subjects. You must release them to me!' The Germans let them go. Angel returned them all to Budapest and put them up in Spanish safe houses. Of course none of these people actually were Spaniards, nor even Sephardim, and none spoke a word of Spanish; so, in case they should ever be challenged, he taught the adults a few phrases, and told the children, 'If someone says anything to you, just say "Buenos días."' When the Russians liberated the city, all went free." (In *Spain and the Jews During the Second World War*, the Spanish historian Federico Ysart claims Sanz was responsible for saving five thousand Jewish lives, mostly Ashkenazim.)

Another diplomat who tried, but was less successful in his efforts to help Jews, was Domingo de las Barcenas, the Spanish ambassador in Rome. Jews were beginning to be deported from Italy when one of Mussolini's military leaders approached de las Barcenas in December 1942. "Even the Jews who are married to Catholics are no longer safe here," he told him. "The Germans are taking them away and will kill them. You must do something." De las Barcenas first tried to find space for Jews in safe houses maintained by various religious orders. Although he was able to place Jews in these houses, they were not saved, because the Italian Fascist forces refused to honor their sanctuary, broke in, and carted off the Jews.

"De las Barcenas now went to the Vatican. He spoke to Monsignor Montini [who later became Pope Paul VI], telling him, 'You can't let this persecution of the Jews continue.' Together they went to the German Embassy, to ask that the Jews be protected. The German ambassador replied, 'I can do nothing, in Berlin no one listens to me.' Later, when Eichmann found out about the meeting, he told Franco, 'We are getting tired of your interference. You have no rights over any Jews except your own.' "

Fifty years later, I was able to find and speak with one Spanish diplomat in Madrid who was directly involved in Jewish rescue efforts. Like several of his colleagues in the Spanish diplomatic corps stationed in Greece, Turkey, and elsewhere, Bejamino Molho, then deputy ambassador to Yugoslavia, provided Spanish passes for many Jews trying to escape deportation to concentration camps while he was posted in Belgrade.

Spain's role in saving Jewish lives during World War II was remarkable in and of itself, but its truly exceptional nature stands out when compared with the lack of response from democratic countries that turned a deaf ear to the increasingly desperate plight of the Jews even after they were fully aware of the deadly consequences of their disregard. The irrefutable fact remains that, although the presence of Jews placed the whole country at risk of being drawn into another war or occupied by Hitler's forces, Fascist Spain, both officially and unofficially, accepted thousands of foreign Ashkenazic Jews within its borders and allowed them to remain until they were able to secure residence elsewhere.

Adding to this paradox are the other two seemingly prohibitive facts that warrant repeating here. Spain itself was in a state of devastation following the Civil War, with hardly enough resources to support its own population. Lastly, the 1492 Expulsion Decree had not only never been formally rescinded, but the law giving Jews legal status in Spain would not be passed for another forty years! Not a likely set of circumstances under which one would expect Jews to find safety, but they did.

To better understand this contradictory set of circumstances and gain insight into the motivating factors behind the actions of those who repeatedly confounded all reasonable expectations, I sought out some of the men and women who risked their own lives again and again to smuggle refugees into Spain and who helped them to survive in numerous other ways. In telling their stories, these people also illuminate the complex human heart of Spain.

Here, too, is the story of the American Jewish Joint Distribution Committee (known as the JDC or Joint), whose brave and selfless operatives worked hand in hand with Spanish authorities who routinely released into their care thousands of refugees caught entering Spain illegally, providing them with necessary (mostly forged) papers and sustaining them until they could find a way out of Spain.

# · 12 ·

# *Lisa Fittko: People Smuggler on Principle*

I first heard Lisa Fittko's name during a conversation with the publisher Mario Muchnik, who brought out the Spanish edition of Lisa Fittko's wartime memoir, *My Way over the Pyrenees* (*Mein Weg über die Pyrenäen*, Carl Hanser Verlag), which won a prestigious prize as the best political book published in Germany in 1985. (The English edition was published by Northwestern University Press in 1991.) "Lisa Fittko is a freedom fighter against Fascism who happens to be a Jew," said Muchnik. "Talk to Lisa. She has quite a story to tell."

Lisa worked with the American-based Emergency Rescue Committee for a few months in 1940–41, smuggling refugees from France into Spain. Operating out of Marseilles, in the Unoccupied Zone, and headed by Varian Fry, a young American with no prior experience in clandestine activities, the ERC was the only organization specifically dedicated to smuggling to safety well-known political refugees: writers, artists, clergy, and union and left-wing leaders. Many refugees were trapped there even before the Germans extended their occupation of France to the Spanish border. Although many of those saved by the ERC were neither famous nor prominent, and most were Jews, the organization's primary task was to save the cream of the European intelligentsia, Jewish or not, people who had become the special targets of Nazi persecution. Best known among the hundreds smuggled to safety were André Breton, Marc Chagall, Marcel Duchamp, Max Ernst, Lion Feuchtwanger, Franz Werfel, Heinrich Mann, brother of Thomas, and Thomas's son, Golo.

Even before she joined Varian Fry's group, Lisa brought about one of the most notorious rescues when she guided Walter Benjamin, the renowned Jewish-German writer and philosopher, over the Pyrenees.

Lisa is tiny and looks fragile. Wispy gray hair frames a long face with strong features and expressive, somewhat sad eyes behind wire-rimmed glasses. She was born in 1909 in a small town that she was reluctant to identify other than to say that it was once part of the Austro-Hungarian Empire and is now part of what used to be the Soviet Union. Her family lived in Vienna until she was twelve years old, when they moved to Berlin. They were deeply involved in the cultural and political life of that city as far back as she can remember. Her father, who viewed war as the worst possible evil, published a small literary magazine with a pacifist slant. Lisa started her anti-Fascist activities in Berlin as a young girl, years before Hitler came to power.

Lisa grew up in one of those Austro-German families that were completely assimilated. They always knew they were Jews, but being Jewish was just not an important factor in their lives. Their values came from humanism, pacifism, and socialism rather than religion. They considered themselves German or Austrian, nothing else.

"It was clear that the Nazi movement was anti-Semitic, although not all kinds of Fascists were against Jews, but we looked upon Fascism in its broader aspects: oppression, suppression of freedom, torture, and terror as means to control dissent. Long before Jews were targeted for systematic persecution, there was a lot of unrest in Germany. Fascists used the dissatisfaction of the masses after World War I ended and began stirring them up."

Lisa told of seeing street rowdiness and vandalism become more frequent and turn more violent. Like much of the rest of the world, she dismissed Hitler as merely a little man with a funny mustache who screamed a lot: "We were not prescient.

"In Berlin I had contact with a Socialist student group, my first experience with 'left-wing' protest. For a long time, relatively few people felt there was anything serious to worry about. Eventually, the Fascists grew more dangerous and I joined the struggle to prevent them from getting stronger."

When Hitler came to power in 1933, conditions changed dramatically. Not long after he was appointed chancellor, when Lisa was twenty-four, the Nuremberg Laws were passed, making it illegal for non-Aryans to attend school, maintain businesses, or practice professions. On April 1 the Nazis called a boycott of all Jewish businesses. That day Lisa's parents decided they could no longer tolerate conditions in Germany.

They said, "We will not stay one more day in a country that allows this to happen." They packed all they could, leaving behind almost all they owned, and fled to Czechoslovakia, never to return to Germany. Lisa emphasized that they did not leave because of foresight. Neither they nor their contemporaries could have known what was about to happen. It was beyond imagining. They did not leave because their lives were in danger; they left *out of principle*.

"My parents tried to persuade me to get out of Germany too,

because they knew I was involved in illegal activities and were afraid for me, but I insisted upon remaining in Berlin. Few believed that this madness would last. I had been involved from the beginning, so I could not just leave, not until I was forced to do so. I had to continue my work."

That work consisted of printing and distributing anti-Fascist literature, pamphlets and leaflets; organizing other dissidents; and hiding and protecting those in danger.

After her parents left, Lisa moved to a neighborhood where she was not known, and refused to register her change of address with the police, as ordered by law. That meant she now was illegal, but it also made her less visible and harder to find. On the street, she did not say hello to people she knew. Mostly, she kept a very low profile. But not always.

"The day Hitler became chancellor I found myself in front of the Reichskanzlei [state chancellery] as the torchlight march began. I can't tell you exactly why I was there. Curiosity. Maybe disbelief would be a better word. I had to see for myself. When Hitler came out on the balcony with President Hindenburg, I was surrounded by people screaming, cheering, giving the Nazi salute. I was amazed to see this huge crowd going along with all of this. I did not join in, not so much as a protest but because I could not believe what was happening. Someone near me noticed that I was not saluting. 'What's the matter,' he asked, 'don't you have an arm? Have you no voice?' "

For Lisa this proved to be a foretaste of what was to come. She was surrounded by a hostile, fanatical crowd, and it was hard to know what to do. Somehow, perhaps because they recognized she was a naive young girl, the crowd opened a path and Lisa was able to get away before things got ugly. Only in retrospect did she realize how potentially dangerous this episode had been.

"We anti-Fascists had not yet discovered how risky it was not to join in. I was lucky that night, but there was another time I could have gotten into real trouble. It was on April 1, 1933, the day the

Nazis organized their one-day boycott against Jews. I was walking past Alexanderplatz and saw a crowd. Storm troopers had surrounded a small shoe store owned by Jews. The crowd was screaming, 'Don't buy from the Jew!' I looked in and saw a terrified young boy behind the counter. I never considered what might happen if I tried to go into the store. I just knew I had to do *something*, so I did it."

As she made her way through the ring of troopers, one of them grabbed her arm. "Are you crazy?" he hissed. When she looked up, she recognized a boy who used to attend some of her anti-Fascist meetings. Defection was something they had to contend with from time to time, Lisa admitted. It was hard to turn down a uniform, a gun, a job, when there was little else.

Lisa broke loose and got into the store. She told the startled boy she did not really need any shoes and didn't have any money. "Pretend I'm here to buy," she said. "I just came to show you you're not alone." They went through with their little charade of trying on several pairs of shoes. Finally she thanked him and walked out through the jeering crowd. Nothing happened. "None of this had been planned. It was a spontaneous reaction: I could not stand what they were doing to this boy."

A few months later Lisa left Berlin. "We had been distributing a lot of anti-Nazi pamphlets and finally three of our people were caught. They had heard a rumor that I had left Germany, so, thinking I was safe, they did what we usually did, blame everything on someone no longer vulnerable to the Gestapo, in this instance, me. They said, 'We are innocent. We didn't know what we were getting into! This woman talked us into it!' "

Only after they were released did they discover that Lisa was still in Berlin. Now everyone was after her. To make matters more difficult, a census was suddenly ordered, with every house and apartment to be searched on a particular day. It was a maneuver clearly designed to flush out those in hiding, especially those in the underground movement. Everybody was ordered to spend that night at the address where they were registered. The small clandestine groups had a hard enough time staying in touch while trying to stay out of sight. Now, it threatened to become even harder.

"The effect on the underground was devastating. None of us could remain where we had been hiding. The people with whom I had been living were afraid and begged me not to return. I hid for a few days with my brother in the apartment my parents had abandoned, was nearly discovered there by the police, and finally decided the time had come for me to leave.

"First I went to a small town in Czechoslovakia, where my parents were living with relatives. But I soon left for Prague, where a lot of my friends in the movement had fled earlier. We had no place to stay and no money. After unsuccessfully seeking support from several refugee agencies, we were finally helped by Czech members of the International Union of Clerical Workers. They provided me, as a refugee, with basic essentials: food and a little money. Many ordinary Czech citizens proved to be quite helpful too. Some allowed me to trade clerical and household services in return for daily necessities. But others, including some of my own relatives, were terrified to have anything to do with me or any of the other refugees."

Lisa finally settled into a large apartment overcrowded with refugees.

"One day, while picking up my mail, I met Hans, the man who was to become my husband. Hans, too, was involved in all sorts of resistance activities, mostly smuggling information and materials in and out of Czechoslovakia."

Eventually Hans's operations aroused the suspicion of an informer on the German side of the border, who reported him to Czech authorities. It was no longer safe for him to stay. He fled to Switzerland and Lisa followed soon after.

They managed to get in, but the Swiss did not provide them with papers, so they were illegal like all other refugees and subject to arrest by local police if they took up residence. Nevertheless, Lisa and Hans remained hidden in Basel for over two years.

Their illegal residence status did not keep Hans from his smuggling activities until the Swiss received a request for the arrest of someone fitting his description. A sympathetic Swiss prosecutor, who happened to be a Social Democrat and a Jew, warned Lisa that Hans was about to be arrested. With the help of some Swiss friends, both narrowly escaped capture and fled to France and from there to Holland.

The Dutch had a reputation for handing illegal refugees back to the Germans, so the Fittkos' stay in Amsterdam was even more risky than in Switzerland. During their year there Lisa spoke to no one except a Socialist couple who befriended them and shared their flat and food with them. She spent much of her time alone, careful to fade into the background, while Hans pursued his resistance work at the Dutch-German border.

By the time Lisa and Hans finally found a way to get into France, her parents and brother had fled there too. The French made their stay as difficult as possible. Like most of the other refugees, they were not permitted to work, so they performed menial jobs that did not have to be reported, like housecleaning and baby-sitting.

As soon as war broke out in September 1939, the French decreed that all men of German origin up to age sixty-five, Jews as well as non-Jews, were to be interned as "enemy aliens."

"Now, 'German' was a loosely defined term. Although we were really Austrian, and the French never recognized Germany's annexation of Austria, for internal security purposes they chose to consider us German. My father was not interned because he was over the age limit, but Hans and my brother were sent to camps. A few months later, when the Germans started their offensive against France, the internment order was broadened to include women. I was put on a locked train and taken to Gurs, a concentration camp in southern France, which was originally used to hold refugees from the Spanish Civil War. Suddenly thousands of women were being sent there. They say that when the commandant of the camp was told to get ready for that huge mass of females, he passed out."

Luckily, Lisa was at Gurs only a few weeks. Conditions were

deplorable. The camp was filthy and the food was terrible. No one knew what to expect. Although Gurs was in no immediate danger from the Germans, there was no way to know how long it would take them to get there. No one knew what to do. The commandant said, "I know I am supposed to follow orders, but who knows *whose* orders?" Afraid to be caught by the advancing German troops, the French officers in charge abandoned their posts and left the camp open and unattended, telling the prisoners, "You are on your own."

Although she had no idea of what she would encounter, with the Germans closing in, Lisa decided to get out. "A friend and I passed the guard at the gate and said, 'Excuse us. We'll be right back,' and he just let us go."

To add to the confusion, the camps had all kinds of Germans in them, including Nazis, who were of course waiting to be repatriated. The Jews and other political prisoners now had to run for their lives, to get away before the Nazis "liberated" them, too. Even before the French army surrendered to the Germans on June 22, 1940, many of those who escaped made their way south, as far away from military action as possible. Since Lisa was in the south already, she made her way first to Toulouse, where she was informed her husband was waiting for her, and then, with him, to Marseilles, the main unoccupied port left in France. Most of the anti-Nazi refugees hoping to get into Spain seemed to be clustered there, sharing information and helping one another. Lisa's brother eventually found her there too. That left only her parents in the Occupied Zone of northern France.

People were willing to go anywhere, even China, but entry visas were hard to get. Hans and Lisa were able to obtain Spanish and Portuguese transit visas. Getting French *exit* visas was another matter. The names of those applying for exit visas were routinely passed on to Gestapo authorities by the collaborating Vichy French. That was something the Fittkos could not risk. It would have been like wearing a sign saying, "Here we are. Come and get us!"

The German authorities demanded that all men under forty-two leaving France by climbing over the Pyrenees be arrested by Spanish authorities, to keep them from joining the Free French forces in England. That did not deter Lisa and Hans. It merely meant they would have to leave France illegally. There were others in the same position who arrived at the same conclusion: get into Spain as quickly as possible. Lisa decided to go to Port-Vendres, a town closer to the border and at the foot of the Pyrenees, to find a way over the mountains.

After making some inquiries, she was directed to Banyuls-sur-Mer, a small village nearby. Monsieur Azéma, the mayor of Banyuls, was an old Socialist who had helped the Republicans during the Spanish Civil War by smuggling in badly needed medical personnel and materials. Lisa was told to contact him and ask for help.

Monsieur Azéma was most cooperative. With the help of hand-drawn maps, he showed Lisa the best way into Spain without running into the Gardes Mobiles patrolling the border.

After meeting with Monsieur Azéma, she stopped off briefly in Port-Vendres before going back to Marseilles to pick up Hans. During the night Lisa was awakened by a knock on the door. When she opened it, she found herself looking into the eyes of the renowned German writer Walter Benjamin. He explained that Hans had told him she was at the border and would find a way to get him out of France. Benjamin added that he had brought along two more refugees, a mother and a fifteen-year-old boy. He begged Lisa to help them.

Benjamin was no stranger to Lisa. He and Hans had spent time in the same concentration camp while she herself was in Gurs. He revealed then he had a heart condition aggravated by years of heavy smoking. Lisa also remembered hearing about an earlier, comic-opera escape attempt when this bespectacled academician had tried to pass himself off as a seaman on an old boat: he was caught, turned back, and somehow he lived to tell about it.

Lisa was not at all sure she could find the way. She told Benjamin she had only a scribbled chart showing the way over the mountains, but if he was willing to take the risk, she would try to find the way with him and his friends. Benjamin agreed.

Lisa arranged to take Benjamin and his two companions to Banyuls-sur-Mer in the morning. Leaving the mother and son behind at an inn in town, she first took Benjamin to see Monsieur Azéma so both of them could go over his instructions, hoping she might feel more confident if two of them were familiar with all the details they had to remember. After again pointing out all the signposts they had to look for, Azéma advised them to first take a practice run to the foothills, return (assuring them it would make "a nice walk"), have a good night's sleep, and take off for the border early the next morning.

Lisa and Benjamin returned to the inn, picked up the mother and son, briefed them, and immediately took off for the hills. To Lisa's surprise, Benjamin had brought along a rather bulky briefcase. When she asked why he needed it, since they weren't really going anywhere until next morning, he said, "This is my latest manuscript. It is more important than my person." He added that he feared it might fall into Gestapo hands, which explained his reluctance to leave it behind, unattended.

They reached their designated turn-around point three hours after they took off and stopped to rest. When it was time to start back, Benjamin, who had been lying down with his eyes closed, did not move. "I will spend the night here," he announced, explaining that this way he would not have so far to go the next day, when they came to join him again.

Lisa was appalled at the thought of leaving him there, alone. She tried to talk him into returning to the inn, warning him about the smugglers and bulls known to frequent the area. Benjamin did not budge. She suspected he must have planned his strategy before they left the inn. She also understood, now, the real reason he had brought along his manuscript. He believed that if he had to start all over next morning, he would never reach Spain. Lisa knew that any additional words would fall on deaf ears. She had no choice but to leave him behind, wondering if she would find him alive the next morning.

When Lisa and the others left the inn the next day, it was still dark. When they reached the clearing where they had left Benjamin, there he was, sitting up, smiling at them!

They began their climb. The road became increasingly steep, narrow, and rocky, and the directions more difficult to follow. Together they puzzled over Azéma's scribbles, and Benjamin was able to help Lisa figure out the way.

The trek over the mountains took much longer than they expected. Benjamin had a theory of resting at intervals, and they followed his theory. Only once did Lisa and the boy have to help him up a steep incline. Then suddenly, they took a turn and there, below them, was the Mediterranean they had left behind when they started out. They had arrived in Spain.

Lisa pointed out that the road into the village below, Port-Bou, was straight downhill. She reassured them they could manage the rest without her, and instructed them to show their papers to the border guards and get them stamped as soon as they got into town. "That should get you safely across Spain to Lisbon. I must go back now. Good luck and good-bye!" For a short time she watched them as they wound their way down. She felt elated. They were safe. Her trip over the Pyrenees was a success. She had also paved the way for her own and Hans's escape. What had taken her ten hours on the way up, now took only two hours going back.

"When I arrived in Banyuls, I found a telegram from Hans. 'Your Portuguese transit visa has expired,' it said. 'Return immediately to renew it.' A week later, while still in Marseilles, I heard that Walter Benjamin was dead."

No one is sure of all the facts, but it appears that when he and the others arrived in Port-Bou, they were informed by the Spanish border guards that anyone without a French exit visa would be sent back to France. It was one of those on-again, off-again regulations

that were mostly ignored by the Spanish but which, on this particular day, was being enforced.

When the Spanish guards ordered Benjamin to return to France,
he must have felt certain that his precious manuscript would fall
into Gestapo hands after all. Lisa found out eventually that, when
the authorities left him in a hotel room with instructions to be
ready to go back to France the next morning, he took a fatal dose
of the morphine he had brought along, just in case. He had prepared for the worst, and, for him, the worst *had* happened.

The Spanish officials were so jolted by Benjamin's death, they
refused to send the others back, orders or no orders. As for Benjamin's briefcase and its contents, they disappeared. The village
registry listed "a case filled with unidentified papers" when his
death was recorded. Forty years later, when Benjamin's literary ex-
ecutor made inquiries about the briefcase, the authorities showed
him the empty storage space and indicated the contents could not
be found. Lisa added, "Twenty years after we had left Europe, I
went back to Port-Bou and Banyuls, to see if some of my old contacts there might know what happened to it, but was unable to turn
up anything new."

Officially, the mystery of Benjamin's missing manuscript has
never been solved.

News of Benjamin's death traveled fast. When Varian Fry, who
had just organized his Emergency Rescue Committee, heard about
it, and about Lisa's finding a way over the Pyrenees, he asked to
meet with her and Hans, and told them about his Committee's
work. "We need someone to take some of these refugees into Spain,"
he said. "More and more of them are getting arrested here. Will
you do it?"

Lisa was not prepared for such a request. She was still devas-
tated by Benjamin's death and just wanted to get away. She and
Hans were ready at last to leave France, with renewed transit visas
through Spain and Portugal. They still lacked French exit visas, and
had no idea where they would end up. But, now that she knew *how*

to get out of France, she and Hans were determined to leave.

"Weren't you afraid of going to Spain and getting stuck there with no place to go next?" I wondered.

"You don't think that far ahead when you are in a trap. All you are concerned with is getting out of the trap. The trap was France. The way out was Spain.

"At first we had a lot of discussions and arguments about Fry's proposition. We asked Fry, 'What about *us*? We are ready to leave *now*. When and how will *we* be able to get out if we delay our own escape?' And he said, 'Whatever happens, I give you my word, the Committee will get you out of France.' I just laughed and said, 'You don't understand, you can't make such a promise. No one has control over the situation down here!'

"Despite it all, my husband and I decided to go back down to the border and take two weeks to find and train someone else to guide refugees into Spain. Those two weeks turned into seven months. We had never planned to stay that long, but that is what happened.

"More and more refugees came. We did not always take them over the mountains, because not all of them were in condition to take the climb. Things became more and more complicated. We had to find creative, alternative methods of escape. There was a railroad worker who agreed to occasionally take some refugees across, hidden in his locomotive. Other times we had to use someone's boat.

"Sometimes people ask me why we stayed with it so long and how I could stand to take those risks. The fact is, it never occurred to me to say no. Like that first time, when Benjamin asked me to help him, all that mattered was that here was this man in need, and I felt I could help."

There were a lot of other rescue groups working out of Vichy France at that time, such as the Quakers, the Joint, the HIAS, to name a few. The British War Office sought to rescue British fliers who had been shot down in France, to get them through Spain to their people in Gibraltar, but Lisa and Hans also smuggled some of them over the mountains, even though they had nothing to do with the British War Office.

"We tried to save anyone in danger, especially those on the Nazi priority list, and we all cooperated with each other. The Committee just kept sending us people that needed to get out."

Because the Fry Committee frequently helped people who were well known and therefore easily recognized, it had to depend, to some degree, on illegal connections and engage in unsanctioned operations. Most of the other refugee organizations appeared to operate legally, had big offices, provided papers, food, and housing, and arranged legal passage into Spain and beyond. The local authorities allowed them to do so; otherwise masses of people trying to get away would have accumulated at the border and created an unmanageable problem. Lisa guessed that Fry's Committee may have been the only clandestine rescue operation, with organized illegal smuggling across the border.

"Even though the Germans had not yet officially occupied Vichy France, French authorities were definitely under pressure to cooperate with them, and they did. Many exceptions existed, such as Mayor Azéma of Banyuls, but many others toed the line. One never knew whom one could trust.

"You have to understand what kind of situation was facing the refugee organizations in Marseilles. Everyone was trying to escape, to find a spot on some ship, some train, to get out of France by *any* means available. Those people were desperate. They would get up in the morning, go from office to office, stand in line, day after day, hoping for a way to get out. All the while the rest of the world was locking them out."

Lisa brought up another aspect of the rescue operation: the commercial smuggling business. A number of refugees, in their shortsightedness, saw it as an opportunity to amass money by selling the services of alleged guides to other refugees for outrageous sums. Some of those "guides" took the refugees to some isolated place and robbed them.

"It was a booming racket, and many such cases are known to me and others working for the AERC. How could they charge large amounts to help others on the run, others like themselves? How could they make a profit business of it? I am not saying they were all like that. Some of them only did the arranging, and French and Spanish smugglers did the actual guiding. But they, those organizer-refugees, took advantage of people in trouble. Several of those in business were caught, turned over to the Germans, and sent to extermination camps. The combination of greed and stupidity can create monsters. It killed a lot of people.

"Hans and I were not paid for what we did. The Committee sent us enough for subsistence and some extra money for those who came to us without any funds at all. You couldn't let them leave France without money for food and shelter in Spain, so we provided what was necessary. We lived rather primitively, wherever we could. It was risky, but there were always people sympathetic to our cause, willing to help."

I wondered why anyone would ever have considered sending political refugees, for even a few hours, into a country where anyone anti-Fascist or left of center was considered "the enemy." Lisa shrugged.

"We have spent the past forty or fifty years asking ourselves the same question: how could we have guessed that labor officials, for example, would make it safely across Spain? I don't know. We just didn't have any other choices. The truth is that the majority of those who crossed the border made it through Spain without any problems, although it did become more and more risky for well-known left-wing refugees, traveling under their own name, to attempt it. Some were caught and arrested, and interned by the Spaniards in various detention camps and prisons, but they were not sent back. The Gestapo, who were stationed on both sides of the border, issued many orders, but, unlike the French, the Spaniards mostly chose to ignore them."

Because the French Gardes Mobiles, under orders from the Gestapo, were watching the direct route to Spain, a more round-about route had to be found. The people of Port-Bou still feel the effects of what happened in their village during those days.

"Since Franco's death, the Francistas, followers of Franco, those who went along with the Germans, are in hiding. They are perse-cuted by the Loyalists. When I went back to Port-Bou a few years ago, to investigate the disappearance of Benjamin's manuscript, I found one woman I remembered. I phoned and asked to see her. 'I will not see you,' she warned me. 'Don't come. I will not speak with you!' I asked her why. 'Because they are still looking for me and everybody else involved.' Until Franco died, in 1975, these Francis-tas had lived in the village, openly, but since then, many have gone into hiding.

"What is true is that although the Gestapo was right there, with their finger on everything, the Spanish authorities, on their own, did nothing to catch any refugees. While some of them did cooperate with the Germans, it was rare and pretty haphazard.

"As for Franco's motives, I don't know. We have all thought about it a lot. Still, none of us is an authority. But there is an inci-dent which might throw some light on it. As I mentioned before, sometimes we were asked to help smuggle out British fliers downed in France. After they somehow managed to make their way across occupied French territory, we would take them across the moun-tains into Spain. We had to be especially careful not to be detected by the French border guards. But once they got to Port-Bou, they went straight to customs. They would sit there, the British fliers, claiming 'prisoner of war' status, demanding to see a representa-tive of their government. Within a day or two, someone from the British Embassy would show up, right under the noses of the Gestapo, and say to the Spanish, 'Those are *our* men,' and off they'd go to Madrid, and from there to Gibraltar, back to their units. I tell you this to show you there were two sides to Franco, and one side was *not* obeying the Germans. Whatever the real reason, to us it meant that Franco, unsure of how the war would end, did not want to create ill feelings between the Allies and Spain.

"Hans and I both did guiding, sometimes alone, sometimes together, and it was always a tricky business. Under the Pétain regime, helping anyone of military age to escape from France was a capital offense. So, had they caught us smuggling anyone in that age group into Spain, which we routinely did, it would have been very bad for us. We were in danger because *everything* we did was illegal, from the French point of view. But you have to consider this danger in the context of the times. Just walking around in Marseilles was dangerous for us, because *we* were illegal. What I am trying to say is it did not matter *what* we did: we were constantly in danger, so much so that it became a normal state for us. Sometimes our brains just blocked it out.

"Our lives depended on good luck, the ability to become invisible, and the help of others. Taking refugees over the Pyrenees became almost like an ordinary job. Except that each time a new group came, two, three, sometimes a family with children; we lived with them, so they became special for us. We could never think of them impersonally, as so much merchandise.

"One also learns to live with tension. What helped reduce that tension for us somewhat was the fact that we had developed a very good relationship with the villagers. We found out later that the whole population of Banyuls was aware of everything that was going on, all our smuggling activities, and no one ever let on."

Before taking refugees over the mountains, Lisa and Hans spent many hours talking with them, preparing them for the crossing. They had to teach them discipline, show them how to act under stress. They also made sure they wore simple peasant clothes and brought along nothing except the kind of bags the vineyard workers carried, so as not to attract attention.

"We had to be careful whom we took on. They had to be in

good physical condition, because the trip over the mountains was hard. A big plus was a positive attitude with confidence that we could make it. It also helped if they were young. A scared, middle-aged person usually took twice as long, and made everything twice as dangerous. Humor helped too.

"Sometimes people had strange panic reactions. One woman loudly demanded an apple, in the middle of nowhere, climbing up toward the pass. Another woman threw herself on the floor and began to scream: 'I am going to die here!' Hans got worried someone would overhear her and everybody would get caught. He grabbed her and shook her hard, and said, 'There is no dying to be done here! Get going!' She meekly obeyed orders and snapped out of it."

Many of the refugees were quite attached to the last remnants of their former lives, after leaving everything else behind, and insisted on bringing along things that were precious to them. Lisa and Hans told them that the mayor of a neighboring village had a small forwarding business, and those who wished to could send their belongings directly to Port-Bou that way.

Most listened to reason. One man Lisa will never forget, a high official in the Weimar Republic, did not. He risked the survival of his whole family and the group to carry with him his fur coat! Since it was summer, the coat made him an obvious target. He was caught, and it took quite a lot of negotiating to get him released.

"At this time, my own parents were still in the Occupied Zone. Once in a while someone among the refugees waiting for their papers in Marseilles would go up to Paris, which of course was very dangerous. But they went anyway, for a variety of reasons, mostly because, like me, they had family there. One of them made contact with my parents, who were staying in a small suburb near Paris. They were well hidden and were afraid to make a move. But a year after Hans and I started working for the Fry Committee, something happened that persuaded us to try to get them out as quickly as possible.

"In October 1941, Fry kept the promise he had made to us when we began to work with him: his Committee bought visas and passage to Cuba for Hans and me. That meant we might have had to leave Europe without seeing my parents, so we began to look for a way."

In 1941 Cuba was just about the only country issuing visas to refugees. The visas were incredibly expensive. The charges were five hundred dollars per visa (four thousand or more in 1991 dollars), five hundred for each boat ticket, and two thousand dollars per person as security deposit to the Cuban government. Clearly, Cuba wanted to make as much money as it could, but at least it was willing to take in some refugees. The United States government did that only rarely, although private Americans, individuals and organizations, contributed large sums to help refugees. (All the money for the activities of the Fry Committee and the Joint came from individual donors in the United States.) In any case, Varian Fry was willing to spend that kind of money to get Hans and Lisa out, and Lisa was determined to see her parents before leaving.

When their departure date drew near, Hans and Lisa contacted a woman in Marseilles who specialized in smuggling people over the demarcation line into the Unoccupied Zone. At first she refused to do it, because by then it had become extremely dangerous. Lisa explained that she and Hans were due to leave for Cuba in a few days and might never see her family again, nor be able to help them afterwards. This persuaded the woman. "I will do it *just this once*, and *only* for your parents," she said. *"No one else."*

When the woman got to Paris, she contacted some of her friends, who in turn told others what she was there for. Suddenly she was besieged by dozens of refugees, pleading with her to help them, too. She was overwhelmed by their desperation and could not say no. She ended up taking on twenty-two Jews!

In the meantime, Hans and Lisa were anxiously waiting for her parents in Marseilles. They had read in the local paper that people caught trying to get over the demarcation line were being shot on the spot.

A few days later the woman returned, alone. She told Lisa and Hans that when she started to take the group over the mountains she kept urging them to spread out so as not to attract attention. Instead, with typical herd instinct, they insisted on clinging to each other. Despite this, she was able to get them across the line, where they were promptly arrested by the police, who sent them back north. Once there, a Nazi officer refused to accept her "load of old Jews," since "Germany was trying to *get rid* of Jews, *not* receive more," and sent them back south! Eventually they all ended up in jail in Mâcon, in the Unoccupied Zone.

With only two weeks left before they were scheduled to leave Europe, the Fittkos mounted a frantic push to get Lisa's parents and the others released. After several more twists and turns of fate, their efforts were rewarded. Just five days before their departure date they were finally reunited in the small town of Cassis. That is where her parents and about two hundred other refugees remained hidden and safe for the duration of the war.

After having trekked over the Pyrenees so often that they could have done it blindfolded, Lisa and Hans were finally ready to do it one last time, alone. But, as so often happened, regulations changed just as they were about to leave. Instead of requiring everyone who wanted exit visas to apply to the Vichy authorities, who would most certainly have turned the applicants over to the Gestapo, new rules made it possible to obtain legal passage out through local officials, who had much less rigid requirements. So, ironically, after helping hundreds of refugees cross into Spain *illegally*, they found they could get there *legally*.

Another fortuitous change in regulations made it possible for each person with legal exit papers to exchange five hundred dollars' worth of francs into American currency. The reason for this was the Germans were still trying to rid themselves of as many Jews as possible, and, since refugees needed negotiable money wherever they went, this arrangement made it possible for more of them to leave.

Because the franc had no negotiable value anywhere except in France, dollars were in great demand on the black market. When they were ready to leave, Lisa and Hans asked the Fry Committee to loan them one thousand dollars' worth of francs for just a few hours, just long enough to perform a bit of black-market magic. They changed these francs into dollars and then back into francs, making a huge profit in the process. They paid back the Fry Committee, provided Lisa's parents with desperately needed funds, and gave some of the left-over francs to close friends. This maneuver, however, created a problem for them later that nearly sabotaged their escape.

At the border, the French guards asked to see Hans's and Lisa's papers authorizing them to take one thousand dollars with them, and to show them the American currency. When the Fittkos opened their luggage and spread their belongings out on the table, the French guard noted that Lisa and Hans had considerably less than the allowable thousand dollars left. Noticing the Fittkos had German passports, he sneered at Hans and shouted that Hans must have given the missing dollars to his "friend, Herr Hitler!"

For Hans, who had been condemned to death in Germany for his anti-Fascist activities and who had spent so much of his life in danger, being accused in this way was intolerable. To Lisa's amazement, her supremely self-contained and self-controlled husband suddenly exploded. He screamed at the French guards, "You want to know *who* gives presents to Hitler? It is *you*, the French, who feed us refugees to Herr Hitler. I am a German, and I fought that murderer while you and your Maréchal [Pétain] were giving him presents!" It was as though a dam had broken, and years of outrage and frustration came rushing out. Here they were, so close to safety yet still not out of danger, and Hans was creating a huge scene, going crazy in front of everybody!

What was particularly frightening was that the customs people still had the Fittkos' luggage. Hidden in their toiletries, in toothpaste tubes, were tiny pieces of rolled-up paper with the names of the top Spanish Republican leaders hiding in France who needed help getting out before the Germans got them. It was the task of Hans and Lisa to get these names into the hands of the Spanish Loyalists in Lisbon who were supposed to figure out how to smuggle their people out of France, through Spain and into Portugal.

By an ironic twist of fate, Hans's outburst actually worked in the Fittkos' favor. He created such a commotion that the authorities of both countries could not wait to be rid of them. With the combined efforts of the French and Spanish border guards and help from other station personnel, Hans and Lisa were literally pushed onto the Spanish train as it was about to pull out.

They stayed in Spain, near Madrid, for one week, and a month more in Portugal before finally leaving for Cuba, where they arrived just ten days before Pearl Harbor. Seven years later they emigrated to the United States.

I wanted to understand what had compelled Lisa into action, even as a very young girl, when so many others chose to remain on the sidelines. Being a Jew had been a fact of life for her, but clearly not the determining factor for her activism.

"Fascism created the climate in which a Holocaust could ignite. What happened in Germany did not happen because Germans were in charge or because Germans are bad people. A tyrant can spring up in *any* country, if the right conditions are allowed to exist. If that happens, action must be taken.

"It is easy for Jews to hate the Germans. They were, after all, the ones who created *that* particular Holocaust, and allowed it to happen on *their own* soil. I understand that hate only too well, and it is easy to justify it. But something happens when we focus only on hate, point a finger at someone else, and fail to examine the broader implications involved.

"Yes, I admit that the Germans have certain traits which make them more susceptible to abusing power, what we call 'the Prussian mentality,' an obsession with discipline, organization, and following orders blindly, a military tradition. But the Germans are not alone. Others also possess these traits. You can go to Poland, to Japan, to Russia, and find those same 'Prussian' characteristics there. What I am saying is that the Holocaust was born in *belief systems and ideologies* which are not limited to any one nationality, race, or religion.

"Prejudice always has and will continue to be directed against some designated group, an ethnic or religious minority, ill defended and easily scapegoated. It is sad that so many people who have themselves been victims of hate and persecution fall into the trap of fixing blame on just *one* group. They point to their victimizers and say, 'If it weren't for *them* the disaster would not have happened.' That's not true. None of us is immune to the poison, just as any one of us can become the next victim. We must all remember that if we allow *even one* among us to lose his or her freedom, *each of us* is in danger."

# ·13·

# Renée Reichmann: Our Woman in Tangier

Ask anyone with any knowledge of Holocaust history to name a hero credited with saving the lives of thousands of Hungarian Jews, and Raoul Wallenberg instantly comes to mind. Another name, far less well known but equally deserving of hero status, is that of Renée Reichmann.

Hungarian by birth, Renée, with her husband, Samuel, and their large family moved to Austria in 1928. After the Anschluss, ten years later, they fled from Vienna to Paris, where they were caught when World War II began in 1939. With France on the verge of collapse, they escaped through Spain to Spanish-occupied Tangier, in North Africa. It is from this unlikely haven that Renée Reichmann ran an innovative and enormously successful Jewish rescue operation with the cooperation of the Spanish authorities.

Operating in some ways like Wallenberg and Angel Sanz Briz, who provided Jews with false Swedish passports and hid them in safe houses, the Reichmanns expanded their efforts to support and gain releases for those already trapped inside the Nazi death machine. Responsible for the rescue of approximately three thousand Hungarian Jews and the sustenance of thousands of others confined in concentration camps, the Reichmann story has all the elements of a legend. Only it is fact.

Today, fifty years later, the Reichmann name is better known for another reason. It has become synonymous with world-class financial power. After moving to Canada in the late 1950s, the Reichmanns transformed a small construction tile manufacturing company into one of the world's largest family-owned real-estate development enterprises. The assets of the Toronto-based Olympia and York Ltd. were, until recently, estimated in excess of six billion dollars.

The Reichmanns are Orthodox Jews. In a time when home life and traditional values are often sacrificed on the altar of success, their involvement in the high-pressure world of international business and finance has not affected the Reichmanns' own strict religious values and sense of family solidarity. They have a reputation for honesty, decency, and integrity. Despite prominence and enormous wealth, they maintain a comparatively modest life-style. Eschewing ostentation and other excesses often associated with their position, most members of this large family are clustered in a middle-class Jewish neighborhood of Toronto.

The family is renowned for its generous support of Orthodox religious institutions, schools, synagogues, and scholarships in the Americas, Europe, and Israel. While these represent a major part of the family's philanthropic passions, the Reichmanns also underwrite many non-religious causes. The field of medicine is one of their most consistent secular beneficiaries; they have helped build hospitals and regularly fund research projects.

The Reichmanns rarely generate personal news and socialize almost exclusively among their own. Gossip columnists have long despaired of uncovering juicy tidbits about them. But when a *Toronto Life* magazine reporter recently dared raise questions about the elder Reichmanns' integrity during World War II with unsubstantiated innuendos, the family instituted a hundred-million-dollar libel suit against all those responsible. "We are doing this only to set the record straight," Paul Reichmann was later quoted as saying.

When I requested an interview with Renée Reichmann, I was asked to send three letters of recommendation, one each from a rabbi, an attorney, and an academician, vouching for my credentials as a professional and reliability as a person. I never received a response after complying, but, since I had several other interviews scheduled in Toronto, I took a chance and called the Olympia and York offices as soon as I arrived in town. I was informed that the matriarch of the family had recently had a stroke, and I was offered an appointment with one of her sons instead.

Albert Reichmann met me in his elegant office early on a Sunday morning. He is a heavyset, mild-looking man, about six feet tall, and much younger looking than his sixty-odd years. I expected him to wear a beard, but the only indication of his Orthodoxy was a yarmulke.

When I expressed my regret at not meeting his mother and hearing her story, he assured me he was old enough to have retained vivid memories about his childhood and his family's activities in Tangier and was quite capable of answering any questions I might have.

"When war broke out in September 1939, my parents were living in Paris with my sister and younger brother. The rest of us, my three brothers and I, were staying with our grandparents in Hungary. Although we tried to join our parents in Paris, the Germans would not let us pass through Austria, so we had to return to Hungary.

"By 1940 things looked very bad for the French, so Mother decided to come and get us. It was a dangerous trip and she did it in a very complicated way, taking us through Yugoslavia, to Italy, through Switzerland, and finally to France. Somehow we made it and all of us stayed in Paris for eight or nine weeks while my parents tried to figure out what to do. Then the news came that the Germans were due in Paris any day."

The family fled to Orléans, about one hundred kilometers from Paris. They brought along a young Hungarian girl who happened to be stranded in Paris and whom Renée Reichmann refused to leave behind, alone. When they got to Orléans they realized the Germans would probably arrive there even before Paris, so they continued on to Bordeaux, keeping just ahead of the advancing enemy troops.

"Trains going south were overloaded and all roads were clogged with refugees, not only Jews but many others running from the Germans, so we rented a truck in Paris and drove to Orléans. I remember the road being strafed by German planes. When we got to Orléans we learned we would not be safe from the Germans there, either. So, we decided to take the train for Bordeaux and from there to Biarritz."

With the Germans right behind them, they quicky realized it was too dangerous to stay *anywhere* in France and concluded the one thing left to do was to find a way out of France and into Spain.

"When Father saw the Germans were coming, he went to Bayonne, closer to the Spanish border. He spoke to the authorities there and asked if he could cross into Spain. After obtaining permission for himself, Father asked, 'What about my family?' and told them he had a wife and six children waiting for him in Biarritz. He never mentioned the extra child. The guard said, 'As long as you get back here before two o'clock, all of you will be allowed through. But remember, if the Germans get here first, you will find the border closed.'

"Father returned from Bayonne as the rest of us were eating lunch. 'There is no time to finish,' he said, 'we must leave immediately.' We managed to get to the border before the Germans and, as promised, all of us were allowed to pass through. The guards noticed the extra child but said nothing. That was late June 1940."

Back then the Reichmanns were just an ordinary young middle-class Jewish family on the run. The Spanish authorities treated them extremely well. They saw how many there were in the family and knew that it was not safe for them to travel through Spain without papers. Since Madrid was the only place they could get passports, they put the Reichmanns on a train after helping them obtain a family compartment so all of them could stay together. All they asked was that the family register with the police immediately upon arrival in Madrid. This they did. Afterwards they applied for passports at the Hungarian Embassy.

"I don't know if my parents had any concerns about Franco. What I *do* know is that they felt that *anything* was better than falling into German hands. They were following right behind us all the way south, so we did not have too much choice. Despite the Inquisition, Spaniards were still considered better than the Germans. Besides, nobody considered Spain or, for that matter Franco, anti-Semitic. A Fascist, yes. A dictator, yes. An anti-Semite, no."

They stayed in Madrid about two weeks. While waiting for their papers, the elder Reichmann tried to find a Jewish community and kosher facilities, but found none. He knew that many Sephardic Jews were living in Tangier, so he decided to go there, instead. After obtaining all the necessary documents, the Reichmann family arrived in Tangier in late summer of 1940.

Before World War II broke out, Tangier was an international city, governed by seven nations but under no one's exclusive control. It was then occupied by Spain, but since it was still considered an international space, provisions were shipped in from all over the world and there never were any serious shortages of food or any other necessities, even during the war. Bread, sugar, and oil were rationed but there was no real hardship. "I remember that we, as children, had a good life in Tangier. We had food, we had all we needed. Mother began her refugee work almost immediately."

In Vienna, long before they had acquired the wealth they now possess, the Reichmann family had been active in the Jewish community, and their home was always open to rabbis who came to Vienna for medical treatment. Thus it was not unexpected that in Tangier their home should quickly become known as a haven for other refugees.

"One day friends of ours in New York [the Kleins, who founded the Barton's candy chain] asked us to send some packages for them to their family in Poland. That was the beginning. Soon we were sending packages of food to refugees in other places, including to some who had fled from France to Spain."

Some of those packages went to people already in concentration camps, but at first most of them went to the Warsaw ghetto. Soon other people heard about what the Reichmanns were doing and began to ask them to send food packages to their families in occupied territories. When the Warsaw ghetto fell, all was quiet for a while. Then everything started up again when the Germans began deporting people from Czechoslovakia.

"The Gestapo used local Czech women to compile the list of deportees. They called these women 'secretaries of death.' My mother had a brother in Bratislava and one of these women passed on to him the names of some of those who had been sent to concentration camps. Eventually she gave him several thousand more names and we started to send food packages to them."

At first local people recruited by Renée worked together to collect food and clothes. Later, Renée began soliciting money to help support her efforts from the refugees of both the Ashkenazic and Sephardic communities, especially those who had come to Tangier and had become prosperous. She was never a woman to take no for an answer, and donations began to pour in.

"It grew in stages, with only my mother, my brothers, sister, and our friends helping. Then we started to write to friends in America to ask if they could help finance the operation. Money began coming from all kinds of sources, especially the Vaad Hatzalah [an Orthodox rescue agency]."

In the beginning, the Spanish authorities were not involved. The Reichmanns first approached the International Red Cross based in Switzerland, asking for help in getting packages to the camps. To their surprise, those in charge of that organization refused to recognize Jewish refugees in concentration camps as "prisoners of war," which tied up all the Reichmanns' efforts in red tape. They also refused to deliver their shipments, and many hundreds of packages got lost.

In turning down the Reichmanns' request, the International Red Cross let it be known they did not approve of the quality of the food being sent. "For example, they complained that the chocolate in the packages was not up to their standards, and that some of the Spanish tins, like sardines and olives, had small stains outside. They did not consider where the food was going, that it was better than nothing, they just destroyed it! I don't know why they did this. No, I don't think it was done with malice, just indifference."

Later there was an investigation, because a lot of criticism arose about the International Red Cross not doing anything to help Jews during the war. This was eventually confirmed by their own investigation. The facts showed that Jews were not a priority for them. "They said they were afraid that if they helped or interceded for the Jews, they might later be prevented from providing other benefits for them. Imagine, they made up this silly excuse! They, themselves, had to admit they just did not help the Jews. Period."

When the International Red Cross refused to cooperate, Renée approached the Spanish Red Cross, which was under government control. Its head, the Conde de la Granja, agreed to help immediately, not by providing merchandise or food but by paying for shipping costs, which saved the Reichmanns huge sums of money. Most importantly, the Spaniards immediately recognized Jewish concentration camp internees as "prisoners of war." (The International Red Cross did not agree to this designation until 1944, more than two years later.)

"The Spanish Red Cross asked how many packages were going to be shipped, gave us fistfuls of their own address labels, without bothering to count them most of the time, and allowed us to use their official stamp to speed up the transactions. Thousands of packages were sent out in this manner. Here, I will show you proof that the packages arrived."

With that, Reichmann opened a desk drawer, pulled out a huge file, and scanned through the mass of documents. He pulled out a Xerox copy showing a rumpled piece of packing paper, creases showing the size of the box it had once covered (about eight by five by three inches), addressed to one of the camp inmates. That name had faded to a blur, but Renée Reichmann's was there, clear, in large dark print as the sender, under the Spanish Red Cross's official imprint, ENVIO PARA PRISIONERO DE GUERRA (shipment for prisoner of war), along with its stamp.

"This was one of many such wrappers returned to us after the war, by those who survived, to thank us for helping them. Sometimes, by the time the packages got to the camps, the people they were meant for were not alive anymore. So other internees took them, and sometimes the Germans kept them. But we have proof that many, many of them reached those for whom they were intended. By 1943, four thousand packages were being sent out every two weeks. Soon after, that number was doubled."

When I expressed surprise that any such packages had ever been received by camp inmates, Reichmann admitted that Elie Wiesel had also challenged him on this issue. "After the war, I showed him proof that it really happened."

He reached down into the file and pulled out several cards. They came from Auschwitz and Birkenau, stamped with swastikas and addressed to "Renée Reichmann, Tangier," written in German, Hungarian, Czech. Reichmann explained that the Germans encouraged the camp inmates to write to their relatives to fool them into thinking they were being well treated. But the Jews knew it was a trick, so they wrote to the Reichmanns instead, because Tangier was far away and a safe place to write to. Had they written to their relatives they would have endangered their lives by letting the Nazis know where to find them.

Those inside the camp and those on the outside developed a secret code, a way to communicate with one another. "People would write us from camp and say, 'Good wishes for Easter.' That meant they needed matzos for Passover, and we would send them matzos. We always sent things to specific people, we had so many names, but they usually shared with others."

First the Reichmanns sent only food. After a while, Renée decided clothing should also be included in the packages. She sent the older children out to solicit for clothing donations from the Sephardic communities of several cities. At first only few among them wanted to be involved, and did not understand the extent of the catastrophe decimating European Jews. Renée found ways to convince them the need was desperate, and got her donations.

Reaching again into his file, Reichmann now produced an official letter in which the Spanish government "authorizes Mme Renée Reichmann to send seven thousand packages to Birkenau, containing one kilo of chocolates and almonds each." He also retrieved some of the postal blanks and the official stamp the post office required in order to send out the packages.

"Look, here I am, stamping the blanks," he said, pointing to a young boy in a faded photograph, perhaps fourteen, fifteen years old, smiling, a stamping tool in hand. More papers appeared. Photos, letters, documents.

Reichmann pulled out several purchase receipts for large quantities of Quaker Oats, almonds, and sardines, along with one of his mother's letters pleading, in broken English, for the Joint to send money to buy matzos to be included in the packages. At first, the Joint turned her down, but later they agreed to pay for much of the food the Reichmanns sent out. Renée eventually received an acknowledgment of her efforts from the Joint, thanking her for her work and concluding with "We are sure you are doing everything to bring aid to the Jews of Europe."

"Just about this time my mother decided to return to Hungary. Obviously, it was another very dangerous trip, but she was never one to worry about danger. Although Mother traveled on a Hungarian passport, she also carried proof that she was working for the Spanish Red Cross. Later, when Germany occupied Hungary, Mother gave the Spanish authorities names of Jews who were in danger there. They issued hundreds of safe-conduct passes for them, which enabled them to go to safe houses provided by Spanish diplomats. (Angel Sanz Briz was involved in this very effort.)

"Mother also traveled to Madrid many times during this period. All this travel was connected with our rescue work, and mostly to get visas for people trying to get out of occupied areas. The head of the US Legation in Tangier, Rives Childs, made connections with the local authorities for her in Madrid, because it was not easy to travel at that time. Later on the Spanish authorities in Morocco were also very helpful."

Renée Reichmann never tired of writing to people, asking for help, and they responded. In one letter she thanked Rives Childs for helping her save twelve hundred people by persuading Spanish authorities to issue them visas and access to Spanish safe houses until they could leave for Tangier. Afterwards she received an answer from Rives Childs: "I think you give me too much credit to attribute their saving to my efforts, because I would never have known about them had it not been for you."

Eventually these letters and others, written by the American Secretary of State Cordell Hull and officials in the American Legation in Tangier, confirmed that the Reichmanns, with the help of Spanish and American diplomats, were able to save no fewer than three thousand Jews.

Albert Reichmann holds Spain in high regard for its role in the rescue of Jewish refugees. "I often think that the Spaniards really exposed themselves to danger helping the Jews. Remember, there were many refugees in Spain. Almost ninety-nine percent of them entered illegally. It would have been very easy for the Spanish authorities to send them back, to say to them, 'You came from France. Go back to France.' And that would have delivered them into the hands of the Germans. They *could* have done that, but they *didn't*. I was told that the Germans asked the Spaniards to turn them over, but they refused to do it.

"We did not encounter any anti-Semitism in Spain. Most of the people did not know Jews, so anti-Semitism was not part of their experience. They only knew what they read in history books. When we were in Madrid my father asked a policeman in the street if he knew where he could find the Jewish community center. My father wore a beard, always had one. Today you don't have to be a Jew to wear a beard, but back then, those who did usually were Jews. The policeman said there had not been any Jews in Spain for hundreds of years and did not recognize my father as a Jew.

"There is no question that Spain tried to help Jews, especially Jews of Spanish ancestry. They did it for others [Ashkenazim] as well, without any intervention from my family or anyone else. Without fanfare. Some European Jewish refugees arrived in Tangier even before we did and also received protection.

"The Spanish are good people. I think they regret what happened five hundred years ago. Very few Hungarian, Polish, Austrian, or German Jews survived the war, because very few Hungarians, Poles, Austrians, or Germans exposed themselves to help Jews. Of course there were others, I don't say there were no exceptions, in Italy, Holland, Denmark, Sweden, relatively few in France. Yes, there were a few exceptions, but the Spanish people are just good people. No, I don't believe it is just for business. I really think they believe a wrong was done long ago and they want to repair it."

Renée Reichmann died in 1989, but her compassionate heroism was publicly confirmed two years later when the Reichmann family prevailed in their slander suit against the *Toronto Life* magazine. As part of the settlement, the magazine printed a full retraction and apology in their March 1991 issue.

# ·14·

# The American Connection: The Joint

When I first embarked on my quest, I had never heard of the American Jewish Joint Distribution Committee. But the more I learned about the horrors endured by those trying to escape the Holocaust, the more I came to appreciate the enormous scope and influence of this privately funded refugee assistance agency. Its operatives seemed to be everywhere, wherever and whenever Jews needed help.

The aims and achievements of the JDC are described in a recent edition of their agency brochure. "In 1914, Henry Morgenthau, Sr., then US Ambassador to Turkey, asked philanthropist Jacob Schiff for $50,000 for the relief of Palestinian Jews caught in the agony of World War I." Soon after the money was raised, seventy-five years ago, the American Jewish Joint Distribution Committee was established to help sustain, rescue, and rehabilitate Jews wherever they were in need or in danger.

"It was once the dream of the JDC's founders that the organization would 'go out of business' once the 'emergencies were over.' That dream was shattered by the realities of twentieth-century Jewish life." The number of people aided by the JDC since 1914 runs into the millions. The motto of the organization is "To save one life is to save the world."

Shortly after World War II began, Dr. Samuel Seguerra, a Portuguese Jew, went to Spain to head up the then illegal Joint. When he met Hans Rosenstiel, a German Jew with a reputation in the community as a workaholic who had lived in Barcelona for several years, Seguerra asked him to join him as his second in command. Seguerra was sent to Brazil a few years later, and Hans took over as head. He worked for the Joint for thirty-six years, till long after the war was over. When he died in 1977, his widow, Paula, took over the few duties left to perform for refugees.

Paula Rosenstiel still lives in Barcelona. Well over eighty years old, she remains spry and alert. She owns her comfortable apartment, and receives reparations and a small pension from Germany that allow her to live in some comfort. She keeps mostly to herself these days, except for caring for the dwindling flock of refugees who still need the Joint's assistance. Although she could not always remember names and the exact dates of events that happened as long as fifty-five years ago, her recall of personal details brought those days alive. She spoke in a charming mixture of high German and German-accented Spanish.

"My brother, Julio Levy, came to Barcelona in 1914 to work in the Solingen steel factory. Many other Germans were here at that time, including Jews. Even though my brother died in 1926, he had many friends here whom we had met on earlier visits. So, in 1933, when we saw what was happening to Jews in Germany, this is where we chose to come.

"We were very lucky, because when we decided to leave Germany, they still permitted people to take out their possessions. So we brought with us all our furniture, everything we owned.

"We never experienced any anti-Semitism here. First of all, we were considered German, rather than Jewish. Because Barcelona was an anti-Franco city for most of the war, and was bombarded unmercifully by the Germans, we suffered because we were Germans, not because we were Jews. No one was interested whether we were Jews or not. But as *Germans* we were the enemy.

"The only time I felt in personal danger as a Jew was when Franco came to Barcelona as conquering hero after he won the Civil War. He marched down the Paséo de Gracia escorted by Falangists [Spanish Fascists] and the German Gestapo. After opposing him all during the war, the people in the streets suddenly became Franco supporters, shouting 'Viva Franco! Viva Franco!' The Gestapo found our tiny little synagogue in the Calle Balmes, broke in, and stole the membership list. They picked out all the German and Austrian names, about twenty of us. Then they came to our houses, looking for us.

"I was home alone. My husband was out of the city, and our son was in Switzerland, where we had sent him during the war because it was so terrible here. They demanded to see our passports and ordered me to come to the German Consulate the next day.

"I don't know why, but when I got to the consulate I wasn't afraid. There were a lot of others waiting but I was the only woman. They kept calling in one man after another. All were German Jews. Then it was finally my turn. They asked me if I was German and if I was a Jew. I said yes. After a few more questions, they told me I could go, but the men were taken to Modelo Prison. When my husband returned, they picked him up and put him in the Modelo with the other men."

Paula and the other wives took turns visiting their men in the prison, standing in line every day with hundreds of others waiting to get in. There was almost no food available, not for the men in prison, nor for those outside. The women bought as much as they could on the black market and brought it to the men.

One day Paula and two other wives asked to see the director of the prison to ask him why he was holding their men.

"*I* am not holding your men," he protested, "the *Gestapo* is. As far as the Spanish government is concerned, there is no cause for these men to be detained. If you want any information about this matter you must go to the German Consulate and ask the chief of the Gestapo what can be done to get the men released."

"So the three of us, another German Jew, a Spanish Catholic, and I, went to the German Consulate. Gestapo Chief Kurtz received us. We asked him why our husbands were being held in prison. He said they were there because they had stolen German property when they left the country, and for that they were going to be sent back.

"We did not argue. We knew it was no use. While the men were in prison, the Gestapo came to all the houses of the Jews whose names they found on the synagogue roster and plundered all they could carry: silver, art, linens, typewriters, radios. I never found out if the Spanish authorities knew and simply were unable to help us, but nothing was ever done about this."

The women knew they had to get help elsewhere. One of them, a Catholic from Majorca, said she would contact her archbishop and ask him to intercede on their behalf. Exactly one month after they were put in prison, the men were released. The most important result was that the men were not deported. But these efforts to rescue Jews were ill organized and not always successful, and remained that way until the Joint was established in Spain. That is when things changed dramatically.

Even though the Joint had to operate illegally, as soon as word about its existence and activities got out, it could barely keep up with the demand for its services. Several thousand refugees came every day, asking for help. Huge lines formed daily outside the Hotel Bristol, where Seguerra had taken a room. Refugees were first asked the usual questions: name, age, place of birth? Last residence? How did they get there? When? Why? Many who came were in bad shape; sick, scared, without funds, in desperate need for everything: a place to live, doctors, medicines, clothes, money, food, jobs, help to get out of jail, transportation.

Everything possible was provided for them. Even showers and baths if the pensions where they were staying had none of those amenities. The Joint also employed about twenty-five refugees to help out in the office, interviewing refugees, taking down histories, and keeping files and records.

Although the Joint operated without official permission during those first few years at the Bristol, no one bothered it at the government level. Nevertheless it was considered prudent occasionally to "take care" of individual policemen to ensure that the refugees would not be deported. Despite this, the fact remains that the police knew very well what was going on and permitted it to go on, illegal or not.

After approximately two years, Seguerra felt sufficiently safe to risk becoming more visible and rented larger quarters, in a building on the Paséo de Gracia. There the Joint shared space with two other agencies: an Italian relief agency and the Quakers. Jews usually came directly to the Joint, but often a husband or wife was Christian, so they went to one of the other agencies for help. Essentially, all three worked together, but the Joint had the primary responsibility and the most requests for aid. It also provided most of the funds to run the rescue operations, with money privately donated by Americans.

One rather famous person who came to Barcelona as a refugee from Paris was the Baron de Rothschild, of the famous banking family. He arrived with his clothes in tatters, after walking over the Pyrenees with his family. His wife, who was not Jewish, had gone on to Lérida with their two children, but the baron came to the Joint's Hotel Bristol offices alone to ask for help. He had a leather belt with gold pieces in it, so he did not require financial support.

What he needed was protection from deportation, because he and his family had come in illegally. To keep the baron safe and hidden from the authorities, Hans Rosenstiel and Seguerra moved him to a very bad section of town called the Barrio Chino, where no one would be likely to look for him and where his wife and children later joined him. After several weeks in hiding they left for Portugal, and went on from there.

The Joint hired men who lived in the Pyrenees as guides to smuggle people across, and not all of them proved trustworthy. Paula recalled two sisters from Germany who needed to be led over the mountains. It was below-zero weather, and halfway through the pass one of the sisters absolutely swore she wanted only to die and urged her sister to go on without her. The other sister did not give in and performed a little dance for her, to make her laugh, to give her the courage to go on. The two guides took advantage of the situation to rob the women, taking their money and jewelry, but they did bring them safely to Spain, whereupon they called the Joint to come to pick them up.

"One of the sisters lost her leg from frostbite, the other one all her toes. My husband and Seguerra went to get them at the border and put them into a clinic to recover. The Spanish doctor here was a great friend to us, and treated all our people with great kindness and generosity. His name was Dr. Figueras. He is still alive, in his nineties.

"Let me tell you about a Russian man whom Dr. Figueras saved. This Russian Jew, who had been here since before the war, was a translator at the railroad company, helping foreign travelers. He had tuberculosis, and was of course very contagious. Although Dr. Figueras was officially forbidden to take this man in, he brought him to the hospital, put him in a private room, and kept him there until he was well enough to leave.

"Dr. Figueras was wonderful to many, many Jews, and worked closely with the Joint. We were great friends with him, my husband and I. He took many risks for us. Once he found out that the nurses, who were mostly nuns, were very anti-Semitic and treated his Jewish patients badly. He risked his position by making a huge scandal over that, and the bad treatment stopped.

"Franco did nothing against us, directly, but once, for a short time, there was a law passed that single men who were here without Spanish entry visas had to be sent back to France. There were five or six of these men, who had been living in pensions, with our help, for some time. The Spanish police took them and escorted them to the French border. When they got there, the French refused to accept them, because the men had valid exit visas from France and thus French authorities had no reason to take them back. So, the Spanish police had no choice but to take them back, and sent them to the Miranda de Ebro detention camp.

"When we found out where our men were, the Joint arranged to have them released and placed in a medical clinic, giving all kinds of fake reasons for getting them admitted. The doctors were aware of this arrangement. So was the police, and still they did nothing to stop it. We visited the men in the clinic and helped them there until we could get them the necessary papers, forged of course."

"Hitler demanded repeatedly that the list of all the Jewish refugees living in Spain be turned over to him. Franco refused, but Jews lived in fear that he might still do so or that the Germans would invade the country and find the list. Our suitcases were always packed; we never knew when we might have to flee.

"Franco personally did very little concrete for Jews, except for some Sephardim. I remember one day a whole trainload of them arrived in Barcelona. They had been given Spanish passports on Franco's orders, because they had proved Spanish ancestry. Other than that, Franco did nothing directly for Jews that I know about. What he *did* do was look away and mostly leave us in peace."

Although Señora Rosenstiel had first been reluctant to talk about her activities during the war, she eventually felt comfortable enough to write an introduction on her personal card to help me get access to the Joint archives in New York, and she urged me to look up several document files she had recently sent there.

On my return to New York, I immediately went to the Manhattan headquarters of the Joint.

Inside, it was easy to get overwhelmed by the mass of documents stacked in hundreds of files, but Denise Gluck, the Joint's archivist, quickly relieved my anxiety. All I had to do was ask for a name or a particular period in a specific location, and someone knew just where to find what I was looking for. However, as I plowed through dozens of documents (lists of names and figures, eyewitness reports on conditions in camps and safe houses, photographs, missives from diplomats complaining their hands were tied, pleas for everything from money, food, and clothing to affidavits and safe-conduct passes, threats and warnings of impending disasters unless drastic measures were implemented immediately, reports describing frightening circumstances of refugees being threatened with expulsion or worse, as well as grateful acknowledgments for assistance received), I found myself getting more and more frustrated by one-way communications to which I could either not find the original query or the response. Many of the letters were addressed to or from a Mr. Herbert Katzki, then the head of the Joint office in Lisbon.

When I asked Denise Gluck to help me find the answers to some of Mr. Katzki's incomplete exchanges, she suggested, "Why don't you ask him yourself?" Since most of the letters in question were written to and from Lisbon in the early forties, I calculated that Mr. Katzki, if he was alive, had to be in his late eighties.

Mr. Katzki was indeed alive and in his office: a dapper, tall man with twinkling eyes behind thick glasses, bending over a deskful of papers and files, he was not at all disturbed by my unscheduled interruption.

He admitted that the Joint had become an addiction for him early in life. After signing up for a one-year work stint, he got hooked:

"Once you get started in this business, you can't get it out of your system," he explained. So, fifty-odd years later, here he was, still actively involved.

"So much of what I am finding here seems to contradict what I have been told by refugees and others I interviewed who were in Spain during the war," I told Mr. Katzki. "Some of the letters sound like real panic responses describing terrible conditions. They seem to indicate that most refugees had a very difficult time in Spain, were severely harassed by Spanish authorities, and were in constant danger of being either deported or imprisoned. Several of the letters spoke about the desperate need for visas, money, and passports, because conditions were so dangerous. How do you explain that?"

"Remember," Katzki explained, "even people with Spanish passports, the Sephardim, knew they had only transit visas, good for maybe three months or so. Even *they* were expected to leave Spain as quickly as possible. Spanish police occasionally came knocking on our door, asking, 'When are you moving these people out?' The refugees with papers had to register with the police and report to them periodically to get their visas extended, so the police knew exactly who was here and how long they had been here. Under those circumstances I can imagine being asked 'Hey, when are you moving out?' could provoke a lot of stress for those refugees who had no place else to go. Some people panicked and wrote to us, and we in turn wrote to New York, to let them know what was going on.

"When complaints like that appear as they do, they always make things sound worse than they really were, because you read them all in a bunch. Those, the ones you saw, were from the handful of people who bothered to write to us, describing what happened to them. But the bulk of the people there, including the ones you interviewed, never wrote us, because things were going well for them. Of course some bad things *did* happen. Some people *did* have a hard time. But many more were helped than not."

"When was the Joint given permission to operate legally?"

"I don't believe the Joint was ever officially given permission to operate openly. One day the police broke in to Joint headquarters when the offices were closed for a state holiday and carted off boxes of documents and all the typewriters. When we protested, all that was stolen was promptly returned. After that incident Seguerra simply decided that we were so well known that there was no point in trying to hide any longer. The lines of refugees waiting to get help could hardly have been more visible. Everybody knew why they were there and what we were doing. Besides, since the Joint was taking financial responsibility for the people we were helping, and taking a burden off the Spanish authorities, it was not as risky to be visible as was first believed." The police just closed their eyes to what was going on. That is when Seguerra moved out of the Bristol and took larger quarters, on the Paséo de Gracia. There were no problems with anyone after that.

Even though he was stationed in Lisbon, and most of those trying to leave Spain had to go through Portugal to reach an exit port to the Americas, Katzki admitted it would be hard to guess exactly how many refugees had passed through Spain.

"It must have been in the thousands, but don't ask me to particularize it. Seguerra had an arrangement with the border patrol, so that anytime refugees came over the mountains and turned themselves in to authorities, they would call him. 'Hey, Seguerra, we got some more for you, where do you want us to send them this time?' They just wanted someone to take them off their hands and keep them out of jail. Sometimes Sammy would send someone to the border to get them."

Asked what he knew about Franco's official attitude toward Jews, Katzki replied; "Franco was very sympathetic toward Hitler and what Hitler wanted to do. But when Hitler tried to get Spain to enter the war on his side, Franco kept dragging his heels. Yes, he may have been sympathetic toward the Germans, but he was not anxious to get involved in another war. Eventually the Spaniards could see how things were beginning to turn. Franco wanted to wait and see what would happen, what to do.

"I remember the day in December 1941 when the US came into the war. We were in Lisbon at that time, and we were sure Hitler would immediately march across Spain to get to Gibraltar and come right into Portugal. Everyone assumed that because of the close relationship between Franco and Hitler, Hitler would get free access to Spain and then take Portugal. But that never happened.

"If we look at it as objectively as possible, the Spanish people's attitude vis-à-vis refugees wasn't bad at all. Anyone with any kind of passport would simply run around to their respective consulates, the Polish, Belgian, French, British, and the consulates would put in a claim for papers on their behalf. The ones who had problems were the stateless people. They had no consulate to go to, so the Joint became their consulate. We gave them the same kind of assistance an embassy would give their own nationals. But we did not want to duplicate services. We helped those who had no one else to help them. The Jews, the stateless, and some, like the Polish Jews who were turned down by their own consulate as 'stateless' even if they could prove they were born in Poland. The Polish Consulate would automatically send them to us. We would send protests, saying that these people were Polish, like their other non-Jewish nationals, but the Polish Consulate said, no, they were stateless, so of course we had to take them."

Many of the other foreign consulates were very helpful, and accepted as their own anyone who had even the most minimal proof of citizenship, providing them with papers and exit visas. But not all were that magnanimous.

"What the Swiss did with refugees was not particularly generous. If people tried to cross the border clandestinely they were routinely turned back to the Germans. The Swiss claimed that they had supply problems and if they had let refugees in they would not have been able to feed them. They pointed out that the Spaniards had liquid borders, the sea, and could import provisions because they had plenty of boats to bring in supplies. They, the Swiss, on the other hand, had a navy of only two boats, in Geneva, and had to drag everything overland. I don't think it is a legitimate argument, from the viewpoint of a welfare worker trying to help rescue people whose lives were in danger. You don't send people back over the border after they have come that far. I say you take them in and figure out later how you're going to feed them.

"But the Swiss were not alone. The Americans did not show themselves very generous either. It started when they turned away the SS *St. Louis,* an ocean liner filled with Jews seeking sanctuary in the US. They sent all the refugees back to Germany, knowing they faced certain death. And America had Fritz Kuhn and his German-American Bund, Father Coughlin, Gerald L. K. Smith, and Charles Lindbergh, with their America First movement, all agitating against entering the war and all spreading anti-Semitic propaganda.

"There was a project I worked on that misfired. Five thousand Jewish children were supposed to come to the States from France. The Quakers and others were involved in placing these children in American homes. All that was needed was permission from the French to let the children go. I went to France to see what I could do. That was in 1942. But then Pierre Laval, the French Nazi collaborator, stopped their exit. Why? Because they were *Jewish* children. Most of these children were killed, but a few escaped and eventually ended up in Spain and Portugal.

"I personally don't know of any refugees having been turned over to the Germans by the Spanish authorities. It probably did happen, but on balance, the border guards just let people in. All I know is that when refugees came over the border, the Spaniards did not know what to do with them. If they had papers or passports, the respective consulates and embassies were called to take charge of their nationals. If they had no papers, they called us. Sometimes, before we could do anything, the refugees ended up in the Miranda de Ebro until we could get them out. Miranda is where you ended up if you had no papers and had no one to stand up for you. Our job was to spring them out of there. It was not hard to get them released. All we had to do was guarantee the maintenance of the refugees, and see some official and let him know we would take care of them. What did we do with them once we got them out? Sammy took over a number of seaside hotels that were empty in off season, and arranged to house the refugees there.

"Sammy Seguerra was a very smooth operator. He had a way of dealing with people, and as a Portuguese he knew just how to deal with the Spaniards. That's all. No trick. He knew what to say to whom and it worked."

In the best sense of the word, I had the distinct impression that Herbert Katzki was no less an operator himself. I saw him as typical of the many special men and women who responded to the crisis of the Holocaust by doing whatever had to be done to save lives, wherever Jews were at risk.

What Herbert Katzki urged me not to forget is that he and the others who worked for organizations like the Joint could not have fulfilled their task without the help and cooperation of the local authorities, who allowed them to operate with minimal interference.

# PART FOUR

# THE
# REFORMERS

# ·15·

# The Winds of Change

When the dust settled after the cataclysm of the 1492 Expulsion, there followed a period of four hundred years during which nobody in Spain openly admitted being Jewish. The goal toward which the Inquisition strove, an eternal and totally Catholic state, seemed to have been reached.

Despite this inhospitable climate, a handful of Jews chose to settle in Spain in the late 1800s and early 1900s to escape persecution in Eastern Europe and Russia. They took every precaution to maintain a low profile, by keeping mostly to themselves and avoiding anything that would draw attention to their presence. As for the Spanish government and the populace, they tolerated the few hundred Jews in their midst so long as they did not make any public display of their Jewishness. A few synagogues existed, but they were illegal, disguised as businesses, with names like "Ben Abraham, Inc.," and their members met in secret. At best, the status of those few Jews was fragile.

Ambassador Shlomo Ben Ami, a scholar and expert on the history of the Jews in Spain, discussed the effect of that four-hundred-year absence of Jews on present-day Spain when we met at the Israeli Embassy in Madrid in May 1990.

The most profound effect was that the Expulsion resulted in a Spanish culture that developed for centuries without any meaningful interrelationship between Christians and Jews. "Unlike any other European country, Spain became a modern nation without Jews. This meant that their image of Jews and Judaism was frozen in the Middle Ages. There exists only the memory of the past, some limited awareness of the contribution made by Sephardic Jews to Spanish culture and a vague sense of guilt over their expulsion."

It was not long, however, before Spaniards realized it was bad for Spain to have expelled the Jews. At first they thought it hurt them only economically, because by getting rid of the Jews they lost their middle class of entrepreneurs. But they soon discovered that the Expulsion also impoverished the cultural life of the country and tarnished Spain's international status and image in the world.

Ben Ami placed this absence of Jews from Spain into a modern European historical context. "One cannot conceive of twentieth-century Berlin without its Jewish presence. While this brought with it the emergence of virulent anti-Semitism, it also included an undeniable awareness of the impact of this Jewish presence on German culture. We cannot think of German culture without Einstein, Freud, Marx, Kafka, and so on. What this means, insofar as Spain is concerned, is that the Spanish attitude toward Jews is not profound. On the one hand, a Jewish presence carries no deep meaning for them and there is no real widespread awareness of the contribution of Jews to their culture. On the other hand, you also find no active, vicious, and malicious anti-Semitism here, as can be found elsewhere. I sometimes refer to this attitude as 'benign indifference.' The French, for example, as well as the Germans, are very aware of the contribution of Jews to French culture. One thinks of Bizet, Proust, Maurois, or Bergson, to name a few. But along with their appreciation comes violent anti-Semitism. Here in Spain, you have neither: no awareness of the meaning of Jewish life in Europe, and no virulent anti-Jewish feelings. Only an intellectual indifference, resulting in ignorance."

In a way that could not have been foreseen, Francisco Franco's 1936 uprising, the event that precipitated the Spanish Civil War, also led to a series of events that would ultimately alter the conditions under which Jews and other non-Catholics would exist in Spain.

After years of absolute power as dictator, Franco made provisions for the return, upon his death, of the Borbón monarchy, which was swept from power in 1931. Skipping over Don Juan, the rightful royal heir and son of the last king of Spain, Alfonso XIII (who had abdicated the throne and fled Spain when a democratic government seized control), Franco chose as his successor Prince Juan Carlos, that king's grandson.

Juan Carlos was still a young boy when Franco brought him back to Spain from Portugal, where he and his family had been living in genteel exile, dependent on the charity of wealthier relatives, and began grooming him to assume the throne after his own death. Perhaps the well-entrenched Fascist dictator believed a return of the monarchy would be the best way to ensure that the centralized, authoritarian state he had created could be perpetuated.

Franco died in 1975, and Juan Carlos was crowned king as planned. But, against all expectations, he soon let it be known that he favored change and progress. Few knew that his father, Don Juan, resigned to the fact that he would never rule Spain, had imbued his son since early childhood with the democratic principles and ideals that he, himself, had hoped to implement had he become king.

The many changes King Juan Carlos brought about soon after assuming the throne did not immediately affect the status of Spain's Jews, who were still considered illegal and were subject to strict scrutiny by a special branch of the Ministry of Justice. But a shift in policy soon became apparent. In 1977 King Juan Carlos appeared at the conference of the World Sephardic Federation, an event that was attended not only by members of the Madrid and Barcelona Jewish communities but by their counterparts in Great Britain, the Netherlands, and other European countries. Three months later, Queen Sofía attended services at the Madrid synagogue.

Then, in 1978, a Freedom of Religion Law was finally passed, effectively abolishing Catholicism's position as official state religion and, by implication, rendering invalid the 1492 Expulsion Decree. Under Spain's new constitution, all religious groups are guaranteed the right to worship according to their own traditions. Synagogues now exist openly, and Jews keep their laws and practice their rituals protected by full civil and legal rights.

Among other liberalizing steps, King Juan Carlos lifted the repressive restrictions on the press and labor unions. Spain's first truly free elections since before the Civil War brought to power a Socialist regime that carried the liberalizing policies even further.

In 1981 King Juan Carlos faced down a group of gun-toting insurgents led by an old-guard Franco fanatic, Colonel Antonio Tejera Molina, who had invaded the Cortes, the Spanish parliament, proclaiming that a conservative military government was taking over. Appearing live on television while the legislators were held hostage, the king refused to give in either to the terrorists' threats or to their demands and exhorted his people to stand fast. He showed he was willing to give his own life to preserve the fragile new democracy, and the coup was broken and order restored in less than one day. The Spanish people have not forgotten his bravery.

Spain has finally emerged from its self-imposed isolation from the rest of Europe. Its economy is booming, bolstered by millions of tourist dollars. There is a new spirit of exuberance everywhere.

Perhaps most important for the future, Spain's universities are bulging with students eager to learn about the rest of the world. After being suspended in a near-medieval twilight zone for many centuries, Spain has made a sudden leap into the modern world.

Franco's death has also led to other policy changes. Soon after he died, the Spanish leaders began to discuss a reconnection to Jews by establishing a relationship with Israel. According to Ambassador Ben Ami, "Their thinking followed two lines. The first was 'It is about time that we correct the error we committed long ago, when we expelled the Jews.' They were not motivated by guilt over the recent Holocaust, but by a guilt five hundred years old! More importantly, they thought, 'We got rid of the dictator, so we must also get rid of his old policies. We should do so by joining the family of European states, by becoming a member of the European community of democratic nations. We cannot be part of that organization if we continue to exclude a nation like Israel." As a charter member of the European Economic Community, Spain established formal diplomatic relations with Israel in 1986.

Despite these political and social changes, the way the average Spaniard perceives a Jew has not changed much. With only twelve thousand Jews among forty million Spaniards, for most the Jew remains an exotic, mythological being last seen in the pages of the Old Testament. The typical Spanish attitude still reflects the virtual absence of Jews from their world since the Inquisition.

Nevertheless, steps are being taken by a brave and dedicated group of Christians and Jews who want to break through this wall of ignorance. Those who now devote themselves to creating a bridge of understanding among the different faiths share a deep respect for the sacredness of everyone's right to follow one's own moral and spiritual convictions. These dauntless men and women have begun the huge and unwieldy task of educating the Spanish people about one another's religious beliefs. Their goal is to create an environment where open dialogue, mutual understanding, and complete religious tolerance can flourish. I call them the Reformers.

What sets the Reformers apart from the others from whom we have heard thus far is that the Christians among them are mostly native Spaniards, while the Jews are either pre–Civil War residents or settled in Spain well after the Holocaust and thus not as refugees. They have not only observed first hand the monumental changes that have occurred in Spain during the more recent past but have taken an active part in bringing about those transformations. Through their eyes we can see what life was like before the changes occurred, for Jews as well as for Christians, while Spain was still in the throes of political, religious, and social evolution, and learn what it took to make those changes happen.

# · 16 ·

# *Carlos Benarroch and Amistad, the Judeo-Christian Friendship Association*

In Barcelona, a city renowned for its individuality, and one that has always valued and encouraged the independent spirit and uniqueness of its people, Carlos Benarroch stands out as an original. This seventy-five-year-old Spanish Jew is Barcelona's Sephardic community's most vocal activist. His life encompasses all the elements with which Spanish Jews have had to live since before the Inquisition: prejudice, persecution, and alienation, as well as the struggle to attain the legitimate rights and respect they are due. Hearing him speak of his experiences makes one aware of the enormous perseverance, courage, and resourcefulness required of Jews to survive as a people.

When the Expulsion Decree forced Benarroch's ancestors to flee Spain in 1492, they settled in Tétouan, Morocco. In 1900, after four centuries of exile, Benarroch's parents decided it was safe for Jews to return to Spanish territory, so they moved to Melilla, an ancient Spanish-Moroccan town perched on the tip of a peninsula stretching north toward the Andalusian coast of Spain, about a hundred miles across the Mediterranean Sea. Carlos was born there, and in 1930, as a young student, he moved alone to the Spanish mainland.

In 1936, shortly after the Civil War broke out, Benarroch was wrongly accused of being a spy, and he narrowly escaped execution mandated by one of Franco's generals, whose anti-Semitic rage he had aroused by boasting to him that he was "a Jew and as Spanish as you yourself, sir!" His life was spared by a Spanish judge and family friend who interceded on his behalf. Immediately drafted into Franco's army and sent to the front without so much as a day's training, Benarroch was lucky once again: his regiment needed someone behind the lines who knew how to use a typewriter, and Carlos happened to be the only one around who possessed that skill. That is how and where he survived the war.

With his unruly white mane, bushy mustache, rumpled attire, and twinkling eyes, Carlos Benarroch resembles an animated reincarnation of Albert Einstein. Even if one knew nothing about him, he would be a hard man to forget. He personifies the archetypal patriarch and exudes the bemused wisdom of a man who has learned to live with, and sometimes laugh at, God's cruel jokes. Padre Joan Botam, a Catholic priest and close friend, later said of him, "This is a man who has suffered a great deal, a man through whose life one could document the entire history of the Jews, from the catacombs to the present."

Like so many of Barcelona's Jews, Benarroch lives in a large apartment close to the Jewish Community Center. His home is a perfect reflection of the man: a dining room furnished with elegant French antiques adjoins a zebra-striped fifties-style sofa set on oriental rugs in the parlor. A large modern painting of Moses on the Mount hangs near a glass vitrine displaying dainty china and framed family portraits. They symbolize Carlos Benarroch's ability to accommodate the opposites in his life.

"I am a crusader for Jewish truth," Benarroch proclaimed with a self-deprecating belly laugh. "I stick pins to explode lies. I protest bad things others print about us. I write letters. I publish articles. I make phone calls. I make a nuisance of myself!"

Benarroch is a familiar fixture on television talk shows, and his byline frequently appears on the op-ed pages of local publications, as he responds to editorials, articles, and other items in the news that offend his sense of justice and fine ear for even the most subtle signs of anti-Jewish prejudice.

There was the time when someone suggested, during a broadcast on which Benarroch was a guest, that the Jews were expelled from Spain "for their own good, to save them from mounting anti-Jewish violence by the Christian masses." Benarroch did not hesitate to point out that the violence from which they had to be saved had been whipped into a frenzy with false accusations by the Catholic Church's religious fanatics.

When a Catholic cleric blamed a recent outbreak of anti-Jewish propaganda in the press on Israel's position on the Palestinian issue, Benarroch was quick to remind him that hostility against Jews antedates that particular conflict by several centuries, and would most likely outlive it by a few more.

He has never hidden his consternation at the Vatican's silence on the slaughter of millions of Jews during the Holocaust. Nevertheless, some of his oldest and closest personal friends are members of the Catholic clergy.

Benarroch's gentle but firm voice often challenges the members of the Spanish Academy, which is responsible for editing Spain's official dictionary, on any word or definition he considers slanted toward a pejorative or anti-Semitic interpretation.

"I am a Jew, but I am also a Spaniard, and proud to be both. It wounds me to see Jews maligned by other Spaniards. Take the word 'Cohen,' yes, like the name. This used to be in the dictionary as a

descriptive noun, and it had a very bad meaning. The definitions
in one old edition of the dictionary are 'Pimp, sorcerer, witchcraft
practitioner.' I had to protest. It is a very negative word, which harms
the image of Jews. It has now been removed altogether in the newer
editions."

Two other words in the dictionary whose definitions Benarroch
wants changed are "Hebreo" and "Passover."

" 'Hebreo' is defined as 'a person who still believes in the law
of Moses,' and 'Passover' is 'a feast Jews used to celebrate,' as though
we have stopped believing in and practicing our religion!" He asked
the academy to please remove the words "still" and "used to," and
hopes they will in the next edition. "When you work with centuries-old issues, a few years doesn't seem so long," he added. "But
every little error matters, because it is part of what creates a false
image of Jews for Spaniards."

"The word 'Sinagoga' used to have three definitions. The first
two were acceptable: 'a place where Jews pray' and 'the site for Jewish religious ceremonies,' but the third describes it as 'a place of
concubinal and conspiratorial assembly.' Imagine! This is the kind
of interpretation that keeps alive the belief that Jews are doing secret, bad things, the kind they used to accuse us of during the Inquisition, like spreading the plague or poisoning wells or killing
Christian babies for their blood. It is subtle but very potent and
perpetuates all those false beliefs, especially in the young." For years
he has been trying to get that third definition changed, and finally
it was done. "But not completely. They just softened it a little.

"Consider the word 'Judiada,' he continued. "Loosely translated it means 'bad omen' or 'bad luck.' The implication is that the
association with anything Jewish is a curse! I am still trying to have
that word excised from the dictionary, but so far, there has been no
action. Anti-Semitism has existed for too long, in too many places.
Negative words like 'Judiada' exist in many other vocabularies, but
anti-Semitism differs from place to place. In the USA, for example, Jews are part of society, and have been for a long time. Lies and

distortions can be told, but are not believed so easily, because there are many people to see for themselves and speak up for the truth. But what do ten or twelve thousand Jews amount to in a population of forty million Spaniards? Here, the Jew must constantly explain himself and prove that the negative assumptions about him are untrue. When someone meets me and says, 'But you don't *act* like a Jew!' I have to say, 'But I *am* a Jew, and *this* is how Jews really act!' It is not easy, but, little by little, Spanish consciousness about Jews will change."

Benarroch does not think the attitudes of present-day Spaniards are shaped or even consciously influenced by the dictionary definitions, but he does believe there is a subtle effect, because they reinforce whatever anti-Semitic propaganda people may have been exposed to in their youth.

Fortunately there are exceptions, people like Sor Esperanza Mary of the Sisters of Zion (a Catholic order of nuns founded by a Jewish convert to Catholicism for the specific purpose of fostering a better relationship between Christians and Jews, *not* to proselytize), who for many years served as the Christian head of an educational organization called Amistad Judío-Cristiana (Judeo-Christian Friendship Association). Padre Joan Botam, a Franciscan priest working with Barcelona's non-Catholic Christians, and two Catholic laymen, the Catalan attorney Antoni de Gibert and a Madrid activist known to all as Señor Doroteo, are the most notable among many other reformers working together to help bring about a change in the relationship among different faiths.

Several years ago, Amistad decided to find out what children in Spanish public schools knew and felt about Jews. Benarroch was then, and still is, the Jewish head of that organization. He and Sor Esperanza went from school to school, asking children a number of questions, such as "Have you ever met a Jewish child?" and "If you ever did, what would you do?"

The response to the first question came as no surprise to them: *not one child* admitted ever meeting a Jew. But neither Benarroch nor Sor Esperanza Mary was prepared to hear how many claimed they would "kill the Jew" or "run away" if they ever met one, although most said they would merely try to "convert him."

When asked who told them things about Jews to make them think so badly of them, the children answered, "The Sisters. The ones who teach us catechism."

"This happened not so long ago," Benarroch emphasized, "*after* the Vatican issued a papal decree that established that Jews cannot be held responsible for the death of Christ. *After* Vatican II. I suspect, however, that nothing has really changed much since then in the schools. It takes the Church a long time to make changes."

With help from Sor Esperanza Mary, he sent the results of the study to the Vatican, "to show how the children were taught to hate, not to love." Without waiting for a response from Rome, Amistad began arranging programs on Jewish subjects for the community. They scheduled conferences and seminars, and taught classes to show what Jews are and what Jews believe. There were classes on Jewish rituals, Jewish traditions, Jewish scholars, the history of Jews in general, and the contribution of Jews to Spanish culture in particular. And the Christian citizens of Barcelona came to hear, in small numbers at first, then larger later—ordinary people curious and eager to learn. They wanted to know what Jews were like.

Benarroch's face lit up as he described how he and the others also go out into the community, to churches, to schools, to seminaries, organizing symposia and dialogues. "I still go into classrooms several times a week. I love to talk to the children. I also invite them to my home. They come with their teachers. I encourage them to ask any questions they want. They ask me about all the old stories they were told about Jews. We often laugh and joke, and together we break down old barriers. They sit on the floor and we talk about how we are alike and how we differ. Just the other day a young girl asked to see photographs of my family, so I brought out an old album and showed them snapshots of my grandparents, where I lived as a boy, our weddings, and other family celebrations. One of the children exclaimed with great surprise, 'But you are *normal!*' Some of them actually expect Jews to have horns, because Michelangelo's Moses has horns! When there are so few of us to point out the misconceptions, how can they learn the truth?"

Listening to the questions the children were asking during these encounters, Benarroch began to suspect that they had not yet been told about the Church's more benign position on Jews since Vatican II. So, recently, he and Amistad decided it was time for another look at what was being taught in catechism classes. He consulted some of his catechist friends, and together they confirmed that the old beliefs were not only *not* being erased, they were *being perpetuated*. The papal writings absolving Jews of guilt in the death of Jesus, which might have helped correct the distorted image of Jews Spanish children grew up with, were not even mentioned.

Sor Esperanza Mary agreed with Benarroch that they could not simply leave the task of educating the children to the schools. They enlisted the aid of Antoni de Gibert to help them solve the problem.

The owner of one of the great private libraries on Judaica anywhere, de Gibert takes pride in the fact that one of his ancestors is in the process of being canonized by the Catholic Church. De Gibert's interest in studying the essence of Judaism and its relationship to Christianity was aroused when, as a young man during the late 1940s, he attended a university conference. While addressing an audience of students and faculty, a high Church official went into a wild anti-Semitic tirade, accusing Jews of everything from killing Christ to being responsible for the Spanish Civil War as partners in an unholy alliance with Communists, Separatists, and Masons, which controlled the opposition to Franco's Church-supported crusade.

De Gibert, a devout Catholic since early childlhood, challenged some of the cleric's statements about Jews, maintaining they were, at best, great exaggerations. But de Gibert's dissent was ignored and his questions went unanswered. This disappointment spurred his lifelong and passionate exploration of the issues that have kept

Christians and Jews trapped in mutual mistrust and social enmity. De Gibert has put his resulting expertise to excellent use as an activist promoting better relations between them.

In 1990, after many years of trying to educate the Spanish public about the essence of Judaism and the nature of Jews, de Gibert joined Benarroch, the Sisters of Zion, and other members of Amistad in a special task: to find a way to put all the information about the Church's new attitude toward Jews into the hands of children in a form they would understand and respond to.

The result of their effort is a small book, simply called *Jews*, which distills the Church's revised teachings, translated from the formal Latin into Castilian and Catalan. Choosing the text carefully, they put the most pertinent quotations in bold print. "Our book is only seventy-three pages long, but it is very powerful. Barcelona's Cardinal Jubany wrote the introduction over his official seal. Among the things stressed in the book is the fact that, contrary to the Church's long-held claim, the ancient covenant between God and the Jews has never been revoked." Elsewhere it speaks about the heroism and martyrdom of the Jewish people since the days of Jesus, in defense of *one* God, a God Jews and Christians share.

The text of *Jews* includes portions of Vatican II's revolutionary decree "Nostra Aetate #IV," which defines the Church's more benevolent position on non-Catholics in general and Jews in particular. It states that blaming Jews for the death of Jesus can no longer be condoned. Other parts explain the relationship between the Old and the New Testament, emphasize Christianity's roots in Judaism, and confirm the Church's disavowal of racism. It concludes with several letters and transcripts of speeches by Pope John Paul II on a variety of issues affecting Jews, and includes two photographs showing him with the chief rabbi of Rome and addressing a Jewish congregation there.

The book's elegant cover shows a stylized menorah on the front and back, and a quotation from the prophet Malachi in Hebrew-style letters: "Have we not one Father? Have we not *one* God?"

Benarroch stressed that the members of Amistad financed *Jews* privately. They plan to send hundreds of copies to schools, seminaries, colleges, and teacher training centers. "We feel that with this little book we will finally reach the young. *That* is where we have to start. Ancient beliefs are so hard to erase, but we cannot give up trying, can we?"

Benarroch reiterated that anti-Semitism in Spain is different from anywhere else in the world. "Although we have relatively few practicing Jews, many, many Spaniards are fully aware they are descended from Jews. They know that their own ancestors had to go into hiding because they were Jews or hide the fact they were Jews by converting. There are moments in history when Spaniards remember to acknowledge their Jewish heritage and act in accordance with it. Hitler's war against Jews was one of those moments when they *did* remember, and when they *acted* on that memory.

"Franco himself knew he came from Jews. Many other well-known persons also have Jewish ancestors. People often come to me and ask me, 'Can you tell me if my name comes from Jews?' Very often we find there are Jews on both sides of the family tree. So many Jews were forced to convert in 1391, 1412, and 1492, it is hard to find a Spaniard who has no Jewish blood in his veins, and this Jewishness has never really been lost.

"It is a very complex situation. Despite everything you hear, I do not believe Franco was an anti-Semite. He was a military man. He was against the Republic. He was a Fascist. He was a dictator. But he, himself, was not an anti-Semite. His friendship with the Nazis was politically expedient and opened the door to political anti-Semitism in Spain, but he refused to implement Nazi racial policies and refused to join Hitler in the big war. The Spanish government has made many gestures toward Jews over the years. And it is beginning to be different now. At least the law is on *our* side now, the government treats us as equals, and we are free to be Jews, to practice our religion openly. But much remains to be done."

# · 17 ·

# *Two Hands-On Catholic Activists: Padre Joan Botam and Señor Doroteo*

One of the most profound changes in Spain since the Civil War can be seen in the drastically altered influence the Church exerts on the moral, social, and political life of the Spanish people. Among those responsible for the changes are a few brave Catholics who worked from *within* the establishment and who dared go against a solidly entrenched religious hierarchy and ultra-conservative traditions to reach out in friendship and understanding to those whom the Church condemned as "infidels." Their methods differed greatly, as did the population to whom they addressed their efforts, but Jews benefited from this activism by Catholics.

Although Franco tried and for the most part succeeded in keeping the Catholic Church's power intact in Spain during his rule, in return for the clergy's support, cracks began appearing in its ranks during the 1950s and 1960s. Dissent was expressed openly by young priests and nuns who welcomed the winds of change emanating from Rome, but to which some of the Church's older and more established rank and file remained frustratingly resistant. As a result, the once all-powerful role of the Church as Spain's official state religion has been steadily shrinking since Vatican II introduced a liberalizing breath of fresh air to the rigid posture of Catholic orthodoxy.

As the Church's iron grip on the Spanish people's religious solidarity weakened, its social and political power base also eroded. This eventually caused Spanish attitudes toward Jews to change as well. Therefore, those Catholic activists who bravely challenged their Church's authority and traditional attitudes during Franco's dictatorship must be acknowledged as heroic allies of Jews, and should be honored for helping bring about the present legal status and freedom of Jews. Padre Joan Botam and Señor Doroteo are but two of many who cared enough to risk getting personally involved in this revolution of the spirit.

It is important to reiterate here that Jews were not the only non-Catholics persecuted or discriminated against by the Catholic Church, before, during, or since the Inquisition. This includes the period of Franco's thirty-six-year rule. Although the Inquisition was abolished and the last public burnings at the stake occurred more than a hundred years before, anyone caught deviating in *any way* from accepted Catholic orthodoxy was branded a heretic, and shared the "illegal" status of the Jews, deprived of the most basic civil rights. Anyone caught supporting the outcasts automatically became an accessory to their "crime" in the eyes of both Church and state.

It is during this period of turmoil within the Church that a young Franciscan priest in Barcelona began to reach out in compassion and conciliation to members of the various outlawed and demoralized Protestant denominations that were persecuted and ostracized by all those professing the only accepted, legal version of Christianity.

At the same time, in Madrid, a devout Catholic layman of Jewish ancestry became concerned over the ignorance and chronic misconceptions about Jews he saw among young Spaniards, and turned himself into a one-man advocate for person-to-person contact with Jews. He endured ridicule and risked alienation from his family and friends to follow his conscience.

Both men, unknown to each other, on separate paths but sharing similar goals, have for years carried on their private and unique crusades for tolerance and understanding.

Because he usually wears casual civilian clothes, there is nothing about Padre Joan Botam to indicate that he is a priest except for the fact that he lives in a parish house next to a large brick neighborhood church in central Barcelona. He has been involved in ecumenical dialogues with non-Catholic Christians since the Vatican II days of the 1960s. He is a close friend of the publisher Mario Muchnik and of Carlos Benarroch, as well as of Sor Esperanza Mary and others involved in the struggle to break through persistent mutual negative projections and prejudices.

He is also a Catalan, which makes him a rebel by birthright, soft spoken but with the unmistakable passion of the reformer in his voice.

Botam described conditions during the Franco days as "a medieval dictatorship in which the Church alone provided the foundation of the state's unity and stability. Thus, all non-Catholics— Protestants, Muslims, as well as Jews—were not only considered infidels but were treated as third-rate citizens. Their non-allegiance to the one state religion made them traitors, enemies of the state. The Spanish constitution branded them 'illegal,' and since they were outside the law, they were given neither the protection nor any of the other privileges accorded those within the law."

All outward manifestations of non-Catholic faiths were forbidden. Adherents could not establish synagogues, churches, or mosques, or have their own consecrated cemeteries. The very practices of their religions were outlawed, and their religious rituals, such as weddings, baptisms, and burials, were considered illegal activities by the state.

Not everybody went along with Franco's and the Church's dogmatic and punitive attitude.

"From the social point of view, some parts of the population were sensitive to these problems. They felt in solidarity with these outcasts, sympathized with them, and tried to help them. But they did this very timidly and in secret, because doing so was seen as seditious. By helping them they, themselves, were breaking the law.

"Worst of all was the fact that there was an ultra-conservative, fundamentalist sector that began to agitate against all those outside the fold. Not only did they refuse to tolerate any opposition, they aggressively persecuted those they perceived as violators of the sacred law. For example, the synagogue here in Barcelona, which at the time existed illegally, was stoned and vandalized on more than one occasion. But Jews were not the only victims. Those fanatics in the Franco regime also mistreated and attacked Protestants. This was a very sad situation, because the police and other established authorities refused to respond or react to these acts of violence. They did not protect the victims, because they lacked legal status, and the government did not recognize them or acknowledge their plight. This presented a terrible moral struggle for all those with a conscience. Whenever something bad happened to any of these people, they had to rely on the few who, out of the depth of their own inner convictions, were willing to help."

The Spanish bishops supported Franco because the Civil War had been perceived by the official Church as a "Christian crusade" to restore a medieval-style "super-Catholic" regime to Spain once the "leftist, anti-religious" Republican government was ousted. "Thus the Church was compromised from the start, and when Franco took control of the country there really was no voice to defend the persecuted minorities, the Jews, Muslims, and Protestants.

"I was a boy when all this was happening and busy with my

studies. I had not yet developed a social conscience, had no sense of history. When I was old enough to take notice, in the late 1950s, Vatican II unfolded. Therefore my awakening as a citizen and as a religious person coincided with those great changes in the Church's attitude.

"During that time a group of us in the Franciscan order decided to join together, in the spirit of Vatican II's ecumenism, to help bring about some changes in the treatment of those outside the Church. We wanted to arouse a degree of sensitivity among the bishops, the priests, and parishioners, some understanding of the problem of persecution and prejudice. We committed ourselves not only to protecting the persecuted, by working directly with them, but to creating changes in the structure of the Church itself by working *from within*. We spoke to the bishops, hoping to persuade them to encourage parish priests to be more aware of and sensitive to those outside the Church, more respectful, more tolerant. That is how the Ecumenical Center of Cataluña was founded.

"That is where my work began, with a small ecumenical group of Christian dissidents: Protestants, Baptists, Evangelical and Reformed Lutherans, Adventists, and so on. We entered into dialogue with this small group of 'outsiders,' and have maintained a close fraternal relationship with them ever since, even though democracy has finally been restored in our land."

Sor Esperanza Mary tried to bring Padre Botam into active participation with Amistad, but he resisted her efforts while maintaining a long and caring relationship with her and others involved with her work.

"As sad as relations between Christians and Jews have been, the discord between the various Christian religions seemed to me, in some ways, even more tragic," explained Botam. "Here we were, the same family, all worshiping the same Lord, all children of the same God, with the same baptism, and yet there is this constant struggle, these wars among us. How can we continue to treat one another that way? So, I told Sor Esperanza, *that* is where my work is, among the different Christians. So she and I were in fact united in our work, I with my Christian ecumenical group, Sor Esperanza in her group of Christians and Jews.

"Sor Esperanza and I have remained close to this theme and this work through many years, although we kept to our own separate arenas. We have survived a tumultuous period, full of madness and ignorance, during which persecution and prejudice were imposed by the controlling majority on every dissenting minority. Because the Catholic Church during that period had all the power and all the resources, these marginal groups were victimized and, without power and resources of their own, found themselves with no one to turn to, no one to intercede for them.

"I will tell you a small anecdote that will give you an idea of what it was like back then. There was this tiny group of Evangelical Protestants who had no place to worship, no church, no chapel, nothing. So, they met in a public park, under the trees, to teach the Gospel, say their prayers, and sing their hymns. This park happened to be within the boundaries of one of the Catholic parishes. Since the entire city was divided into parishes, there was no place anywhere that was not part of a Catholic parish. One Sunday morning some young Catholic boys happened to pass through that park and noticed the activities of these non-Catholic worshipers. Because they had simplistic and fundamentalist attitudes, they rushed to their parish priest. 'Father,' they said, 'we found these Protestants in our park, praying and singing and doing their propaganda! Do you want us to go back and stone them?' The priest coldly responded, 'That is a question one asks only *after* having done the act, *not before*.'

"When I tell this story now, hardly anyone can believe that it really happened. But that is how things were during the Franco years. It was an absurd climate. On the one hand it was due to ignorance. On the other it was directly related to the compromised position of the Church with the regime in power. This was reinforced by Fascist propaganda, which stressed that all those who were not Catholic were automatically enemies of the state: Masons, Protestants, Muslims, Jews, and, in my own case, 'Separatist Reds.' That is what they called all the Catalans who wanted to regain a certain measure of autonomy for our people. Although we were very moderate, unlike the Basques, who have always been militant and want nothing less than total separation from the central government, we Catalans wanted only to preserve our own language, outlawed by Franco, and our culture. For this we were branded Separatist Reds and thus traitors and enemies of the state. The youth that grew up during that time became so infected by that fanaticism that when they attacked any of these branded minorities, they were convinced that they were actually defending God, the state, and even the world against a supreme enemy bent on destroying them.

"I am a Christian, a believer in the Christian faith, which has its roots in Judaism. But I believe there exists in this world a terrible ignorance of one another's values. This is especially true here in Spain. It is not that one has to remain ignorant but, unless one makes a special personal effort to discover what is important culturally, spiritually, and humanly in Jewish traditions, information about all this is not easily available to the general public of this city, of this country."

Botam conceded that considerable progress has been made lately, some major steps taken forward. "Many Spanish politicians have traveled to Israel. Spaniards were awakened to the horrors of racism when they found out about the Holocaust. Many have visited concentration camps. There were also some Republicans who fled to France at the end of the Civil War and joined the Free French to fight the Nazi regime. Many died there. Others were caught and sent to concentration camps. Those who managed to survive returned to Spain and told their stories, how they were but a tiny drop in a sea of Jews trapped in the camps. This has done much to raise the sensibility and conscience of those who heard about it, given them a more humane attitude.

"Now, as to the contribution by Jews to our culture, we must be grateful to people like Mario Muchnik, whose publications have done so much to dispel some of the ignorance on these matters. Many of their books deal with Jewish themes, Jewish issues, Jewish problems, containing information and documentation that otherwise would not be available to us here. We need much more of that.

"But of course these books reach only a small minority, those who show an interest in this subject. As far as the more profound aspects of Jewish spirituality are concerned, the multitude of facets of this enormous richness, I believe we remain, on the whole, quite ignorant about them. In Spain, as in so many other countries, we have our own view of history, our own version of what is true, so we hold onto our unilateral viewpoint. We teach history from our own protagonistic mind-set, according to our narrow ideological and political frame of reference. What happens when we do this is that the humanity we have in common with one another is left out. Without that, is it any wonder we continue to have wars?

"Nevertheless, from my personal experience, I do believe we are making progress. In 1986 the pope called a convocation in Assisi, Italy. He asked all religions to send representatives to pray for peace, justice, and safe ecology. Many responded and a great movement grew out of this convocation. I myself proposed to my bishop that we hold a parallel, simultaneous meeting, bringing together representatives of the various faiths right here in Barcelona. I was put in charge of contacting all the representatives, all the non-Catholics, to ask them to join us. Jews, Muslims, Protestants all responded with great joy to my invitation.

"We called it the Assisi Interreligious Peace Reunion. Thus, I sat in my Catholic church, next to my Jewish friend Carlos Benarroch, and on his side sat a Lutheran minister, and a Greek Orthodox priest sat next to him. The cardinal of Barcelona, although he was the host, sat not up by the altar, as would be customary, and he did not lead the convocation, as was expected. He joined all the others as an equal.

"We approached each member individually, and introduced them one by one. I had the honor of saying, 'May I present to you the leading member of the Jewish community here in Barcelona,' and Carlos Benarroch, wearing his yarmulke, responded with a resounding 'Shalom.' We handed him a microphone and he gave a stirring message about human salvation, and about the fact that his God is not a God of vengeance but of culture and mutual respect, and much more. It was a very good talk. The others followed. Everybody was deeply moved. The prevalent feeling was one of hope. There was a reunion the following year, and others may follow. So you see, after the dark 1940s, there has indeed been a lot of meaningful change."

Señor Doroteo, as he is known to everyone, is a teddy bear of a man in his late sixties: short and stocky, with a ruddy, jovial face. He lives as a layman in a religious community residence not far from Madrid. A lifelong Catholic, he is aware of his Jewish ancestry and has devoted his life to honoring it by studying the meaning and essence of Judaism, traveling to Israel as often as he can afford to go, and teaching Spanish youngsters about their Jewish heritage.

"I have a somewhat different attitude about the subject of Spain and the Jews than the average Spaniard. You see, my family always knew we had Jewish blood, from long ago. We knew from my two surnames. [Spaniards customarily use both parents' family names.] My mother's name is Jewish. So is my father's, which shows that I have Jewish blood on both sides of my family. Most Spaniards do, but normally no one pays much attention to this fact. You *know*, but you ignore it. For me it became important for several reasons."

Doroteo joined the war against Franco at the age of sixteen. Until he met some of the members of the American Lincoln Brigade fighting alongside him, he had never met a Jew. His first concentrated exposure to anti-Semitism came during the war when Germany sent a publication to Spain that summarized all the propaganda messages distilled from German newspapers. Published by the German Information Office, ASPA was printed every two weeks, and its vitriol was carried by Spanish newspapers. Until then, the Spaniards' view of Jews had been mythical. Now, suddenly, it was concrete and personal.

The propaganda was aimed primarily at the young, impressionable reader, and its purpose was to blame the Jews for all the world's industrial, financial, and social problems.

"We were told Jews controlled everything: the banks, industry, trade, real estate, and that they could 'take over' anything or anyone, whenever they chose to do so." Doroteo remembers being indoctrinated with this propaganda when he was a schoolboy. There were also pamphlets and small papers that showed caricatures of Jews with black top hats and big bags of money. Something told him that Jews could not all be the same, any more than Spaniards were all the same. "I was interested in investigating these claims, because I knew it was not possible for *all* members of one group to be rich and powerful. How could it be so? My brain told me this was impossible."

Even as a youngster, Doroteo wanted to know about his ancestral roots and felt no conflict in this need. "Like my parents, I have always been a Catholic, and that is why I wanted to know about my Jewish roots. After all, our Lord was a Jew. As a Catholic, I read a lot and asked a lot of questions, but I had to look for my own answers, because I was not willing to go along with this narrow belief, this limited attitude toward Jews.

"My friends and relatives don't quite know what to make of it all. They often say to me, 'Oh, you and your Jews! Don't you ever get tired of learning and speaking about Jews?' And I answer, 'No, I am not tired.' And they ask, 'Don't you get bored going back to Israel again and again?' And I ask, 'How could I get bored there when there is so much to see, to learn?' They ask these questions and hear my answers, but they stay my friends and I stay theirs. They hold their beliefs from what they were taught when they were youngsters. That is why I so strongly believe that children must be taught the real truth early, while they are young, before their minds close up."

By traveling to Israel, Doroteo saw for himself. As part of his search, he studied as much as he could about the Inquisition. "Bad as it was, most people do not know that the Spanish Inquisition was not as bad as the one in England, for example. The torment of persecution in Holland, France, Germany, and Belgium was far worse. Basically, the Spanish Jews were told they had a deadline by which they had to make a decision: 'Convert or leave. If you leave, you may take with you all you own except for gold. You will remain free until you leave. If you decide to stay, you must convert to Catholicism.'

"It was different in other countries. For example, here is what happened to Jews in England. Anytime King John needed money for his treasury, he would call the leader of the local Jewish community and demand tribute in gold. 'Remind your people that they are merely guests in my country and they have to pay taxes if they want to stay.' The Jewish leader answered that there was no more gold left, that his people had been taxed until there was no more. The king sent a message to the Jewish community stating that their leader would be held hostage for taxes due, and proceeded to pull out the Jew's teeth, one each day, until all the ransom was paid. The Spanish Inquisition did not use such crude methods. And the persecution here was not against Jews per se, but against pretenders only, those who claimed to be converted but remained 'Secret Jews.'"

It is clearly a moral struggle for Señor Doroteo to reconcile his Jewish blood with his faith and his allegiance to the Catholic Church and come to terms with the Church's violent history of persecuting Jews, but he proved he was no mere apologist for the Church.

"Many reasons are given to explain the Inquisition, but the truth is that the main purpose for expelling Jews was that the Church, the state, and the people wanted the property the Jews owned. By expelling them, they were able to confiscate and expropriate their land. If they could prove that the converts remained Secret Jews, they could also take away their land. And sometimes their lives."

Asked what he had learned by meeting Jews and interacting with them, Señor Doroteo replied, "What I felt most strongly when I first went to Israel was that everything the Jews had achieved there was deserved. They had worked so hard for it all and achieved a miracle. They deserve to be there. Everything bad that happened to them was because of the terrible misinformation others taught about Jews in schools, in traditional education. That is where it all starts. They deserve to have a place of their own, a place to be safe."

One of the ways Señor Doroteo counteracts the impact of the distorted view of Jews that Spanish children are taught in school is by taking as many as possible to Israel and acting as their guide. By now, Señor Doroteo has taken several groups of youngsters to "meet Jews." Money alone keeps him from doing it more often. "I dream of the day when I can take another group, to show them what can be brought into being from nothing. So many are curious about Israel now. I think it is more important for ordinary people to go there, to see for themselves, instead of reading what historians have written."

On the subject of the role Spain played in the rescue of Jews during World War II, Señor Doroteo could only guess. "Somewhere around seventy thousand Jews were saved in Spain during that time. I believe that most Spaniards did not know how many Jews were living among them, because everything was done very clandestinely, in secret. Information about the influx of Jews was mostly for foreign consumption and not presented to the Spanish public as an official attitude. Usually Jews were moved to larger cities, where they could be more easily hidden.

"Do I believe active persecution of Jews is likely to occur again in Spain? Of course, what happened before could happen again, anywhere, but I doubt it would happen here, in Spain. Why? Because we know more now. We have acquired some knowledge, some culture. We have learned something from our past. Much is still missing, but I do not believe I am wrong to say that it will not happen here. If more people traveled to Israel, as I do, and saw how hard the Jews work, they could not help but become friends. Even brothers.

"Now there is a strong campaign against Israel. Even the smallest thing is blown up big in the press. Many countries have fallen into this trap, in Europe, South America, and even in North America. A cousin of mine who lives in Uruguay sent me a sign he has seen posted everywhere: IF YOU WANT TO DO SOMETHING FOR YOUR COUNTRY, KILL A JEW! I am afraid that if world propaganda against Jews continues escalating, there is no way to predict how far this could go. But I don't think it will go that far here. For that to happen, the movement against Jews would have to be supported by the leaders, not just the people, as it was in Germany, and before that, in Spain and elsewhere. Now, our leaders are not predisposed in that direction, and neither are our people."

Señor Doroteo stopped, reached into his pocket, and handed me a small pamphlet. "I have written this for our [Madrid branch of Amistad] center. It is called *My Jewish Brother*. It went out in our monthly bulletin to our entire membership. Basically, it stresses that I love Jews because Jesus was a Jew. I love Jews because the Virgin Mary was Jewish. I love Jews because the Apostles were Jews. I love Jews because Jesus taught us to love, and to hate no one. That is the real essence of my religion."

# ·18·

# Samuel Toledano
# and Mario Muchnik:
# Two Jews Who Choose
# to Live in Spain

When Samuel Toledano and Mario Muchnik settled in Madrid and Barcelona, respectively, they were not fleeing a war, like so many other Jews before them. They could have chosen to live anywhere in the world, but they chose Spain as their home.

Samuel Toledano is a prominent Sephardic Jew who has lived in Madrid since the early 1950s. He can trace his ancestry back to Yusef Toledano, the father of Rabbi Daniel Toledano, who left Toledo with all the other non-baptized Jews who chose exile over conversion in 1492.

A tall, elegant man in his fifties, Toledano converses comfortably in English and several other languages. Born in Morocco, he has lived for over thirty years in Spain and is a major power behind the changes in attitude toward Jews. He knew Franco well and is

247

influential in religious, financial, and political circles. Recognized as the most eloquent spokesman for the Jewish communities in Spain, he travels widely and frequently finds himself the focus of international media.

"It is not at all unusual for Shabbat candles to be lit by Spanish families whose ancestors converted to Catholicism centuries before. They do it out of respect to their past. With all the intermarriages over the centuries, practically all Spaniards have at least one Jew in their family tree. You must realize that more Jews converted than were massacred or fled the Inquisition.

"Sometimes I am asked if Spain is still anti-Semitic. This is not 1492! That was five centuries ago. Perceptions do change. Perhaps there is some anti-Semitism here. But anti-Semitism here is different, unlike anywhere else. If you wanted to be cynical, you could say that there is no real anti-Semitism in Spain because there were no Jews here for over four hundred years.

"Take the average non-Jewish American. His attitude toward a Jew is generally more antagonistic than that of a Catholic Spaniard. This is certainly so on a social level. There is no social anti-Semitism here, the way it exists everywhere else."

Toledano told of attending a major university in Paris, where there were only three other Jewish students in a class of 220. During his three years at that very elitist French school he was not invited once to the home of any of his 216 non-Jewish classmates. They were polite to him in school, but the minute school was over, they ignored him. He suffered deeply from this kind of anti-Semitism in France. Toledano also spoke about spending the early part of his childhood in French Morocco. When the Vichy puppet government's anti-Semitic laws were instituted, the French extended these laws to French Morocco, although there really was no valid reason for them to do so.

"They did so with obvious pleasure and satisfaction. Nothing like this ever happened in Spanish Morocco, despite Hitler's pressure to get Franco to fall in line. The Spaniards did not allow French anti-Jewish laws to be enforced in the French schools of Tangier, which at that time was under Spanish rule, even though those schools were clearly part of the French system.

"You could not join certain clubs in England if you were a Jew. This does not happen in Spain. You can join the most exclusive club here, as long as you can pay the membership fee. I have never felt any social anti-Semitism here. I have many Spanish friends. I never feel with them as I do with my French friends. Today, in Madrid, I am a member of a prestigious French club, because I have the same degrees as they do and because I come from the same level of French society. But I am always the outsider, because I am a Jew. This does not exist with the Spaniards. I have excellent Spanish friends, real friends. It never crosses their minds, 'You're a Jew, therefore you're bad.' They either like you as a person or they don't."

Mario Muchnik lives in Barcelona. A small, bearded man with a quiet, deceptively self-effacing manner, he came to Spain from Argentina in the mid-1970s. We met at the offices of Editores Muchnik, a Barcelona publishing house he founded, which has a reputation for championing controversial authors and causes, presenting its readers with conflicting points of view that defy simple solutions.

Mario pulls no punches when it comes to his personal opinions about any subject, sacred or not, particularly relating to Jews and Israel. Much of his efforts have gone into exhorting Spaniards to acknowledge their multicultural heritage and clarifying for them the difference between "Jews, who are members of an ethnic group," and "Israelis, who are citizens of a political state."

Despite his upbringing in a religious home, Muchnik is a self-proclaimed secular Jew. He objects to being pigeonholed as a Jewish publisher, and points to the fact that only a handful of his hundreds of titles are on Jewish subjects. "I am a publisher who happens to be a Jew," he argues when others draw obvious conclusions about his reasons for including in his publication roster works by and about Jews, Israel, and the Jewish-Palestinian conflict. "Those issues are of general interest for the serious reading public. Other publishing houses here also put out books on similar subjects, but, because I am that rarity, a Jew in Spain, I am labeled a Jewish publisher."

Despite his protestations, he is deeply concerned about the status of Jews in Spain and other matters that concern them. In 1983 he wrote a book for Spanish children called *Jewish World: A Personal Chronicle*, in which he answers questions from a seventeen-year-old Spanish girl who knows nothing about Jews.

"The main role for intellectuals is to be critical of society. This does not mean to speak badly, but to analyze deeply. One of the problems in Spain is that the schools and teaching here are terrible. There is a need for total reform of the educational system. As far as the 'Jewish Problem' is concerned, Spanish children should be told, 'You come from three different roots: Arab, Christian, and Jewish.' Therefore, teaching should not be *about Jews, per se*, but about *roots: about who you are*. They must be taught about their multiple social, ethnic, and religious origins, which are distinctly different for the people of Spain than for those of France or Germany, for example.

"Until 1492, there was coexistence among Arabs, Christians, and Jews. Thus, in Spain, *everybody* is an Arab, *everybody* is a Christian, *everybody* is a Jew. Until that is recognized, there will be a 'Jewish Problem' in Spain. We are keeping alive a historic lie if we keep denying it.

"The Jews in 1492 Spain were a very important minority, playing a vital part in Spanish identity, culture, and economy. They were thrown out. When Spaniards realize that there is a history in their behavior and in their perception of themselves, which cannot be cut away surgically, they will start to have a different relationship with every Jew. Spaniards should know about the Jews and care about the Jews because *they are Jews!*"

Muchnik explained that things are different in Spain today for several reasons. One is the influx of Jews from Latin America, refugees from dictatorships there, who have found a place in Spain and have contributed a new element to Spanish society. Not only because they are Jews, but because they are *Ashkenazic* rather than Sephardic Jews. This has changed the viewpoint of many cultured Spaniards, most of whom had never met *any kind* of Jew-in-the-flesh before.

Another event that had a huge effect, Muchnik added, was a television show called "Holocaust," which was broadcast throughout Spain in the early 1980s for five consecutive weeks. "I remember walking into bars frequented by working-class people, around ten P.M., and everybody was sitting there, hypnotized by the TV screen. The show was corny, commercial, like "Roots," a machine to make us cry, but when it was on, the streets were empty. Everyone went to watch "Holocaust" in religious silence. The reaction was immense. It forced everyone to look at what went on then.

"It was the first time Spaniards learned what happened to Jews during the war. Until then, not only the Holocaust but World War II itself was something they knew hardly anything about. During Franco's times, the war was something that happened to others in faraway places, far from any of Spain's concerns. War films were seldom shown in Spain during the war, especially if they showed the Allies as the good guys and the Nazis as the bad guys."

Muchnik is just as concerned about ill treatment of Arabs in Spain as of Jews. One view he finds very disturbing is that the Jew is considered so much superior to others, particularly to Arabs. "I have talked to Spanish journalists, for example, who told me, 'You Jews are *so intelligent*,' and I would answer back, 'Listen, I could introduce you to a couple of Jewish acquaintances of mine who are not intelligent at all. I can also show you some Jews who are pretty bad guys.' Then they didn't have much of a comeback except to admit that there is no real reason to discriminate against other people, Arabs for instance."

Muchnik feels that much needs to be done to improve the relationship between Jews and Spaniards. "Educational reform is necessary for changing cultural 'embeddedness.' In Spain many are illiterate. If they are not illiterate, they are bigoted; if they are not bigoted, they are indifferent. You have no idea what this country would be like without Vatican II! Children still play with dolls called Matajudíos (Killers of Jews)! Many priests are still anti-Semitic.

"When a Fascist goes around saying, 'Down with the Jews,' I am not worried, because people can identify him as an open bigot, so what he says does not have much of an impact. My worry is about an educational system that encourages and supports children in their anti-Semitic views. Just as they don't know about Jews, they don't know what anti-Semitism is. We have purposely pushed the 'Jewish Problem' out of the closet to bring about greater awareness of it. I am personally responsible for pointing out to Spaniards that it is possible to be anti-Semitic without having gas chambers—for example, by condemning the Israeli bombing of Iraq's nuclear plant as a barbaric act while refusing to label the Munich Arab terrorist attack a barbaric act."

As an example Muchnik told how Max Mazin, a prominent Jewish refugee financier and longtime resident of Madrid, almost became the victim of terrorists who bungled the job and killed someone else instead. *El País*, a popular daily newspaper, wrote about the incident in a typically anti-Semitic manner: "The victim was an architect, *mistaken for the Jew*."

"They did not say whether the victim was a Christian, Jew, or Arab. They did not identify Mazin's profession. Only that he was a Jew. I wrote a letter protesting the inconsistencies, and *El País* printed it. I write letters to publications. That is how I help raise the Spaniards' awareness of anti-Semitism."

Muchnik revealed that during Franco's time, 80 percent of the schoolchildren went to church-run private schools. There really was no public school system. Therefore, most intellectuals, even liberal thinkers, went to church-run schools, and the "Jewish Problem" manifests itself today even among these intellectuals. "Their anti-Semitism is based on *ignorance*. That has to change."

# PART FIVE

# SECRET JEWS

# ·19·

# *Old Friends*

In the spring of 1939, a few weeks after the end of the Spanish Civil War, two young doctors found themselves working side by side in an ill-equipped infirmary in a small Andalusian (southern region) town. One was an American Jew, whose idealism had led him to volunteer for a medical relief mission to Spain. The other, a Spanish Catholic, had arrived at the infirmary more by an accident of geography than from political conviction. In the aftermath of that bloody war, the infirmary was swamped by an endless stream of wounded and starving patients.

The two doctors worked long hours under trying conditions. Though neither knew the other's language at the start, necessity forced them to learn. By the time the American left to return home six months later, they had learned to converse comfortably. What's more, they had become friends, and they maintained a correspondence over the years. But it wasn't until the late 1980s, when the American returned to Spain for the first time, that they saw each other again. Almost fifty years had passed; they had learned much about each other in their letters, but the American still had one question on his mind that he had never asked.

They met at the Spaniard's summer hacienda, surrounded by vineyards and olive groves and furnished with enough antique saints and crucifixes to give it the air of a medieval monastic estate. As it happened, the house was not very far from the old infirmary.

The two men reminisced as they sat sipping brandy and smoking cigars. The American studied his host a moment, then he said, "I've been meaning to ask you this for a long time. Your family name is common among Spanish Jews. Were your ancestors Jews? If they were, does that not make you a Jew too?"

The Spaniard laughed. "Of course I'm not a Jew. My family has been active in the Church for many hundreds of years, and I count among my relatives priests, nuns, and even a bishop or two! We are as Catholic as Catholic can be. But my roots, my roots, dear friend, are a different story." He paused, sipped his brandy, and thought about what he was going to say next. When he spoke, his voice was soft, barely above a whisper. "I do not talk to others about this, you understand, but since you asked and since we have known each other for so long, I will show you something." He reached out to his friend. "Come, follow me."

He led his guest through long corridors, past a flower-filled atrium to another part of the hacienda, and into a narrow, dark room, then closed the door behind them. The room had no windows. He lit the candles in several wrought-iron candelabra, filling the room with soft light. Shelves of books lined three walls. One wall, of ancient red brick, was bare, except for an arched niche covered by an iron-studded wooden door that was secured with an antique padlock.

The Spanish Catholic faced the American Jew. "Whenever I

am troubled or need help, I pray to the Virgin Mary or to Our Savior Jesus Christ or to the saints. I say the rosary and go to Mass." He paused, looking directly at his friend. "But if all else fails, I come here." Saying this, he took a large iron key from his pocket and unlocked the door to the niche. He pulled out a tooled leather box, lifted the cover, and removed a threadbare tallit and a set of ancient phylacteries. (The tallit is a prayer shawl and the phylacteries are small leather amulets containing passages of scripture. Both are traditionally used by pious Jews during prayer.) After gently unraveling the long, thin, fragile leather straps of the phylacteries, he carefully bound one of the amulets to his forehead and the other to his left arm. Then he draped the timeworn tallit over his shoulders and turned to face his startled friend.

"After I try everything, I do this." He turned to the wall and began to bow and rock back and forth slowly, with great reverence. The sounds he made were a low, rhythmic, wordless singsong. With the language of his body he re-created the age-old manner of Jewish prayer.

Eyes wide with wonder, the American watched. As soon as the Spaniard fell silent, he asked, "Where did you learn to do this?"

"My father taught me. His father taught him, and so on into the past. I teach my sons, and I can only believe they will teach theirs."

The American shook his head in disbelief. "May I?" he asked, reaching out to the ancient symbols of his people's faith.

"Of course, of course, please."

The Spaniard allowed his friend time to touch each piece. "They are very old," he said, "perhaps five hundred years or more. We must preserve them very carefully, they are part of our family treasure."

The two men looked at each other for a long time, both now aware of the bond between them that had for so long been unacknowledged. Then, without another word, the Spaniard took off the phylacteries and shawl. He carefully rewrapped them, returned the box to its niche, closed the iron-studded door and snapped the padlock shut. His secret was safe again in its ancient hiding place.

# · 20 ·

# *My Marrano Soul:*
# *Matthew's Story*

The story of the two doctors came to mind in the fall of 1989 when I attended a lecture by a young genealogist and expert on the history of the Jews in Spain, who claimed he could trace his own family back to the fourteenth century there. I expected no more than a brief overview of the most important contributions of Jews to the cultural life of Spain during the Golden Age, and highlights from Inquisition records of Jews getting burned at the stake. What I got was far more than I bargained for.

The lecturer, a slight man in his early forties, had the dark hair, intense eyes, and aristocratic nose of the quintessential Spaniard. A certain sadness about him was not dispelled even as he spoke animatedly about his heritage.

Addressing a small audience in a suburban Los Angeles synagogue, he described what life was like for Jews in Spain during the many centuries they lived there. He spoke about the impact of the abrupt change facing them in 1492, what it meant to have position, to be educated, to own property, and suddenly to be given the ultimatum: convert or lose all your possessions and leave Spain forever.

He painted a graphic picture of the ironic fate of those who chose to convert and stay in Spain. Instead of improving their lot and affording them some measure of safety, their conversion immediately placed them under the strict scrutiny and control of the Catholic Church and the Inquisition. Thus, those who wanted to observe their Jewish laws and practice their ancient traditions had to find creative ways to avoid being found out, always at grave risk to their lives.

As I listened to the young lecturer, the Golden Age, the Inquisition, the Expulsion, and the experiences of the Secret Jews came alive as never before.

He began with a historical overview of medieval Spain.

"We often speak about the Golden Age, when three major world religions are said to have lived peacefully together collaborating to create art, literature, and science unequaled in volume and quality anywhere else in the world during that era. But there really were two Golden Ages: the first one with Jews and Moors, who had conquered much of the peninsula, working together in southern Spain—Granada, Seville, Córdoba, and part of central Spain. Then, later, as the Christian forces reconquered the land from the Moors, a joint effort between Jews and Catholics in central and northern Spain—in Castile, Catalonia, and especially Toledo, called the Jerusalem of Spain. Together these two Golden Ages spanned about seven hundred years.

"My own family's history starts in the late 1300s, in Toledo. We were there long before, but our property records begin only after that. For many generations we were scribes, translating legal documents into Castilian, Latin, and Arabic. We also interpreted dreams. We owned orchards and vineyards, had large families, were respected, and lived well.

"Since the Church disapproved of Bible study by all but the clergy, to discourage dissent and make the faithful more dependent on it for guidance, priests were free to interpret scripture without fear of challenge. Thus it was easy to stir up the emotions of the faithful by describing the passion and death of Jesus in gory detail, stressing that Jews were responsible for the suffering of the Savior. On Ash Wednesday in 1391, rampaging mobs killed four thousand Jews. Among many others, the entire eight-hundred-year-old Jewish community of Barcelona was wiped out in one night. All Barcelona's synagogues were destroyed and its Jewish population was either killed or dispersed, never to regroup or recover.

"For a whole year after that, there were daily persecutions in the Jewish communities throughout the peninsula. Some of the great saints of that day made their reputations by persuading huge numbers of Jews to convert. Saint Vincent Ferrer alone is credited with forcing seventy-five thousand to be baptized. One hundred fifty thousand Jews in all, including my own family, succumbed to this pressure to convert during that year. Fifty thousand were killed. The rest, in the thousands, either went underground or lived in fear of continued persecution.

"The Iberian peninsula, in those days, had very large Jewish communities. Seville alone had twenty-four synagogues! Most of those who converted, like my own family, really remained secret, invisible Jews."

"The baptismal book shows we were converted in 1391, and refers to us as 'Those who walk among the great in the courts of kings.' But Christians as well as unconverted Jews called us Marranos, a nasty word that means swine. No one really trusted converted Jews. 'We know you're sneaking kosher food and burning candles on Friday night,' said the Catholics, and the unbaptized Jews condemned them, saying, 'You should have died rather than convert. You're a Marrano because you're really a Catholic and only pretending to be a Jew.' But the baptized Jews insisted: 'We're still Jews.' They called themselves Anusim, the Forced Ones, which, while it gave the desired connotation, was not as widely recognized a term as Marrano. Everyone knew what *that* meant!"

As the young genealogist relived his family's history before my eyes, it was evident that he was ambivalent about identifying with his Marrano forebears: he frequently vacillated between "we" and "they" as he spoke about his long-dead ancestors.

"Look," he said, with a hint of defensiveness in his voice, "you must try to understand, put yourself in their place. The police would come down the street and say, 'Anyone who is not baptized is forbidden to own property.' Let's assume you own five hundred acres of orange groves, what are you to do? So your brother decides to get baptized, to keep the family property intact. *He's* the one who gets to keep the orange groves, but at least it's still in the family. My family kept their property and they always married other Jews who were also baptized. We simply learned to keep the law of Moses in secret.

"Then it was decided that, for better protection, one man in each family should become a priest. That way, when you went to confession, *he* is the one you went to and no one would know what you were saying. Priests had legitimate reasons for keeping secrets. The confessional seal gave them that right. They were also allowed to keep Hebrew texts without arousing suspicion. This whole underground system of Judaism was created to get around the civil laws whose only purpose was to oppress us and force us to convert. We learned to be very clever. No one caught on for a long time.

"My family intermarried with another prominent Marrano family with eight sons. One of them was 'el escribano real' (royal scribe) for King Alfonso; another became vice chancellor of the court. Luis was treasurer to the king of Navarre. Fernando became the vice rector of the University of Zaragoza; Don Martin was Admiral of the Aragon Fleet.

"Many in my family chose to go into the Church as priests.

Some even became bishops, so they could still better protect their own. They believed their high position as princes of the Church would protect them from the Inquisition, but often it did not: all converts were always under scrutiny."

Some converted out of conviction, and several among those became the Jews' most zealous persecutors. Among the better-known Jews who converted was Pedro de Aranda, bishop of Calahorra, and Juan Arias de Ávila, archbishop of Segovia. Hernando de Talavera became archbishop of Granada and confessor to Queen Isabella when he was just a priest.

Another of the apostates was Moshe Esfaradi, who, upon his conversion, became Petrus Alfonsus. Like so many other Jewish scholars, he had been a Talmudist rabbi and physician, who became a member of the Catholic clergy. He is renowned for his *Dialogue Between Peter and Moses*, an argument between Judaism and Christianity, whose outcome was clearly dictated by the convert's new convictions.

Another well-known convert was Abner of Burgos, a disciple of the Kabalistic (mystical) school of Judaism, who, as the priest Alfonso de Valladolid, led a public disputation between the two religions, an exhibition mandated by the Catholic Church to discredit and humiliate Jews. One of the most infamous of these disputes was led by Pablo de Santa María, formerly Rabbi Shlomo Hallevi, who became the bishop of Burgos. Although the conclusion was preordained, this spectacle, the Disputación de Tortosa, lasted almost two years. One of Pablo de Santa María's former disciples, Joshua Halorki, asked him why he converted. The answer must have been convincing, because, after agonizing over his decision for twenty years, Joshua Halorki converted as well, taking the name of Jerónimo de Santa Fé. Immediately after his conversion he turned on the Jews with a vengeance and became one of their most formidable enemies.

It should be noted that the Jewish theologians who participated in these disputes did so only because they were forced to do so, knowing full well they were being used in a propaganda show they would never be allowed to win. Among the many calculated disadvantages facing the Jews during the disputes (whose prime intent was to demoralize the Jewish community and shame its members into capitulating to conversion) was the fact that they could be burned at the stake if they attacked Catholic dogma. Thus hampered in their defense, the Jewish protagonists often appeared weak and indecisive to their own people. The Catholic Church's tactic unfortunately succeeded in devastating the Jews, and many chose to convert.

The one Jew who was ever allowed to defeat his Catholic opponent in a religious dispute was a great Talmudic scholar from Gerona, Nahmanides (Moses ben Nahman Gerondi, also known by the acronym Ramban,), who enjoyed a favored position at the court of King James I. In 1263, Paolo Christiani, a Jewish apostate who was determined to justify his own conversion, challenged Nahmanides to compare the relative truths of Judaism and Christianity. The king granted Nahmanides full freedom of speech prior to the contest, which was held before him and his court in the Cathedral of Barcelona. During the four-day-long dispute, Nahmanides impressed all present with his great knowledge and debating skills. After his victory, Nahmanides was awarded three hundred pieces of gold by the king, but won the envy and enmity of the Dominicans, who succeeded in forcing him into exile at the advanced age of seventy years. He spent his remaining years in Jerusalem.

Despite serious defections among the Jews, the great majority of those who agreed to be baptized did so for expediency only. "You must understand," explained the lecturer, "in those days, most of those forced to become Christians did not take their conversion seriously at first, and nobody expected to have to stay Catholic for very long. They felt that, eventually, the rules would change, and besides, nobody really meant it when they converted. 'I may be baptized,' they said, 'but I'm still a Jew. What's a little holy water to a Jew?' So we went to Mass on Sundays to make the police happy, and when everyone bowed, saying 'Mea culpa,' we bowed and said 'Aleynu,' then went home and said prayers to ask God to forgive us for going to church. That is when the Kol Nidre, the All Vows prayer traditionally said on the eve of Yom Kippur, was first said, to let God know that we didn't really mean to keep all the baptismal vows we had to swear to when we converted. We also relied on a Talmudic rule that allows breaking a law—murder, adultery, and blasphemy excepted—to save a life, even if it's our own.

"The baptized Jews got to keep their positions and their property, but the 'old' non-convert Catholics made life very difficult for them. They continually demanded bribes for everything, and assigned the converts nasty jobs like collecting taxes in the 'Juderia,' where the unbaptized Jews lived, to create ill feeling between them.

"In 1478, nearly a hundred years after the mass conversions of 1391, a prominent baptized family was caught celebrating a Seder. The Church officials were outraged. They said, 'How can we trust you? After all these years you are still acting as cheating, sneaky Jews! Your sons are becoming priests, performing marriages, hearing confessions, giving communion, but *inside*, you remain Jews! By absorbing you, *we* are not destroying *you, you* are poisoning *us!*'

"That's when they became really afraid of us, and that was the year when Queen Isabella called in the Holy Inquisition to clean things up.

"The inquisitors soon concluded that unbaptized Jews were a bad influence on those who had converted, and kept them from being assimilated. They began to examine all the old record books in order to identify the baptized Jews, so that they could keep an eye on them."

Here the lecturer pointed out an interesting fact about Spanish architecture: "All the churches from that period have tall towers. One of the duties ascribed to the local priest was to climb up the tower on Friday nights and check out whose chimney had no smoke coming out of it. 'That's a Jew,' the priest would say. 'Never mind what he says or what it says on his door, *that's* a Jew in there who won't light a fire on the Sabbath.'

"They would send the priest to that house to say to the owners, 'Mr. and Mrs. Mendoza, we *know* that you are good Catholics, and that you go to Mass and confession, but we know you have Jews in your family. Your mother and father were Jews, so please, just to show us what good Catholics you are, prove your good faith by lighting a fire for us.'

"They would do these things to put the Marranos on the spot, to trap them. They would separate families and question them and tell them the others had confessed, to break down their unity. They turned families against one another, especially children, whom they tricked into thinking they would be helping their parents by cooperating. Many of them fell for the ruse and spilled everything."

Soon the inquisitors began to burn Marranos alive. On February 6, 1481, Seville was the site of the first of many *autos de fé* (oddly, meaning acts of faith), public executions of those convicted of the crime of secretly adhering to their ancestral beliefs. By 1488, four thousand "new Christian" families, aware that their conversion had served only to increase their danger, not lessen it, had fled Spain.

It is important to remember that, while individual members of the clergy could use their position to whip the faithful into anti-Semitic frenzies of persecution, as they did in 1391, the Inquisition itself had no direct jurisdiction over Jews, just over Catholics. So the only ones the inquisitors could legally hound and bring to trial for the "crime of Judaizing" were the newly baptized "Conversos," whom they suspected of keeping Jewish laws in secret. Those who chose to remain Jews, despite the hostile climate, remained outside the Inquisition's authority, unless they were caught proselytizing.

Despite the Inquisition's efforts, King Ferdinand and Queen Isabella eventually arrived at a fateful decision: the *one* sure way to absorb the baptized Jews was to get rid of the unbaptized ones, whom they accused of contaminating the new converts. Some historians claim that when the Expulsion Decree was about to be signed, Abraham Senior and Isaak Abravanel, two rabbis who were held in high esteem at the royal court, pleaded with the Catholic monarchs to reconsider their decision, offering them a fortune in gold in return for a reversal of the order. Tomás de Torquemada, Grand Inquisitor and behind-the-scenes instigator of the Expulsion, is said to have overheard the discussion and burst into the chamber, brandishing a crucifix. "Judas sold Jesus out for thirty pieces of silver. Will you do the same for thirty thousand? Well, if so, here he is. Barter him!" With that he threw the crucifix on the table. That settled the matter.

The decision stood. "Once the Jews are gone," the king and queen assured each other, "the 'Conversos' will fall into place, go to Communion and Mass." The decree stipulated that anyone still unbaptized by the end of July 1492 had to leave Spain. Abraham Senior, much younger than his colleague, decided to convert and remain in Spain. Isaak Abravanel, remembering the life of hiding and subterfuge his family was forced to endure after his grandfather, the renowned Samuel Abravanel, converted to save them from a pogrom, refused to submit, even when threatened with having his little grandson held as a hostage by the court. He succeeded in rescuing the boy and led a large group of Jews into exile in Italy.

"No one was allowed to take out anything of value, like precious stones or gold, only whatever household goods you and your donkey could carry. They did allow you to sell your property, but since everyone knew you had to leave whether you sold anything or not, no one paid much for a Jew's property, unless a baptized relative bought it. 'When things blow over, we'll return and we'll get back our land, our orchards and vineyards,' they thought, 'and then everything will get back to normal once more.' But that's not what happened. Those who left never came back." (Recent research challenges this assertion and shows evidence that several thousand Jews did return after a few months, and were allowed to reclaim their property, albeit only after they agreed to convert.)

The suffering of those who chose exile has been described in several diaries. Unscrupulous merchants took advantage of the desperate Jews by charging them exorbitant sums for carts, horses, and vessels for passage out of Spain. Robbers attacked them and took what little they had salvaged even before they could leave the country.

The account by one Rabbi Yehuda is particularly harrowing. Bubonic plague erupted among the two hundred fifty Jews aboard their ship after they began their sea journey, and they spent months searching for a port that would grant them asylum. Their ship was taken over by pirates, who robbed them of all their belongings and left them stranded and without provisions in the port of Málaga. That city's authorities forbade them to disembark, and when the ship was unable to set sail, they sent priests who threatened to starve the passengers unless they submitted to baptism. Many died, and one hundred converted before they were finally able to continue their journey to Morocco.

As Señor Doroteo had reminded me earlier, the scope of the Spanish Inquisition tends to obscure the fact that Spain was neither the first and only, nor the last country to expel its Jews. What the young genealogist pointed out was that, while other countries also occasionally forced Jews to leave, *their* Jews soon trickled back. Spain thought of itself as "muy Católica," more Catholic than anyone else, so when "super-Catholic" Spain expelled its Jews, it meant for them to *stay out.*

"Who, other than Spaniards and their descendants, have names like Jesús, Cruz, or Jesús María? Not the Italians, not the French. Look at Spanish sacred art. Nowhere are crucifixes bigger, bloodier, more explicit than in Spain. They wanted to show how 'muy Católicos' they were.

"Many of those who became such 'super-Catholics' were Marranos who put off the Church's spies by asking, 'Would I name my son Jesus if I were not the most Catholic of Catholics?' What they were really saying was 'You can see we're good Catholics, can't you?

So leave us alone.' All the while they were keeping their Jewish laws and holding onto their Jewish traditions. When a Marrano kissed the foot of the Madonna by his front door, who would have guessed that a mezuzah (a small tube containing a parchment scroll of biblical passages) was concealed in the foot?"

If the Church and the Catholic Monarchs thought they had solved their problem by getting rid of the unbaptized Jews, they vastly underestimated the determination of half of the Jewish population, not only to remain in Spain but to hold onto their commitment to tradition and the law as Secret Jews. Instead of a simplification, things became much more complicated, and the inquisitors had to step up their Marrano-hunting efforts.

"Detailed Inquisition records are housed mainly in Spain and at the Vatican. Anyone can go there and look up a date and read, word for word, what transpired on a given day, because the inquisitors had to keep exact accounts of everything that happened. If someone screamed, they had to write, 'He screamed.' If a woman fainted, they wrote, 'She fainted.' It's all there. All the names, the dates, the baptismal records, marriage books, they are all preserved, with little notes in the margins, like 'Jewish family.'

"The Church gave out a set of guidelines to help Catholics recognize Jews hiding in their neighborhood, so they could denounce them. In part, it advises:

> If you see that your neighbors are wearing clean and fancy clothes on Saturdays, they are Jews.
> If they clean their houses on Fridays and light candles earlier than usual on that night, they are Jews.
> If they fast for a whole day, until nightfall, they are Jews.
> If they refer to Queen Esther [a biblical Jew in a foreign land who kept the truth of her religion secret from those around her and who became a champion and inspiration for Marranos], they are Jews.
> If they eat unleavened bread and begin their meal with celery and lettuce during Holy Week, they are Jews.
> If they say prayers facing a wall, bowing back and forth, they are Jews.

If they prepare meat in a special way, draining its blood and cutting away fat and gristle, they are Jews.

If they avoid eating pork, rabbits, eels, or other scaleless fish, they are Jews.

If you observe them sitting on the floor, eating eggs and olives and throwing morsels of bread into the fire upon the death of a relative, they are Jews.

If they name their children after personages in the Old Testament instead of saints and never say "Glory to the Trinity," they are Jews.

"The Inquisition was not paid by the Church. It was seen as performing a service for the community, so the community was expected to support it. The inquisitors had a quota to fulfill in order to stay in business, but they did not think they were being unethical. They really believed that heretics were posing a grave danger to the faithful, and it was their job to find them and get rid of them."

As Señor Doroteo admitted, one major factor that provided the Inquisition with widespread and enthusiastic public cooperation proved to be an irresistible incentive: if a neighbor turned in a suspected Jew and the Inquisition found him guilty, that neighbor got to split his property with the Inquisition.

"Although other heretics, such as Christian deviants, were also hunted, most of those singled out for persecution were Secret Jews, like my family, and they caught a great many of us. I have read the record of the trial of Elvira del Campo, whose husband was Alonzo de Moya. Their names don't sound it, but they were Jews. In 1569 it took the Inquisition two years to get her to admit that she was not eating pork. For two years they kept telling her, 'All your neighbors say that you have never been seen eating pork,' and she admitted that this was true but swore that she was a good Catholic in spite of it. She had statues of the saints and the Virgin throughout her home, and all her children went to church, she assured them. 'So what if I don't eat pork?' But they said, 'We know all about you. Your parents were Jews.' Then they told her they would torture her until she admitted her guilt."

According to Roman law, back then, a tribunal did not need any witnesses or evidence to convict someone as long as a confession was obtained. Roman secular law allowed torture on suspicion alone. Jewish law, on the other hand, required independent proof in order to convict someone of a crime, which made a confession obtained by torture invalid. Although the Church hierarchy in Rome insisted that confessions and conversions obtained by torture or death threat were unacceptable, the Spanish Inquisition's enforcers used whatever means they deemed necessary to extract confessions, and then persuaded their victims to confirm that their confessions, and any resulting conversions, were obtained without duress. Sometimes this ruse backfired when the confessions and conversions were publicly repudiated.

"Back to poor Elvira. They strapped her to the rack and stretched her arms and urged her to confess the truth. She screamed and screamed and admitted that everything they said about her was true, but insisted that she refused to eat pork simply because it made her ill. The inquisitors rejected that reason as invalid, because they were looking for a religious motive. They kept on torturing her and she said yes, yes, she did refuse to eat pork, but swore she did not know why.

"By law the torture had to be stopped at night, and was resumed afresh each morning. This went on for two years. By then her arms were coming out of their shoulder sockets, and finally she admitted that she refused to eat pork 'to keep the law.' Now they were finally satisfied: they had their valid confession, and now they could convict her and pass sentence on her.

"Elvira was not burned at the stake. Once a confession was obtained, the Inquisition could impose such innocuous sentences as having to wear a bell around the neck for seven years or not being allowed to wear shoes for several months. But this kind of 'easy' sentence would apply only to the first offense. If you were ever caught again and found guilty, that was it: you were burned at the stake.

"Families of the condemned were required to watch the *autos de fé*. If they refused, they were in danger of being accused of also being Secret Jews. Family members were also expected to bring the wood for the fire. Some were asked to bring dry wood, the rest, green wood. The condemned were given a chance to recant while tied to the stake, awaiting the flames. Those who refused were burned slowly, with green wood. If they recanted, they were still burned alive, but were given dry wood to speed their agony. If they recanted and agreed to kiss the cross, they were accorded the special grace of being garroted before the pyre was lit. Drums and loud songs were used to drown out the screams of the dying.

"Several bishops and archbishops, including some in my own family, were arrested during that time, but the Inquisition was not allowed to judge these princes of the Church, only the pope was. So, to avoid the humiliation of a trial of a high Church official, the accused were sent to Rome and kept in prison at Castel' Sant Angelo until they died. But the inquisitors back home sometimes demanded that the bones of one of the ancestors be dug up and burned publicly, in the place of the accused, to officially brand them heretics." (Exhuming and burning the bones of a dead relative when the accused was unavailable for actual execution, or already dead, was a common practice. The king himself dared not intervene when Bishop Arias of Ávila, the grandson of Jews, demonstrated his Christian zeal by insisting that the bones of Ferdinand's own Jewish grandmother be exhumed and burned!)

Eventually it became impossible for a converted Jew or descendant of Jews to become a priest. As late as 1877 a candidate for priesthood was denied entry to the seminary because two hundred years earlier his ancestors were burned at the stake for practicing Judaism after baptism. "You might still be one of *those*," he was told.

"Many who refused to convert went next door to Portugal, hoping to wait out the repressive Spanish laws. But soon they, too, were faced with the same problem. When the impoverished royal family of Portugal wanted to marry into that of their wealthy Spanish neighbors, they were ordered by Queen Isabella to rid their country of all infidels or the marriage would be called off. She let it be known she would not allow even one of her daughters to marry any of their princes until Portugal was free of Jews.

"The Portuguese rulers responded by ordering all Jews to assemble in Lisbon and forcing them to be baptized. That of course meant that the Inquisition soon followed. Forty nuns were burned to death there in 1673 because they admitted they had been keeping kosher and Shabbat and were caught with a mezuzah."

The persecution and execution of Jews continued for centuries. Cecil Roth, in the *Encyclopedia of Judaism*, quotes another historian's figures in describing the extent of the Inquisition's persecution: "From 1481–1521, 28,540 were burned alive, 16,520 were burned in effigy, and 304,000 were 'penanced' for suspicion of Jewish practice." Records show that the last *auto de fé* occurred on June 26, 1826, in Valencia. The victim was an old woman accused by witnesses of having had "carnal knowledge of the devil" and "laying eggs with prophesies written on them." The Inquisition was finally disbanded in 1834.

The young genealogist went on with his story: "Most of my own family left Spain in 1501 because persecution by the Inquisition had become too severe. They fled first to Portugal, then to the area that later became Italy, and finally to Savoy, whose cardinal protected us. Savoy was absorbed by France in 1860 and my family remained there because the French had a non-religious government, and were in frequent dispute with the Catholic Church over property and tax matters. My grandfather felt he would be safe from anti-Semitism there. Then the Dreyfus Affair erupted (a celebrated 1894 case when a Jewish officer was falsely accused and convicted of treason, only to be exonerated later), and it proved to my grandfather that social anti-Semitism can be as bad, even worse, than the religious kind. He left France in 1902 and brought the family to America."

As the lecture drew to a close, I felt a wave of overwhelming sadness. With so much fear, so much pain, how can those who shared this horrendous history as adversaries ever transcend their past and learn to trust one another? I was also left with a strong sense that the lecture had been carefully edited for this particular audience of Jewish suburbanites.

Eager to hear more, I called the lecturer the next day. After briefly describing my own background and my project, I asked to speak with him privately, hoping to explore some of the details he might have left out of the public presentation. He agreed to be taped as long as I did not identify him by name. I shall call him Matthew.

As we discussed Matthew's lecture, I wondered when the descendants of the Marranos who fled the Inquisition finally felt safe enough to come out of hiding and cast off their Catholic cover. I was totally unprepared for Matthew's answer.

"What makes you think they have? Most people don't realize that Secret Jewish, or Marrano, families exist in many places throughout the world, yes, even today. There are secret synagogues where secret rites are being performed. Secret Jews meet, carry on their Jewish traditions, intermarry only among their own. And they go to church. They are afraid to give up the front of being Catholic. They may not be active Catholics, but they don't feel safe without their Catholic cover.

"People keep asking Marranos why we stay hidden, today, why Marranos choose to remain invisible as Secret Jews. After all, we don't have to worry about the Inquisition hunting us now, do we? They don't understand that Marranos never feel it is safe to come out. Those Marranos who fled to Holland during the Inquisition, in the early 1500s, stayed hidden there for four hundred years. In 1920 most of them finally decided it was safe to come out openly as Jews. Twenty years later nearly all were killed in the Holocaust. Those who kept their cover did not need false baptismal certificates to escape death. They survived.

273

"Marranos stay hidden for many reasons. One is that we lived in Spain for centuries as Spaniards. We had Spanish names, looked Spanish, with all the rights and privileges of Spanish citizens. Suddenly we were told, 'You are *not really* Spaniards, you are Jews, get out!' It happened to German Jews, too. With German names like Goldstein and Rosenberg, they were suddenly told they were not Germans. A Marrano may not feel in danger all the time, but he always feels better knowing that if some Jew-hating mob ever chased him down some street, a Catholic neighbor who is a Secret Jew will take him in.

"For years our children have been taught by nuns and priests, taught catechism and Catholic prayers. To counteract this we keep trying to sneak them some Hebrew prayers and Jewish customs. We discovered long ago that it is best to wait until the children are old enough to understand our situation before we tell them they are really Jews. So, when they turn twelve or so, Grandma sits them down and explains what it means to be a Marrano. She warns them, 'You must never let anyone know about this, it has to stay *our* special secret.' The trouble is that, by then, it is often too late. 'Why are you telling me this?' they want to know. 'I'm a Catholic, I'm not a Jew!' Sometimes they turn against their families and betray them to their priest as impostors, to prove what good Catholics they are.

"Marranos have never been fully accepted by Jewish communities, anywhere. We are told, 'You're not Jews, not *really*,' and we cry, 'What do you mean, we're not Jews? We died, were burned at the stake because of our faith!' But we continue to be excluded and have only one another for support.

"At Marrano meetings, one of the main topics is: 'When will the Jewish community finally understand us, understand our history? When will they stop shutting us out, when will they stop judging us?' After all those years of being a Marrano, all of us begin to feel like variants, like zebras. The white horse looks at us and sees only the black stripes, and disowns us; the black horse sees only the white stripes and asks, 'Why are you white?' Neither side trusts us, neither side lets us in. They treat us as though we do not exist. But we do exist, whether they like it or not. *Zebras exist!*"

Something about Matthew's story did not fit. A piece of the puzzle was missing. He kept talking about Marranos as "we," yet he was obviously no longer under cover. Were he and his family Jews, Catholics, or Marranos?

Thus confronted, Matthew revealed that all the other members of his family have remained Marranos, practicing Judaism in secret as their ancestors had five hundred years ago in Spain. Moreover, true to Marrano tradition, *he* was the one chosen by his paternal grandfather to be "the priest of his generation" when he was a young boy. He was educated in American Catholic seminaries and universities, and holds degrees in theology and canon law. Through all that he studied Jewish scriptures, held on to his Jewish faith, and kept the Jewish laws. Sundays through Thursdays he officiated as a priest. Friday evenings and Saturdays he was a Jew, attending Jewish services, participating in Jewish practices.

Then things changed. Although his Jewish ancestry was known to his Catholic colleagues, rumors about his ongoing outside activities began to surface with increased frequency. He had always managed to keep Friday nights and Saturdays free for his Shabbat observances, but his superiors began to assign him arbitrary duties on those days. He knew questions about his duality and the pressure to explain himself to Church officials would not abate and his life was bound to become more and more complicated.

Two years ago it became clear that his position in the Church was becoming increasingly suspect. After eleven years as a priest, he left his prestigious position as vice chancellor of a major diocese, resigned the priesthood, cut his ties with both his Catholic and Marrano communities, and left town. He is practicing Judaism openly for the first time in his life.

. . .

It is not surprising that when anyone hears his story, Matthew immediately becomes the focus of a lot of interest and curiosity. Once they know the facts, people look at him as if he were a walking, talking anachronism. But, for Matthew, this fascination masks a deep mistrust and skepticism. Much to his surprise and chagrin, he finds he must be as careful now as when he was a Secret Jew, and he is reluctant to reveal anything personal during his lectures.

More than anything, after burning his bridges behind him, Matthew wants to become part of a Jewish community. So far, none has welcomed him unconditionally. When he tried to join an Orthodox synagogue, one of the rabbis said he could accept him as a Jew only if he submitted to the traditional conversion rite, the Mikvah (the ritual bath by which non-Jews wash off all impurities before conversion to Judaism).

"I told him, 'I am a Jew, I have always been a Jew! This is an insult!'"

Matthew wants to put to good use, for the benefit of his own people, his experience and knowledge of Jewish law, Sephardic history, and ecumenical activism. Although he says that his status as a practicing Jew under Marrano cover has long been an open secret among his city's Jewish leaders, no concrete employment has materialized from within the community.

The main stumbling block seems to hinge on Matthew's providing proof that his family did, in fact, maintain its Jewish integrity over the years. To verify this he would have to show that Jewish laws were kept by the family, that marriages within the family occurred only among Jews and according to prescribed rituals, that circumcisions were performed according to custom, and so on.

Matthew responds with exasperation. "How come they can't understand? As Secret Jews, during the early years, with the Church spying on us everywhere, we did the best we could under the circumstances. Often we did not have rabbis to minister to us and we were forced to hold onto our traditional beliefs, rituals, and practices by passing them from generation to generation by word of mouth and example. Of course, some of these traditions got lost or underwent changes along the way. Some of the practices of Marranos today would hardly be recognized by traditional Jews. But does no one see any value in the fact that we tried so hard to hold on to our faith and our heritage under such difficult conditions? Is no one willing to make allowances for the circumstances under which we were forced to live or to show respect for the traditions of secrecy bred into us over the centuries?"

Paradoxically, another obstacle in the way of Matthew's acceptance by the Jewish community is the close ecumenical relationship established between Jews and Catholics in recent years.

"How would *we* feel if one of our rabbis suddenly admitted he had always been a secret Catholic and were hired by *them*?" one of the leading local rabbis asked when I called to enlist his help. Several others who knew and respected Matthew as a Secret Jew have been either unable or unwilling to champion his cause now that he has unmasked himself. In their eyes he has gone from being a Secret Jew to being a "phony priest."

Most of Matthew's educational and work history is limited to his experience in the Catholic Church, and could not be supported by references. After all, he could hardly ask his bishop for a recommendation once he admitted having been a practicing Jew while pretending to be a Catholic. Besides, his diocesan expertise would be considered irrelevant by the Jewish community. Thus handicapped, he was turned down repeatedly for all but very short-term jobs, for which he was vastly overqualified.

Then, one day, Matthew was finally offered a prestigious administrative position with the Sephardic community of a large city. After undergoing hours of interviews, he was assured that no one being considered for the position came anywhere close to his own expertise and that all questions about his qualifications to perform well in that role were satisfied. All that was needed to secure a nod from the board of directors, he was told, was proof that he was, indeed, descended from a pure and uninterrupted line of Jews, hidden or otherwise! They demanded to know the names of his family members, past and present, their place of origin, the course of their emigration, and any other pertinent records and information to verify his claims as a bona fide Marrano.

For weeks Matthew agonized over what to do. If they were satisfied with his qualifications for the position, why did they need to verify this ancestral background? Did they want to use him as a rare specimen on exhibit, like a freak in a side show? One rabbi considering his employment told Matthew, "Whenever I meet with you I feel I'm looking at somebody who has just stepped out of a history book."

Matthew offered assurances that, as a genealogist, he would have no problem corroborating all his claims. But to do so, he would have to go against every principle traditionally held by Marranos. He would also have to betray his own family.

In a letter to the Sephardic authorities in which he finally turned down the position, Matthew wrote the following:

"Marranos, by definition, are Secret Jews. The main reason we have survived all these centuries is because we have refused to 'come out' into the open. This, of course, has made us suspect in the eyes of both Catholics and Jews. With this suspicion and mistrust we have had to live.

"I am very dedicated to preserving Sephardic history, culture, music, language, and literature. I see it a great honor to be offered this position and I think you know my administrative skills would be most professional.

"However, revealing my Marrano background in depth, exposing my family's customs to the scrutiny of others, even though they might be well-intentioned individuals and sincerely interested, is something I am unwilling to do. To reveal family secrets goes against my Marrano soul. I cannot be the one to expose my ancestors or in any way unmask my living relatives.

"There are many Gentiles today who cannot understand the

preoccupation of Jews with the Holocaust. Such persons do not understand how the Holocaust colors much of modern Judaism, like fallout after a nuclear blast, which lingers for centuries in the atmosphere. So, too, not many Jews can fathom the loneliness and isolation of a Marrano, when, even within our own family, we can never be sure whether someone will betray us out of fear, greed, envy, hatred, or stupidity.

"My family and I have been scrutinized, interviewed, investigated, examined, and studied by individuals and committees, by priests, by rabbis, by scholars, and by neighbors for centuries. Those of us whom God gave the gift of clever speech were able to side-step questions, talk our way out of tight spots. Those of us who made a false step, perished.

"Somehow the inquiry you propose still echoes to me of the Inquisition. I may be guilty until proven innocent or innocent until proven guilty. Or I might be authentic until proven inauthentic or inauthentic until proven authentic. In any case, there will be questions and more questions and then there will be a decision. About me. About my family. This is a price too high for me to pay.

"If your Sephardic community wants my involvement with your project, good. If they want someone who is competent and who has a deep love and knowledge for such a project, then let them turn to me. I have no wife or children to distract me from a total commitment to the task. But my Marranism, other than a passing fact about me, should not play a role in the performance of my duties or affect my relationship to anyone.

"I know that your stated goal is to simply verify the facts about my past, and then to go on. But I am telling you that I am very experienced as to the reaction of Jews and Gentiles to Marranism. The skepticism never ends but only spreads, until ever more and more proof is demanded.

"When scientists want to find out what makes a bird live, if they dissect the bird they may find out all about it, inside and out, but in so doing they have killed it. It is the same with a Marrano.

In satisfying another's curiosity or in verifying his reality, the Marrano has been put through the Inquisition. *Again!* This is our weak point, but it must be dealt with.

"I want no more inquisitions. I have been through Roman Catholic seminary board inquisitions, before bishops, priests, fellow seminarians, roommates, and co-workers. I have been through diocesan inquisitions before the Bishops' Council. I will not sit through any more inquisitions, even Jewish ones. *Especially Jewish ones!* Jews, above all, should respect my sentiments."

It is a struggle for Matthew to keep from sinking into depression. He also misses the power and prestige he enjoyed as a priest. "When a priest leaves the Church, there is nothing he can take along, no severance pay, no references to help him survive in the secular world. He has lost his community, his family, his support system. And his credibility."

Matthew does not earn enough from his lectures and genealogical research to afford a place of his own, so he shares someone else's home. He mows lawns for extra money and borrows a car to get around. He monitors all calls before answering the phone and uses a postal box for his mail. He has mastered the art of hiding. He longs to be an active, involved member of a Jewish community, but the rejection by his own people has wounded him deeply and is eroding his resolve. He is beginning to wonder if staying a Secret Jew might not have been the best solution after all. At least he would still have the support of his Marrano family.

# ·21·

# Crypto-Jews of
# the American Southwest

Matthew's story had such a profound effect on me that it altered
the course of my search. I felt a connection to him and his people
that went far beyond sympathy or care. Instinctively identifying
with him as a spiritual brother, I decided to learn more about the
Secret Jews he claimed were scattered throughout the Americas. If
I could find evidence of others like him, it would further reveal the
living consequences of the events that happened in Spain so long
ago. Perhaps I would meet American counterparts to the Chuetas
of Majorca, a community of Marranos who, after centuries of secrecy, have recently made tentative moves to embrace their Judaism
openly.

I soon discovered that others had preceded me in searching out
the descendants of Spain's Marranos in the New World. In *Pioneer*

*Jews: A New Life in the West,* Harriet Rochlin interviewed a Marrana related to a long line of Secret Jews whose family members were recipients of a land grant issued by Spanish conquistadors in the 1500s. After centuries of secrecy, this woman finally decided to come out openly as a Jew. Although she now regrets her decision to emerge from the safety of her Christian cover, after first generously sharing her story, she remains the leader of a small group of former Marranos in New Mexico. Her very existence, however, supports Matthew's story.

Rochlin's work was only the first of many sources that led me to learn more about modern-day Marranos. In recent years, numerous scholars have begun the task of researching the religious backgrounds of many Hispanics living in the American Southwest, and an amazing story of major proportions has come to light. Today there are thousands of Hispanic Catholics who are Secret Jews, called Crypto-Jews. In New Mexico alone their numbers are estimated by some researchers to be at least 1,500 families. The strength of their connections to Judaism and their own awareness of it vary greatly from family to family, and even among individuals in the same family. Some of the Jewish customs they continue to observe have been so modified over time that they are barely recognizable. Nevertheless, these customs persist. And after twenty generations of secrecy and persistence, many of these people are now coming forth to reveal their true identities and struggle with the implications of their dual religious inheritance.

In January of 1991, the "International Conference on the Inquisition in the Americas and the Hidden Jews of the Southwest" at the University of Arizona in Tucson drew nearly four hundred scholars and researchers from all over the United States, several Latin American countries, Spain, and Canada. The papers and seminars dealt, in part, with the conditions under which the Marrano tradition crossed the Atlantic as soon as the New World was "discovered."

The year 1492 was the most momentous in Spanish history for many reasons. Aside from the fall of the Moorish kingdom of Granada and the subsequent unification of Spain under the Catholic Monarchs, followed by the Expulsion, there was Christopher Columbus's historic expedition of discovery that would change the world.

Columbus bears one of the most famous names in history, yet we know little of his background with certainty, including his ancestry. The Italians, calling him Cristoforo Colombo, claim him as theirs, but the Spaniards, who know him as Cristóbal Colón, say he was a Spaniard. What *is* known is that Columbus left on his first exploratory voyage at midnight, on August 2, 1492, the last day Jews were allowed to remain in Spain, that several men among the crew were of Jewish descent, and that some of them were believed to have been Marranos. Based on these facts and a lot of conjecture, several arguments have been made (none of which is taken seriously by historians) to demonstrate that Columbus himself was, or at least may have been, a Marrano, and that his real goal was to find a safe place for Jews.

Perhaps we will never know the precise nature of the prior relationship between the voyage of Columbus and the plight of the Spanish Jews, but we do know that as soon as the New World was discovered, Spanish Jews (professing Jews, Marranos and true "Conversos") migrated in great numbers. They journeyed to whatever regions of the New World were opened to settlement. In 1521, Hernando Cortes conquered Mexico, then known in Europe as New Spain, thus providing a new magnet for refugees.

By 1539 the drain of intellectuals, professionals, and artisans had become such a threat to the well-being of Spanish society that King Ferdinand issued a decree prohibiting all newly baptized Christians from traveling to the New World, but by that time there were Jews of one sort or another all over America. According to one chronicler, by the mid-sixteenth century, 25 percent of the Spaniards living in Mexico City were Jews, and if Marranos were counted, Jews would outnumber Catholics. A century later, there were fifteen synagogues in Mexico City and about a dozen more scattered through New Spain.

In the beginning, Jews were treated with tolerance, and many rose to positions of power and wealth. But when they grew too strong, the Inquisition crossed the sea and continued its work in the New World. In 1571 the Inquisition came to Mexico. The governor of New Leon, Luis de Carvajal, was called before its tribunal because he failed to turn in his two sisters, who had been found to be Secret Jews. He died in prison as a Converso. Between 1589 and 1596, nearly two hundred people were tried for the crime of Judaizing. Records show that Jews were burned at the stake in Peru as late as 1736.

As a result of this new persecution, the Marranos migrated in large numbers from the urban centers of colonial Mexico to the unpopulated frontier territories, which now constitute the Southwest of the United States. Here they built small self-sustaining communities and continued to practice their religion. But over time, their clans grew to include Catholic Spaniards, with whom some of them intermarried. Some people also intermarried with the local Indians. Since these settlers were cut off from other Jewish communities, and forced to practice their religion secretly, their religion itself underwent changes.

The Tucson conference touched on these early factors, but its main focus was the present-day descendants of those early Secret Jews. Until recently, not much was known about contemporary Marranos in America. Although a few have opted to reveal themselves openly, most still insist on keeping their practices and their ceremonies secret, protected from the scrutiny and betrayal of outsiders. They guard their dual identities as though their lives depended on keeping their Christian cover.

Nevertheless, signs of their presence have become increasingly more visible. As stories of unlikely and unexplained practices by otherwise unexceptional Christian Hispanics in the Southwest surfaced, they attracted the interest of the academic community. Historians like Drs. Stanley Hordes, Frances Hernandes, Judith Laikin Elkin, and Tomas Atencio have written about Crypto-Jews in the Americas and confirmed their existence in numbers far greater than anyone expected. What has become increasingly clear, confirming Matthew's story, is that hundreds of descendants of Jews who were forced to convert during the Spanish Inquisition are still struggling to come to terms with long-buried fragments of their Jewish past.

The wide spectrum of Secret Jews whose ancestors settled in the territories claimed by Spanish conquistadors (once called New Spain, but now Mexico and parts or all of Texas, New Mexico, Colorado, Arizona, and California) falls into three main categories.

The first group lives outwardly as assimilated Christians, but still practice an array of Jewish customs without recognizing them as Jewish in origin. The members of the second group acknowledge their Sephardic heritage and think of themselves as Jews (a fact they hide from all except "nuestra gente," our own people), despite their solid Christian affiliations, and despite the fact that their secret Jewish practices have undergone so many transformations that they bear only marginal resemblance to traditional Jewish customs. Those in the third group find themselves somewhere in between: true believers in Christian dogma, but nevertheless acknowledging their Jewish roots and holding on to some Jewish traditions.

Dr. Judith Laikin Elkin, president of the Latin American Jewish Studies Association, believes that the Marranos' need to remain hidden is validated by their persistent fear of persecution. She also holds that the main legacy of the Inquisition in the New World was the legitimization of the persecution of Jews: its sacred mission made Jew hunting an honorable pursuit.

Several facts support this assertion. The Catholic Church not only followed the colonizers west but often provided the colonizers (as exemplified by Padre Junípero Serra, the Franciscan priest who established the now famous missions all across California). Because these "Soldiers of God" came to bring the "True Faith" to the Indians, to pass on their culture to the "unschooled savages," to teach them valuable skills and civilized customs with which to replace their primitive ones, who would dare quarrel with *whatever* means were used by the *one* organization charged with ensuring that these noble goals were reached? No one seemed concerned that this meant the destruction of entire civilizations and the murder or enslavement of millions of people. As the Church's legal and moral watchdog, the Inquisition was supposed to maintain God's holy mandate. Thus, ever since the fourteenth century, when the Spanish Inquisition's prominence and power rose to its highest level, *the persecution of Jews has been linked to these commonly accepted and socially admirable aspirations.* Like Matthew and his family, the descendants of those Jews who suffered this widely sanctioned persecution are still, to this day, infected by the fear that plagued their ancestors centuries ago.

Ben Shapiro, a researcher whose radio documentary, "The Hidden Jews of New Mexico," was aired on National Public Radio in 1988, tells many stories that reflect the anti-Semitism encountered by New Mexican Hispanics with secret Jewish roots.

Typical of these is the story of the Secret Jew and the priest. The priest shows a beautiful flower garden to the Secret Jew. He describes each lovely flower as a different aspect of the Christian faith. The Jew sees a scraggly cactus off to one side of the garden and asks what it represents. That, explains the priest, represents Judaism. The Jew reminds the priest that none of his beautiful flowering plants would naturally survive in an arid climate under a burning sun, but his cactus would not only survive, it would thrive.

The discovery of a Jewish past is sometimes very traumatic for Hispanics who have lived a lifetime believing they are Christians. For those who live in a conservative Catholic society, finding a Jewish skeleton in their closet often raises uncomfortable questions and creates unexpected problems, not the least of which is the fear of persecution. As Hispanics in an Anglo society, they maintain they have to cope with enough prejudice without adding anti-Semitism to their burden.

Shapiro tells what happened when one woman discovered the inscription "Somos Judíos" (We Are Jews) in a small prayerbook she inherited from her grandmother. Horrified, she tried to hide the book, and complained it was "burning" her hands. "Please, dear Jesus, don't let it be true," she prayed. "Don't let us be Jews!" Eventually she decided to study Judaism. Although she had considered herself a devout Catholic, she was attracted to the Mosaic law and the absence of idols, and became a Jew.

Professor Stanley Hordes tells of a Crypto-Jew whose family became terribly upset when their home was raided by the parish priests one day, searching for evidence of Jewish practices. "The way he spoke about it you would have thought it happened yesterday. The fact is it actually happened sometime back in the 1800s. He stressed that his family hasn't been the same since."

Hordes went on: "Shortly after Shapiro's "Hidden Jews" program aired on NPR, a woman called me at night, all agitated. Why? Because she had recognized some of the practices described as those she observed her family practicing. She was terribly upset at the very thought she might be a Jew! 'I have these horrible feelings,' she said. 'I must talk to you.' When we met I asked her if her father ever prayed in a secret place. She burst into tears. It all seemed to open up such painful wounds. She had to come to terms with it alone."

Many Crypto-Jews run into trouble with other family members, those who refuse to accept they are Jews, who deny it, who want to keep their Jewishness hidden, who are afraid to "come out."

In an article in the November 11, 1990, issue of the *New York Times*, Kathleen Teltsch quotes Rabbi Isaak Celnik, of Albuquerque, New Mexico, as saying that during his twenty years of service to the community, it is only during the past two or three years that a few Crypto-Jews have actually attempted any contact with him, and only after observing him carefully at a safe distance, for a long time. If and when they finally attend services, they sit alone, in the rear, apart from the rest of the congregation. On rare occasions he is invited to officiate at prayer services in one of their homes, usually "because some elderly relative wants to renew ties to the ancient faith."

Rabbi Celnik also confirms what Matthew, Rochlin, and Shapiro articulated: "These people have lived with fear so long they still look over their shoulders. They are conditioned over centuries to be suspicious and alert." He claims that although there are some Crypto-Jews attending Catholic services who want to return to Judaism, many others prefer to hold on to the two traditions and seem to have no trouble integrating the two and feeling part of both. The most troublesome is a third group, who feel vengeful toward those who openly embrace Judaism. They present a real threat. Some of those Jews are "afraid of their own cousins," he says.

Shapiro tells that most Crypto-Jews become very agitated at the very idea of revealing their ethnic background, turning hostile and defensive when questioned. "They'll kill you, even today, if you stir up trouble among the Hispanics," a woman told him. "It can happen again, that's why we do it secretly." One boy became very angry when his grandfather told him he was a Jew, after being taught as long as he could remember that Jews were "Christ killers." Eventually the grandfather convinced the boy to allow him to "un-baptize" him by pouring water on the boy's head and saying, "Now you are no longer a Christian."

Others, once they have made the discovery, take pride in their Jewish heritage. They do all they can to discover what they can about their past, and to understand its meaning. They read books, they ask questions. They analyze the mysterious rituals and customs performed by their families, trying to trace back their origins in Jewish practice and thus make them meaningful parts of their everyday lives.

The Reverend Symeon Carmona, a very unusual Crypto-Jew, was the subject of an article by Demetria Martinez in the *Albu-*

*querque Journal* of July, 27, 1986. Like Matthew, the Reverend Carmona became a priest. Like Matthew's family, his ancestors had converted during the Inquisition in Spain and practiced their Judaism in secret for generations while professing Catholicism outwardly. When he was twelve, he was told he was a Jew, and for years he struggled to come to terms with his spiritual and ethnic duality.

He describes his efforts to decide which of his two heritages to choose as "a heavy trip." His family members were very conservative Catholics, confused and disturbed by the turmoil created in the Church by the Vatican II reforms. When he attempted to join a Jewish congregation, he was made to feel out of place and uncomfortable by its mostly Eastern European membership.

An interest in Russian history and language led to his joining a Russian Orthodox study group that met regularly. That aroused an interest in Orthodoxy and more intensive study with an Orthodox priest. He was drawn to the exquisite rituals and precise rules of its ancient traditions.

Before long he made the decision to become a Russian Orthodox priest. His brother soon followed him into the Church, as a monk. They share a house next to the church whose members Father Carmona serves in the Albuquerque barrio.

They do not hide their Jewish heritage. The Virgin of Guadalupe shares her space in their home with a Star of David in the stained-glass entrance door. Father Carmona said that carrying the Gospels to the altar each day reminded him of the reverence he saw accorded to the Torah when attending Jewish services: "This and other traditions of Russian Orthodoxy convey a sense of living, unchanging traditions, the kind I grew up with as a Jew and a Catholic."

Father Symeon Carmona is self-taught, speaks Greek, Latin, Hebrew, and Spanish, and reads and writes Egyptian hieroglyphics. He estimates that in New Mexico alone there are about 1,500 Crypto-Jewish families who have kept their origins secret. He explains that Hispanics have hidden their Jewish roots because "Hispanic culture tends to ostracize those who are very different." Anyone

Spanish is automatically presumed to be Catholic, he said, and a Jew cannot even get credit at the grocery store. And yet, he added, he feels himself to be very much part of his world. "We have to live in the barrio . . . live with the people, laugh and cry with them. . . ."

Dennis Duran is a young corporate official who lives in Santa Fe, New Mexico. His story is representative of many of his peers.

"My name shows that I am of Hispanic descent. My father is a Mormon and my mother a Roman Catholic. I went to church until I was a teenager, but soon thereafter lost interest in going. For several years I was not involved in anything religious. Then, while a university student, I took a class in comparative religion. As we explored the different faiths, it struck me that all the Christian religions had their roots in Judaism. So, I decided to explore this further. I soon became involved in a more serious study of Judaism. Eventually I decided to convert, to become a Jew. My family did not oppose my conversion. They simply accepted it, telling me that if that made me happy, it was all right with them.

"Only later, as I learned more about Jewish practices and symbols from my readings in Jewish writings, I noticed strange differences in the tombstones in the private cemetery where members of my own family are buried near Santa Fe. Those of my own people are all clustered in one section. I recognized that some of them had carvings that seemed to be of Jewish origin.

"When I questioned my parents about this, I was given no satisfactory answers, so I decided to explore my ancestry through a study of our genealogy, which I can trace back for fourteen generations."

Duran told of finding tombstones bearing none of the traditional Christian symbols. Instead, he found clusters of tombstones facing east, with Stars of David and six-pointed lilies carved into the stone. "I found at the head of one grave a large obelisk covered by something resembling a tallit, fringed at the bottom, all in stone. Again and again, I noticed graves with small, round pebbles on them, evidence of a practice customary among Jews who wish to leave evidence of their visit."

In a remote cemetery far from any habitation he discovered another curiosity. Not only were the tombstones decorated with Jewish symbols, but there was a water pump at the entrance. Since there was no vegetation of any kind that required irrigation, why had someone gone to such trouble to provide for water? Duran thought it was for washing hands, an old Jewish custom upon entering and leaving a cemetery.

Duran's research has been extensive. He has collected data suggesting his ancestors came to New Mexico from Mexico in 1598. In all probability, these ancestors were Marranos. His findings are of interest to historians, but for him they are personal: "That is how I discovered, fifteen years after *choosing* to become a Jew, that my roots are Jewish."

Maria Stieglitz, another contemporary researcher in this field, reported some of her findings in "New Mexico's Secret Jews" (*Lilith*, Winter 1991). She found numerous examples of practices that identify certain Hispanics as Crypto-Jews.

Many of her subjects, recalling their childhood, spoke of seeing special ways animals were butchered, being asked what they had eaten before visiting Grandma's house so meat and dairy foods would not be mixed, and regular bread being replaced by flat round crackers shortly before Easter. Others remember receiving coral jewelry to ward off evil, and seeing Stars of David, menorahs, the Hebrew letter "Shem," and other such non-Christian signs on family tombstones. All the boys in the family were circumcised by a doctor when they were eight days old. Yet they were all raised as devout Catholics and, because everyone with whom the family associated followed the same customs, none of these practices aroused any questions or curiosity until they were adults, if then. They just assumed that these practices were part of their mixed heritage, which included Hispanic Catholicism and American Indian blood. The twenty-year-old son of one Crypto-Jewish woman found some clarity in this unlikely mixture: "We're Jewish-Catholic-Indians!"

The status of Secret Jews is a complex issue.

Rabbi Marc Angell, of New York City, was quoted in the *El Paso News*, March 31, 1991: "The very nature of Crypto-Judaism makes it difficult for today's descendants to establish an ancient link." He further explains that "feeling" they and their ancestors are Jews is not enough to establish that they in fact *are* Jews. "If they can prove it," he adds, "I'll be glad to accept them."

Professor Hordes responds, "I think the fact that Orthodox Jews will not accept Crypto-Jews as real Jews and demand they convert is an insult. Of course, I speak as a historian, not a rabbi, so I don't have to deal with this directly, but I am personally offended by this demand. Here are these Jews who went through all these sacrifices to keep the fires going all these years. They should not be made to go through all this." Professor Moshe Lazar of the University of Southern California, who has lectured widely on the history of the Jews of Spain, appears to share this feeling. "I consider them heroes and martyrs," he said recently, referring to Secret Jews, whom he refuses to call Marranos.

Hordes told one woman, after she was turned down by the Orthodox rabbinate, that the Conservatives would accept her. In a response reminiscent of Matthew, she replied, "I am a Sephardic Jew. For me 'Conservative' does not exist. I have always been a Jew. I don't need conversion."

If nothing else, the Tucson conference has corroborated Matthew's authenticity, validated his responses, and proved his fears were grounded in a tradition sanctified by the blood of his ancestors. Perhaps, in time, as more is learned about Marranos, Crypto-Jews, and their tragic past, more Jews will come to share the feelings of Andre Sassoon, vice president of the International Jewish Committee, Sefarad '92, as he welcomed the support and participation of the Southwest Secret Jews: "We [Jews] are a tolerant people. Personally, whether someone is truly a Jew or not, only God can judge, and not mortals."

# *Postscript:*

## New Beginnings,
## Temporary Endings

The process of exploring the past and reconnecting to my Jewish roots proved to be far richer than I had imagined. It forced me to look at what it means to be a Jew, and why we Jews, in the face of relentless persecution, have managed not only to survive but to retain our unique identity with such fierce determination and pride.

It also led me to dicover a deep kinship with my spiritual brothers and sisters, the Marranos, who struggled so valiantly to hold on to their Jewish identity and heritage, when doing so presented a daily threat to their survival, and to their present-day descendants, the Crypto-Jews, for whom real acceptance in a secure environment remains an elusive dream.

• • •

In order to formalize and experience more fully my reconnection to my Jewish self, I felt I had to go to the one place in this world where a Jew is not an outsider: Israel.

As soon as I had settled into my hotel in Jerusalem, I walked all the way to the spot where, I was told, I would have the finest panoramic view of the Old City. The sky at dusk was full of wild, gold-tinged clouds, and there, across a deep gorge, was Old Jerusalem, surrounded by its massive stone wall. For a long time all I could do was stand there, overwhelmed, taking in the familiar skyline with its domes and towers shimmering in ever-moving patches of light. It was so much more beautiful than I had imagined. This wall, unlike the one in my long-ago dream, had no cracks, but its open gates invited me in.

I spent the next few days walking the streets of the Old City, and saw why Toledo is called the Jerusalem of Spain: both are built from the same golden-hued stone that makes the cities glow even when the sun does not shine. I explored every narrow cobblestoned street, despite the Intifada, poring over ancient artifacts and books, steeping myself in history, breathing in the pungent, spicy smells coming from tiny food shops tucked in alley doorways. Wherever I went, I felt the ghosts of the past walk with me.

When I got to the Western Wall and saw the throng of Orthodox Jews praying before it, the old feeling of alienation, of not belonging, again enveloped me. For a long time I stood apart, reluctant to get close. When the crowd thinned out I slowly walked up to the wall and passed my fingers over the worn stones. I was intensely moved by a sense of history, of continuity that unites all Jews in this unique place. I was also painfully aware that I did not know what to do, what to say, what to pray. Even the tears burning my eyes did not flow freely. In this holiest of places for Jews, I was a stranger.

Earlier I had written two wishes on a piece of paper I wanted to tuck into a crack in the wall. I stopped to add a third: "Next time, I want to feel I belong." Among the thousands of paper wishes I found a tiny open space and inserted my own, pushing it in firmly so it would not fall out.

When I returned to Jerusalem eighteen months later, and once more visited the wall, I no longer felt like a stranger. Since then I have joined a small, somewhat unorthodox congregation whose rabbi uses modified rituals, incorporating meditation, chanting, traditional as well as contemporary music, and wonderfully evocative parables, to ease me gently into my slowly evolving Jewish spirituality. I was born a Jew. I now live as a Jew.

It took me well over four years to come to the last page of this book, but that does not mark the end of my quest. Writing it has opened closed doors, revealed long-hidden secrets, released repressed feelings, taken me back to childhood haunts and to foreign places, and introduced me to so many fascinating people who have become my friends that there is no way the adventure could possibly end here, even if I wanted it to. But for now at least, the circle is complete. The past and present have finally come together, inside and out. There remains still more to be done, but I know at last who I am, and my heart is at rest. My silver filigree mezuzah, which I bought in Jerusalem last year, is affixed to my front doorpost.

# *Epilogue*

Although I began my quest without a clear agenda beyond exploring my past, each trip to Spain, and each new experience with the people I met there, convinced me that a real change in the relationship between the Spanish and Jewish peoples was possible. Today, with only a minuscule Jewish population in their midst, most Spaniards still carry distorted stereotypical images of the Jew. The time to heal old wounds, to sweep away obsolete myths, to clear the way for a genuine rapprochement between our two peoples is long overdue.

Even before I began my journey, I suspected that the reigning monarchs of Spain were favorably disposed toward Jews. This impression was confirmed in 1987 when King Juan Carlos and Queen Sofía were invited to a special ceremony at Temple Tiferth Israel in Los Angeles. His Majesty's appreciation of the role of Jews in the historic fabric of Spain and his hope for a reconciliation between the Spanish and Jewish peoples was clearly spelled out in the following excerpts from his address to the Sephardic community.

"How can we not, on this momentous occasion, recall the role played by the Jewish community throughout centuries of Spanish history? Its contribution to letters, science, and the arts during the Middle Ages, and the beauty of the synagogues, such as that of the Tránsito or Santa María la Blanca in Toledo, constitute a legacy in which we all acknowledge the rich variety of the Jewish culture and traditions.

"The search for an identity and respect for the traditions that characterize the Jewish people have been forged in the setting of countless adverse and difficult circumstances: unjust and unnecessary expulsions, persecution and intolerance, culminating, more recently, in the tragedy of the Holocaust. From all this adversity, the Jewish people were able to draw teachings with a view to consolidating their faith and their traditions, in an exemplary struggle for their survival.

"Today's Spain is proud of its close kinship with the [Jewish] community, which has contributed in a very special way to the prosperity of this great country.

"I should like to convey to this community the greeting of a Spain which in full conscience assumes responsibility for the negative as well as the positive aspects of its historic past. This is also a unique opportunity to emphasize the will for peace and friendship that animates the Spanish people, who see this community as part of its own history."

Later I wished I had taken the opportunity during this visit to thank King Juan Carlos for the role played by the Spanish people in saving the lives of so many Jews during the Holocaust, and personally to express my appreciation to him and his queen for their efforts in creating an atmosphere of freedom and openness, which has dramatically changed the official status of Jews in Spain.

I was given that opportunity four years later, in early June 1991, when I was granted an audience with both the king and the queen at their private country residence near Madrid, the Palacio de la Zarzuela.

Tape recorders and cameras were not allowed, and note-taking discouraged. Much to my surprise, the royal couple had been well briefed about my book, and considerable time was spent on discussing its content. I found both to be deeply concerned with the lingering impact of the more negative aspects of our peoples' joint history.

When I mentioned that I feared that most Spanish children were taught very little about their Jewish heritage, Queen Sofía assured me that many of these issues were now being addressed in television programs, and in classes and seminars focusing on the contribution of Jewish scholarship and art to the cultural history of Spain that are being offered at schools and universities throughout the country.

When I asked the king if there was any truth to the rumor that he might declare the Expulsion Decree a "historical error," Queen Sofía interjected with a smile before he could answer: "I bet Elie Wiesel persuaded you to ask this question!" After I admitted I had never personally met the winner of the Nobel Peace Prize, the king replied that, had *he* been the ruling monarch in 1492, he would not have issued that decree. "It is an unfortunate event in Spain's past that can be neither denied or erased."

While discussing a variety of other related subjects, the queen mentioned that she and the king were planning a trip to Israel during the quincentennial year, adding that they would be the first Spanish monarchs to ever do so.

When I realized that the ten-minute audience I was allotted had stretched to nearly an hour, I asked His Majesty to write a few words expressing his thoughts on the relationship between Spaniards and Jews today, five hundred years after the Expulsion, for inclusion in this book, and he graciously agreed to do so.

Two months after that conversation, in late August 1991, the Spanish Embassy delivered the following statement by His Majesty King Juan Carlos, on crested stationery and personally signed.

In 1992 Spain commemorates Sefarad'92, an event which has very special connotations for the Spanish as well as the Jewish people, whose ancestors had to leave Spain in 1492, a land they loved and where their culture blossomed for so many centuries. This anniversary is a good occasion to consider the negative impact of intolerance and prejudice, prevailing in Europe during that time, and above all it is an occasion to pay tribute to the golden age of Spanish Jewry.

The poetry of Yehuda Halevy, the scientific and philosophic innovations of Maimonides, and the profound contribution to astronomy by Abraham Zacuto, just to cite a few names, are inscribed with golden letters in the books of literature, philosophy, and science. We should also remember the example of tolerance and peaceful coexistence given by Jewish, Christian, and Islamic communities in Toledo, which made that city one of the most extraordinary centers of culture during the twelfth and thirteenth centuries.

This book also contributes to our common history with a very important and not very well known chapter. By means of personal accounts we are told how the lives of many Jews were preserved during the Second World War, when thousands of foreign Jews were sheltered in Spain or granted asylum in Spanish embassies throughout the world. Although these episodes could be considered a historical paradox, considering the situation in Spain at that time, they are in fact not so surprising, because they originate in a profound historical connection.

The Expulsion of the Jews in 1492 did not sever the link between Spain and the Jewish world. Jewish culture was kept alive in Spain thanks to Crypto-Jewish families, and outside the boundaries of the peninsula, first in the Mediterranean basin and the Near East, and later in the Spanish territories of North and South America. While Spain was taking its language and culture to the New World, the dispersed Sephardim disseminated their culture to the far corners of the globe, a legacy for which the Spanish people should be thankful and proud.

I still remember, with great emotion, the warm welcome that Queen Sofía and I received in 1987 at the Sephardic Temple in Los Angeles, which marked the official reencounter between the Spanish crown and some of our most beloved brothers and sisters. Since then, the Spanish and Jewish peoples have rediscovered the best side of our common past; my son, the Prince of Asturias, had the pleasure of awarding the Humanities Prize, which bears his own name, to the Sephardic Community.

Finally, I want to give my warmest thanks to Trudi Alexy for her decisive contribution to a better understanding of our two communities, by writing a book that will certainly constitute a discovery in the year commemorating the discovery of the New World.

Signed: His Royal Highness, King Juan Carlos I

On October 7, 1991, King Juan Carlos was awarded the Elie Wiesel Foundation Humanitarian Award. What follows is an excerpt from the address by Elie Wiesel during the award dinner.

As a Jew, I am committed to the memory of our history, the history of Israel and therefore to its right to live and fulfill its destiny in security and peace.

As a good Jew, I believe in the obligation to remember. We remember the good and the bad, the friends and the foes. We remember that during the darkest era of our recent history, Spain gave shelter to countless Jews who illegally entered its territory. And I remember that five hundred years ago, clinging to their faith, Jews were forced by your ancestors to leave Spain. Could they have imagined that their descendants would meet five centuries later in an atmosphere of tolerance, understanding, and friendship? History does have imagination as well as memory.

In 1950, when I visited your still-tormented country as a young correspondent for an Israeli paper, I had an eerie feeling that I had been there before. Many places seemed familiar. I thought I "remembered" events, names, experiences. . . .

When I came to Toledo I thought I could hear—some 850 years after his death—Yehuda Halévy's powerful poem of nostalgic love for Jerusalem: "Libi ba-mizra'h ve'anokhi besof maarav": My heart, said he, is there in the East, but I am here, at the other end of the West. . . . Barcelona evoked for me the great thinker Nahmanides. It was in that cathedral that he defeated Paolo Christiani during their famous disputation. Granada? I knew the city from Shmuel Hanagid's war poems. Abraham Ibn Ezra was born in Córdoba. . . . I have always been particularly fond of him. He was a fatalist, who believed he was meant to be poor, always. In one of his songs he wrote: "If I were to sell candles, the sun would never set; if I dealt in funeral shrouds, no one would ever die . . . As long as I lived."

Oh, yes, Your Majesty, I think of Spain and I see the noble figures of Menahem ibn Saruk and Joseph ibn Abitur, of Shlomo ibn Gabirol and Maimonides. How poor Jewish philosophy and poetry, and philosophy and poetry in general, would be without their legacy.

The history of your people, Your Majesty, and mine, have registered many moments of glory. . . . Three religious communities lived and worked and dreamed together in Spain for many, many decades. . . . But our past also contains moments of despair. When I think of the great luminaries of medieval Spain I cannot help but remember the Inquisition and its flames . . . the public humiliation of Jews who wanted to remain Jewish . . . the Expulsion and its endless procession of uprooted families in search of new havens. . . .

*Still, while no man is responsible for what his ancestors have done, he is responsible for what he does with that memory.*

Your Majesty, what you have done with yours is what moved us to honor you tonight.

We honor your convictions and beliefs, your principles and ideals, we honor your commitment to humanity.

Having witnessed the evil in fascism and dictatorship, you chose to bring democracy to your nation by restoring its taste for religious freedom, political pluralism, and social justice.

Your personal courage in opposing the attempted coup d'etat won you the admiration of free men and women the world over.

We applaud your wisdom in separating religion and state, your compassion . . . your sensitivity to and concern with Jewish fears and hopes . . . your emphasis on symbols. . . . Your decision to visit a synagogue next March, on the five-hundredth anniversary of the Expulsion Decree, offers proof that Spain, represented by Your Majesty, has overcome its past and faces the challenges of the future. That is a noble gesture that will remain in our collective Jewish memory forever.

# Acknowledgments

This book would have remained an unrealized dream without the help, support, and encouragement of the many wise and generous individuals I encountered throughout the four years it took to complete the research, translate and transcribe the interviews, and knit it all into a viable, readable document. I am deeply grateful to them all.

I am most profoundly endebted to the sixty persons (the rescued, rescuers, historians, diplomats, and members of the Christian and Jewish communities in Spain, Canada, Israel, and the United States) who so graciously shared their memories, impressions, and expertise with me. Although I was unable to include all the stories, each of their contributions broadened my understanding of the personal element in the history of the Jews in Spain and helped to make this task an unforgettable experience for me.

*Stephan Zusman, Ph.D.*, nurtured the creative, adventurous spirit in me and dared me to reach for the brass ring when I believed it was beyond my grasp. He was the first to validate my quest.

*Monica Andrews, Ph.D.*, interrupted her doctoral studies at Harvard University to work with me during the crucial formative months of the research. It was her vision, her enthusiasm, and her creative mind which helped broaden my private quest into a public document. When lack of funding for the project forced her to return to her studies a few months after we began working together, she remained available, ready to listen and make suggestions. Her contribution was invaluable.

*Bob Goldfarb* convinced me I had a publishable book long before there was a book to publish. On countless occasions his calm and cool-headed reframing of what I perceived as insurmountable obstacles saw me through a crisis and kept me on course. His optimism and great expertise as a literary agent enabled me to survive the publishing minefield more or less intact. It was he who convinced

*Al Zuckerman*, of Writers House literary agency in New York, to accept me as a client. Al used his clout and persuasive negotiation skills to get a major publisher to make a substantial financial commitment long before my work was completed.

*Philip Turner*, my first editor, deserves special thanks, as well as a medal for bravery, for bringing a stubborn, opinionated, and untested writer under his expert wing. His interest in the subject and recognition of the universal theme behind my personal journey first brought this book to the attention of the publishers. His enthusiasm sold them. His perseverance brought us halfway through, when he was suddenly and unexpectedly removed from the project. I will always be grateful to him for giving me my first professional break as a writer.

*Gail Winston*, my last and primary editor, had the thankless task of taking over and reframing the focus of a book which had been shaped by another editorial team. Her solid know-how and fine ear made the transition a creative adventure. Her sensitivity and warmth quickly created a climate of cooperation and trust. I consider myself lucky to have had her guidance and wise counsel.

The following leaders in the professional community were among my first active boosters, expressing their support verbally and/or writing letters of introduction which lent legitimacy to my work and helped open doors. Each of them shared my hope that this study would add a meaningful chapter to the growing historical record focusing on instances of humanity amid the horrors of the Holocaust.

*Lucky Altman*, Director of Interreligious Programs, National Council of Christians and Jews, Los Angeles, California;

*Rabbi Harold Schulweis*, Temple Valley Beth Shalom, Encino, California, Founding Chairman of the Foundation to Sustain Righteous Christians;

*Eva Fogelmann, Ph.D.*, consultant to the Jewish Foundation for Christian Rescuers/ADL, in New York, and the director of the Rescuer Project, a study of three hundred rescuers and survivors from Nazi-occupied Europe;

*Drs. Sam and Pearl Oliner*, founders of the Altruistic Personality and Prosocial Behavior Institute at Humboldt State University, Arcata, California, and authors of *The Altruistic Personality, Rescuers of Jews in Nazi Europe.*

*Rabbi Ted Falcon, Ph.D.*, psychologist and founder of Makom Ohr Shalom Congregation, Tarzana, California.

The following knowledgeable colleagues and friends read parts of my manuscript and provided valuable suggestions and editing help: *Leonard Felder, Ph.D., Evelyn Virshup, Ph.D., Beverly Matthews, Zella Brown, Harriet Rochlin, Gerry Monosoff*, and *Victor Raphael.*

The librarians and archivists whose names follow contributed their patience and expertise, making my research infinitely easier: *Denise Gluck, Harvey Horowitz, Rozlyn Weiss*, and *Judith Greene.*

*Sarah Feldman* and *Beth Luttrell* generously donated uncounted hours transcribing many of the dozens of ninety-minute audio tapes.

## Acknowledgments

Four persons deserve special mention for their unique and very personal contributions:

*Jackie Pizante,* my friend, secretary, and all-around guardian angel, provided her loving presence and moral support during the writing of this book. As she has for years, she was there for me whenever I needed an encouraging word to keep me sane, or a helping hand to pitch in when I felt overwhelmed. I have long ago despaired of evening out our account: I will be in her debt forever.

*Florabel Kinsler, Ph.D.,* director of "Café Europa," a support group for elderly European Jews in West L.A., provided crucial connections to people who made invaluable historical contributions to the research and showed, in a thousand ways, that she supported my work.

*Donald Goodkind* allowed me to use his personal computer when my own word processor proved inadequate for the job. He is indeed true to his name.

*Ron Rozanski* spent hours patiently teaching me how to use new, more efficient software, which greatly simplified the writing.

Last but not least, a very special thanks to:

*Ambassador Nicolas Revenga,* in Madrid, then Executive Secretary of Sefarad '92, Spain's Consul General in Los Angeles, the *Hon. Pedro Tamboury,* and his able successor, the *Hon. Eduardo Garrigues,* his secretary, *Chony Fernandez,* and the rest of the consular staff, who shared my vision and whose influence wrought miracles for me, including an audience with Their Majesties the King and Queen of Spain.

*Patricio Maillard* and *Gabriel Perez,* past and present regional managers of the United States Western States operations of Iberia Airlines, who demonstrated their company's support for my project long before I could impress them with a publisher's commitment. They provided several complimentary flights to Spain and Israel, with no strings attached. I never told them I would have flown Iberia even if I had had to pay my way: they are a wonderful airline.

# Index

# About the Author

Trudi Alexy is a family therapist specializing in art therapy. She was born in Romania and sheltered in Barcelona for part of World War II. She lives in Los Angeles.

978-0-595-41159-7
0-595-41159-2

CPSIA information can be obtained at www.ICGtesting.com
Printed in the USA
LVOW12s1109300314

379521LV00002B/566/A